D0107429

Alaska

John Murray
Photography by Don Pitcher

Additional writing, editing, and photography
by
Nick Jans

Compass American Guides
An Imprint of Fodor's Travel Publications

Alaska

Third Edition

First published in 1997
ISBN 0-679-00838-1

Editors: Kit Duane, Nick Jans, Cheryl Koehler, Penn Jensen
Managing Editor: Kit Duane
Creative Director: Christopher Burt
Designers: Christopher Burt, Deborah Dunn
Map Design: Mark Stroud, Moon Street Cartography
Production House: Twin Age Ltd., Hong Kong
Manufactured in China

Compass American Guides, 5332 College Avenue, Suite 201, Oakland, CA 94618
10 9 8 7 6 5 4 3 2 1

The Publisher gratefully acknowledges the following institutions and individuals for the use of their photographs and/or illustrations on the following pages: **Jean-Michel Addor** pp. 26, 38 bottom (courtesy Ken Berger); **Alaska Aviation Heritage Museum, Anchorage** p. 246; **Anchorage Museum of History and Art** pp. 22, 23, 24, 25, 27, 29, 35, 39, 45, 47, 48, 49, 52 (top, middle, and bottom), 53 (top, middle, and bottom), 85, 98, 100, 102, 111, 136, 146, 154 (top and bottom), 155, 156, 239, 296, 326, 335, 337; **Bancroft Library, U.C. Berkeley** pp. 20, 29, 32 (top and bottom), 42, 69, 101, 103, 118, 121, 336; **Brad S. Lomazzi, Western Railroad Collectables** pp. 38, 120; **Byron Birdsall** p. 150; **R.D. Caughron** pp. 257, 259; **Paul Chesley** p. 77; **Kit Duane** pp. 201, 205; **Robert Holmes** pp. 72, 74; **Kerrick James** pp. 222, 256; **Nick Jans** pp. 43, 60, 61, 63, 80, 228, 281, 283, 286, 287, 289, 292, 302, 303, 305, 307; **Library of Congress** pp. 31, 34, 37, 119, 242; **Barbara Rowell** p. 69; **Galen Rowell** p. 71; **U.S. Coast and Geodetic Survey** p. 114; **Underwood Photo Archives, San Francisco** pp. 36, 51, 123, 251, 300, 347, 353; **Washington State Historical Society,** Tacoma p. 33 (top). We also wish to thank: **Jamie Bollenbach** for "Art and Culture in Anchorage," "Alaska Politics," and "Anchorage Bars and Nightlife," in addition to his expert reading of the book; **Nick Jans** for "Arctic Seasons" and "Wolves Are Listening," both excerpts from his book, *A Place Beyond,* and for his essay, "Bush Etiquette;" R. D. Caughron for "Climbing McKinley;" **Mina Jacobs** and **Walter Van Horn** of the Anchorage Museum of History and Art; **Amy Bollenbach** of Homer for her contributions; **Candace Coar** for proofreading; **Denise Lido** for indexing; **Julie Searle, Jan Hughes,** and **Philip DePetra** for research.

Dedicated to four great Alaskans:
Joe Firmin, Lynn Castle, Billy Campbell, and Michio Hoshino

CONTENTS

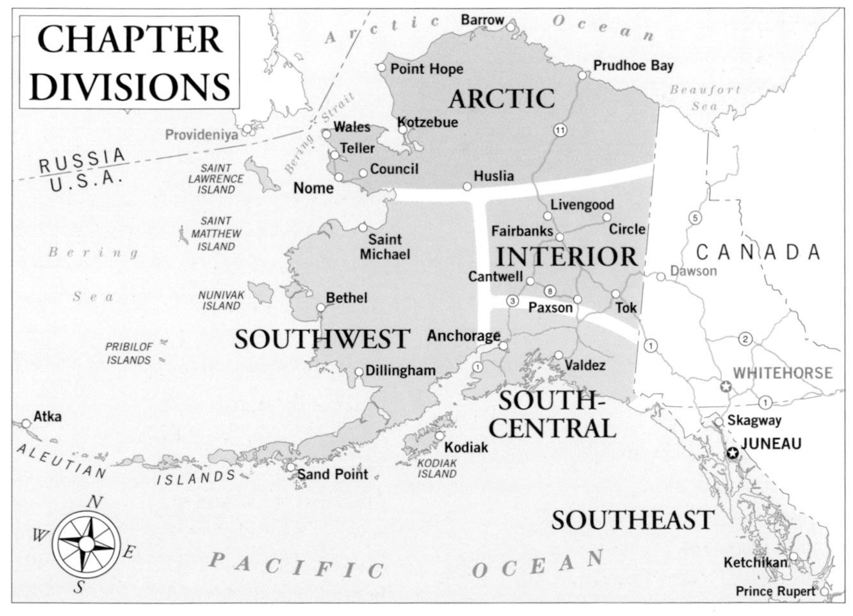
CHAPTER DIVISIONS
Arctic Ocean
Barrow
Point Hope
Prudhoe Bay
ARCTIC
Beaufort Sea
Bering Strait
Wales
Kotzebue
Provideniya
Teller
RUSSIA
U.S.A.
SAINT LAWRENCE ISLAND
Council
Nome
Huslia
Livengood
Fairbanks
Circle
SAINT MATTHEW ISLAND
Saint Michael
INTERIOR
CANADA
Dawson
Bering Sea
Cantwell
NUNIVAK ISLAND
Bethel
Paxson
Tok
SOUTHWEST
Anchorage
PRIBILOF ISLANDS
Dillingham
Valdez
WHITEHORSE
SOUTH-CENTRAL
Atka
Skagway
JUNEAU
Kodiak
ALEUTIAN ISLANDS
Sand Point
KODIAK ISLAND
SOUTHEAST
N
W
E
S
PACIFIC OCEAN
Ketchikan
Prince Rupert

Literary Extracts

Topical Essays

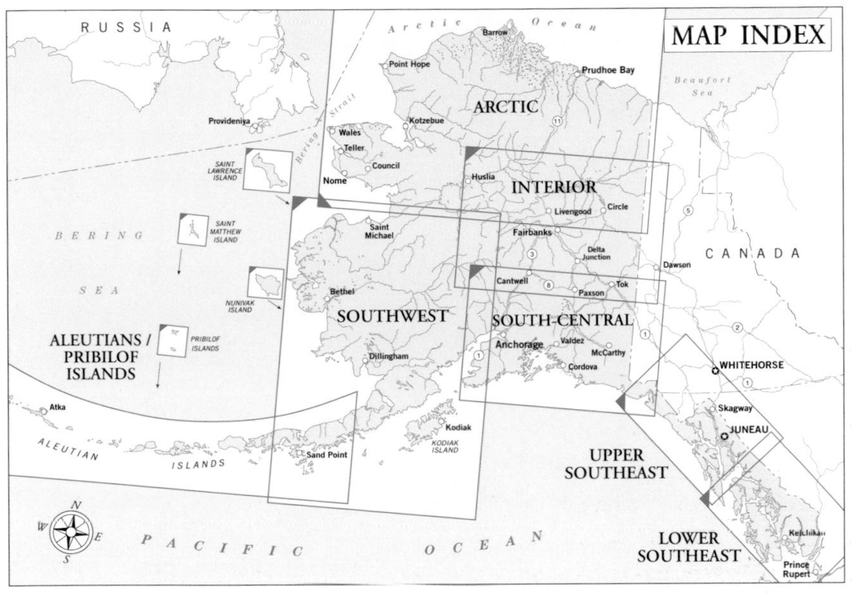
MAP INDEX
RUSSIA
Arctic Ocean
Barrow
Point Hope
Prudhoe Bay
Beaufort Sea
ARCTIC
Provideniya
Bering Strait
Wales
Teller
Kotzebue
Council
Nome
SAINT LAWRENCE ISLAND
Huslia
INTERIOR
Circle
Livengood
Fairbanks
Delta Junction
Dawson
CANADA
SAINT MATTHEW ISLAND
BERING SEA
Saint Michael
NUNIVAK ISLAND
Bethel
SOUTHWEST
Cantwell
Paxson
Tok
SOUTH-CENTRAL
Anchorage
Valdez
McCarthy
Cordova
ALEUTIANS / PRIBILOF ISLANDS
PRIBILOF ISLANDS
Dillingham
WHITEHORSE
Skagway
JUNEAU
Atka
Kodiak
KODIAK ISLAND
ALEUTIAN ISLANDS
Sand Point
UPPER SOUTHEAST
PACIFIC OCEAN
LOWER SOUTHEAST
Prince Rupert
N
W
E
S

Maps

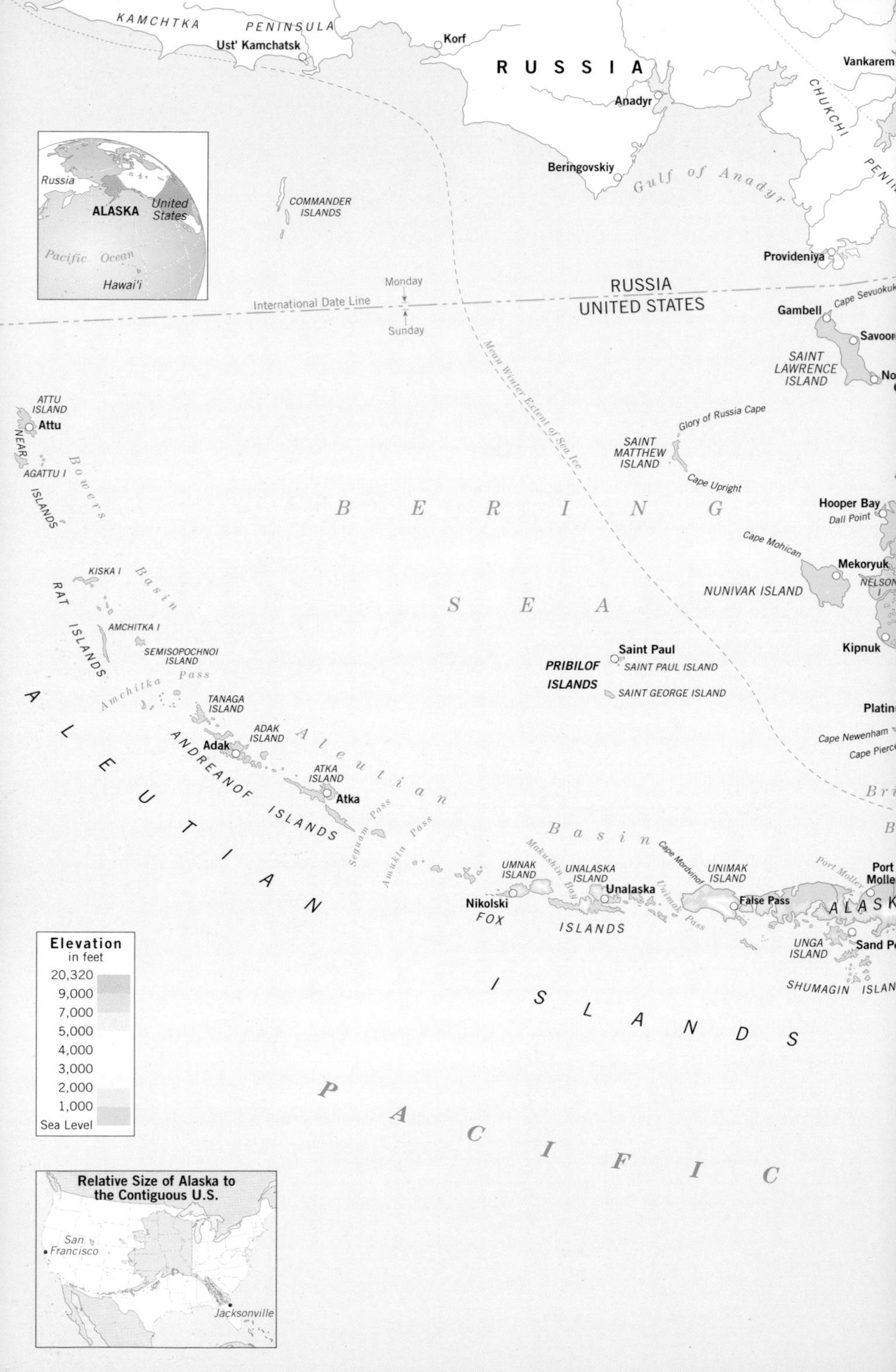

KAMCHTKA PENINSULA
Ust' Kamchatsk
Korf
RUSSIA
Vankarem
Anadyr
CHUKCHI
Beringovskiy
Gulf of Anadyr
Provideniya
COMMANDER ISLANDS
Russia
ALASKA
United States
Pacific Ocean
Hawai'i
Monday
International Date Line
Sunday
RUSSIA
UNITED STATES
Gambell
Cape Sevuokuk
SAINT LAWRENCE ISLAND
Mean Winter Extent of Sea Ice
ATTU ISLAND
Attu
NEAR
AGATTU I
ISLANDS
Bowers
Glory of Russia Cape
SAINT MATTHEW ISLAND
Cape Upright
BERING
Hooper Bay
Dall Point
Cape Mohican
Mekoryuk
NUNIVAK ISLAND
KISKA I
RAT ISLANDS
Basin
AMCHITKA I
SEA
Kipnuk
SEMISOPOCHNOI ISLAND
Amchitka Pass
Saint Paul
PRIBILOF ISLANDS
SAINT PAUL ISLAND
SAINT GEORGE ISLAND
TANAGA ISLAND
ALEUTIAN
ADAK ISLAND
Adak
Aleutian
ANDREANOF ISLANDS
Cape Newenham
ATKA ISLAND
Atka
Seguam Pass
Amukta Pass
Basin
Cape Mordvinof
UMNAK ISLAND
Makushin Bay
UNALASKA ISLAND
Unalaska
Unimak Pass
UNIMAK ISLAND
False Pass
Port Moller
Nikolski
FOX ISLANDS
UNGA ISLAND
SHUMAGIN
Elevation in feet
20,320
9,000
7,000
5,000
4,000
3,000
2,000
1,000
Sea Level
ISLANDS
PACIFIC
Relative Size of Alaska to the Contiguous U.S.
San Francisco
Jacksonville

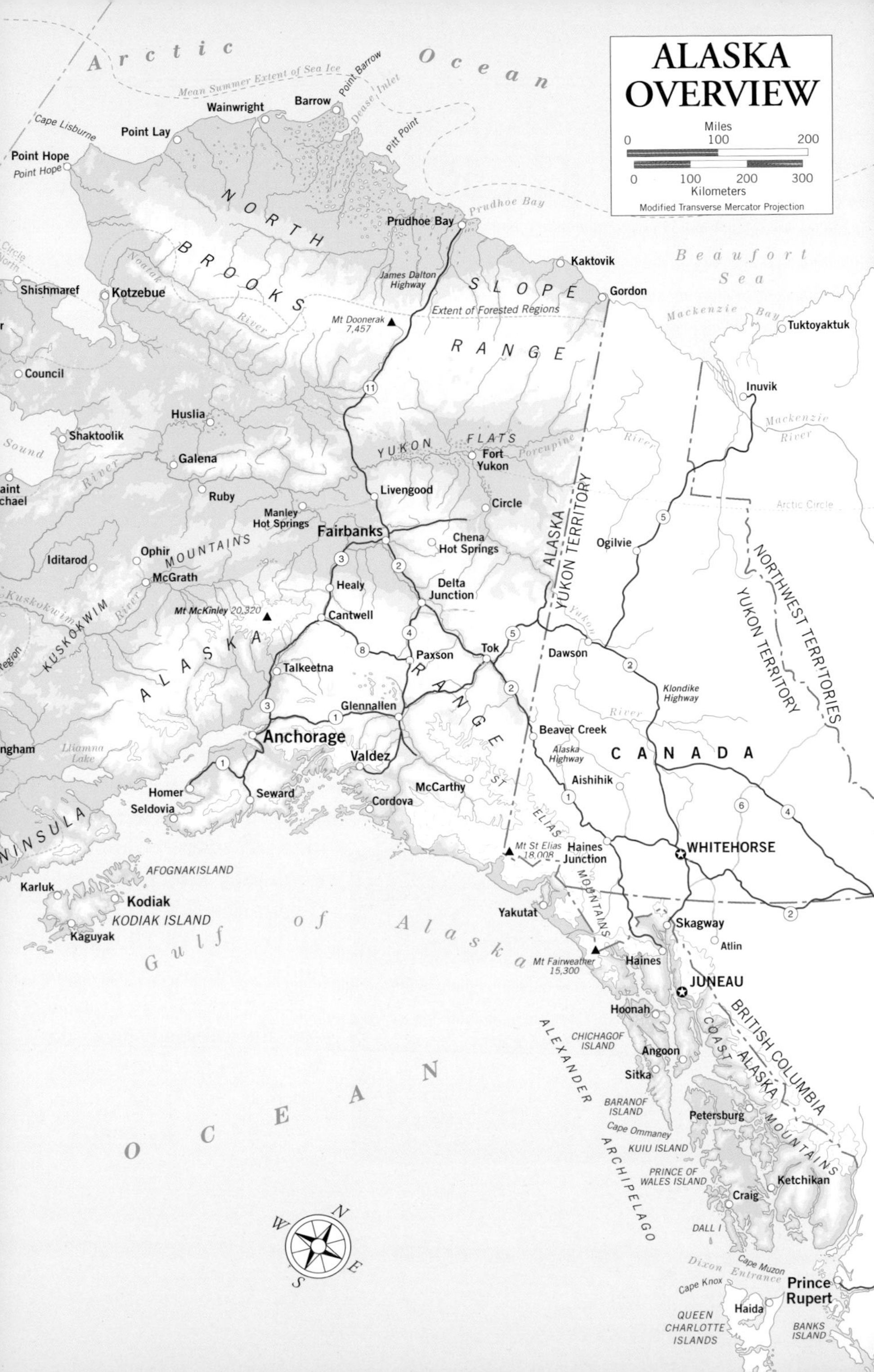

ALASKA OVERVIEW
Miles
0 100 200
0 100 200 300
Kilometers
Modified Transverse Mercator Projection
Arctic Ocean
Mean Summer Extent of Sea Ice
Beaufort Sea
Mackenzie Bay
Gulf of Alaska
OCEAN
NORTH SLOPE
BROOKS RANGE
YUKON FLATS
ALASKA RANGE
KUSKOKWIM MOUNTAINS
ST ELIAS MOUNTAINS
COAST MOUNTAINS
ALEXANDER ARCHIPELAGO
CANADA
ALASKA
YUKON TERRITORY
NORTHWEST TERRITORIES
BRITISH COLUMBIA
Arctic Circle
Extent of Forested Regions
James Dalton Highway
Klondike Highway
Alaska Highway
Mt Doonerak 7,457
Mt McKinley 20,320
Mt St Elias 18,008
Mt Fairweather 15,300
Barrow
Point Barrow
Wainwright
Point Lay
Cape Lisburne
Point Hope
Dease Inlet
Pitt Point
Prudhoe Bay
Kaktovik
Gordon
Tuktoyaktuk
Inuvik
Shishmaref
Kotzebue
Council
Huslia
Shaktoolik
Galena
Ruby
Manley Hot Springs
Livengood
Fort Yukon
Circle
Fairbanks
Chena Hot Springs
Ophir
Iditarod
McGrath
Healy
Delta Junction
Cantwell
Paxson
Tok
Dawson
Ogilvie
Talkeetna
Glennallen
Anchorage
Valdez
Beaver Creek
Aishihik
Homer
Seldovia
Seward
Cordova
McCarthy
Haines Junction
WHITEHORSE
Yakutat
Skagway
Atlin
Haines
JUNEAU
Hoonah
Angoon
Sitka
Petersburg
Ketchikan
Craig
Prince Rupert
Haida
Karluk
Kodiak
Kaguyak
AFOGNAK ISLAND
KODIAK ISLAND
CHICHAGOF ISLAND
BARANOF ISLAND
Cape Ommaney
KUIU ISLAND
PRINCE OF WALES ISLAND
DALL I
Cape Muzon
Dixon Entrance
Cape Knox
QUEEN CHARLOTTE ISLANDS
BANKS ISLAND
Iliamna Lake
Noatak River
Yukon River
Porcupine River
Kuskokwim River
Mackenzie River

OVERVIEW

ALASKA

A SUBCONTINENT THAT straddles Asia and North America, Alaska is larger than Texas, California, and Montana combined. At its center is the mighty Yukon River and 20,320-foot Mount McKinley. Grizzly bears fish in salmon-choked streams, polar bears sun themselves on icebergs, whales breech, and migrating tundra swans fly past vast herds of caribou. Even in urban Anchorage, an unspoiled landscape is close at hand.

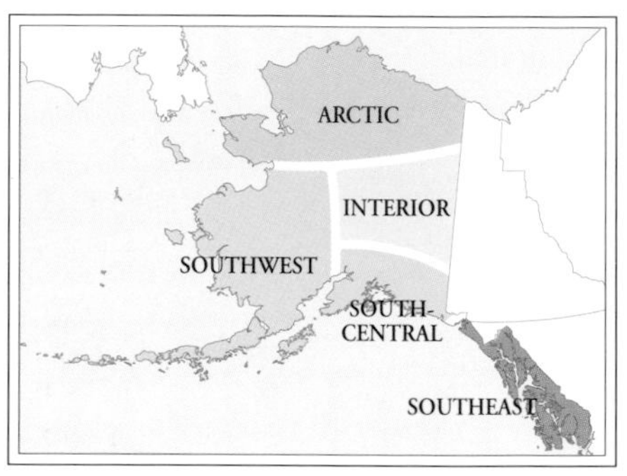

◆ SOUTHEAST AND THE INSIDE PASSAGE *pages 84–143*

Along Alaska's southeastern panhandle lie thousands of forest-draped islands and small towns set on emerald-green bays. Ferries and cruise ships ply the Inside Passage, passing islands and fjords where whales breach and bears can be seen fishing in coastal waters. Nearby small towns offer fishing tours and "flightseeing." Trading posts sell Eskimo and Tlingit art. Juneau, America's only state capital inaccessible by road from the mainland, enjoys the most spectacular setting of any American city. At the Panhandle's northern extremity is magnificent Glacier Bay.

◆ SOUTH-CENTRAL *pages 144–209*

With a population of over 250,000, Anchorage is a bustling metropolis with good restaurants and modern accommodations. Alaska's largest city, it serves as a jumping off point for excursions to Denali National Park, the beautiful Kenai Peninsula, and Prince William Sound.

◆ THE INTERIOR *pages 210–271*

Embracing mountain and taiga, the heartland is home to magnificent Mount McKinley (Denali), the highest mountain in North America. Grizzlies and brown bears, wolves, caribou, moose, and Dall sheep inhabit the national park that surrounds it. Fairbanks is the Interior's only city. The area's most famous sport is mushing, or dogsledding; its most popular sports are salmon fishing and big-game hunting which are as close as the nearest bush pilot's plane.

◆ ARCTIC ALASKA *pages 272–315*

Tundra stretches in a great arc along the Arctic Ocean from the Bering land bridge—where hunters of the Asian steppe crossed into North America 30,000 years ago—to Barrow, where the sun doesn't set 83 days of the year. Home to Inupiat (Eskimo) culture, enormous herds of caribou, and polar bears who live on the ice floes, this vast and empty space has undeniable magic for those who experience its wildness. Remote villages, national parks, and wilderness lodges in this area are reached via the Dalton Highway or bush plane.

◆ SOUTHWEST *pages 316–347*

This enormous expanse of land remains pristine and remote. Here are active volcanoes, vast areas of tundra, the Aleutian Islands inhabited by millions of seabirds, and seas crowded with walrus, seal, and whale. Kodiak Island, thought by early explorers to resemble Ireland, is home to the enormous Alaskan brown bear.

THE GREAT GIFT

My prayer is that Alaska will not lose the heart-nourishing friendliness of her youth—that her people will always care for one another, her towns remain friendly and not completely ruled by the dollar—and that her great wild places will remain great, and wild, and free, where wolf and caribou, wolverine and grizzly bear, and all the Arctic blossoms may live on in the delicate balance which supported them long before impetuous man appeared in the North. This is the great gift Alaska can give to the harassed world.

—Margaret Murie, *Two in the Far North*

The Mendenhall Glacier near Juneau in Tongass National Forest serves as a dramatic backdrop to a field of Nootka lupine.

INTRODUCTION

ALASKA REPRESENTS ONE OF THE LAST unspoiled wildernesses on Earth, a vignette of the primordial world. Imagine tens of thousands of caribou streaming through mountain passes, dozens of brown bears fishing rivers thick with salmon, or flocks of amber-horned sheep grazing above a glacier larger than Rhode Island. As volcanoes vent ash and smoke, the ghostly green northern lights dance among the stars. In Alaska you will see North America in its morning freshness when the rivers had no dams and the trees had yet to feel the ax, and not one animal had ever heard a human voice. You may feel that you've gone back in time, that you're seeing the world as you did as a child—when everything was still new, and wonderful, and incredibly big.

Everything in Alaska is off the scale. The state sprawls across 21 degrees of latitude and 43 degrees of longitude. Consider that for a moment. The state is more than 2,400 miles across and 1,400 miles from north to south! From the Alaskan island of Little Diomede, the nearest Russian territory is less than three miles away. In other places Alaska is almost 1,000 miles west of the Hawaiian Islands. And yet, in its southern extremity, Alaska is only an hour's flight from Seattle, Washington. If the state were to be superimposed on the lower 48 states, the southeast tip would rest along the Georgia coast and the Aleutians would extend past Los Angeles into the Pacific Ocean. If you explored 100 acres a day, picking flowers and noting animals and rocks, it would take you more than three million years to cover the state.

In Alaska are the largest bears in the world, the biggest salmon in the world, the largest national parks, forests, and wildlife refuges in the world, the largest gatherings of bald eagles in the world. And so on. Alaska is not so much a continental peninsula as it is a massive sub-continent. It extends far into the Pacific, nearly to Asia, and, in terms of fauna, flora, and geography, is sometimes more Siberian than North American. Yet, virtually every ecosystem can be found in the state, from shadowy rain forest to dry frigid tundra, from apocalyptic volcanic wasteland to bird-filled salt marsh, from spectacular glacial fjord to rolling subarctic taiga.

The Alaska Range stretches across a vast area of interior Alaska.

The purpose of this book is to guide you through a state that overwhelms even lifelong residents. Because the state is so large and the recreational opportunities so diverse, this book is, of necessity, selective rather than comprehensive. What I have tried to do is give you the benefit of my half-dozen years in Alaska, a period during which I traveled from the frosty arctic coast to the forested tip of the Kenai Peninsula, from the wind-swept Canadian border across the interior wilderness, from a nameless mountain in the Arctic Refuge to the crowded streets of Anchorage.

Although travel in Alaska is accomplished quite simply via the excellent road system, I would also encourage visitors to leave the roads and hike in the backcountry, or take an hour-long flightseeing trip, or float a river, or hire a fishing boat at one of the many seaside villages. In this way you will see the "true Alaska," a timeless, beautiful realm beyond the reach of civilization, a realm where you may watch two bull moose lock antlers in the twilight, or catch a glimpse of a wolf pack patrolling their home territory, or spot a humpback whale breaching in a remote bay.

"The spell of Alaska," Ella Higginson wrote in 1908, "falls upon every lover of beauty who has voyaged along these far northern snow-pearled shores . . . or who has drifted down the mighty rivers of the interior which flow, bell-toned and lonely, to the sea . . . . No writer has ever described Alaska; no one writer ever will; but each must do his share, according to the spell that the country casts upon him." This book has been written in the spirit of Higginson's eloquent passage. Alaska is a place that will change you forever, if you let it, and each must, as Higginson suggests, experience that change in a different way. For me, the joy of Alaska has always been in the small things—picking wild blueberries on the tundra domes around Fairbanks in the fall, feeling the sharp tug of a salmon while fishing the Kenai, spotting a bald eagle as it glides through the clouds, watching the delicate auroras play against the January constellations, listening to a wolf serenade the moon in the Alaska Range. In after-years such memories return, reminding me of the rare abundance and innocence that are wild Alaska. Come now, and let us together roam this incredible state, which is as much a state of mind as it is a state of the Union.

◆ Author's Acknowledgments

I have many thanks to give. First a word of appreciation to my good friend Jeff Gnasse, who put me in touch with Kit Duane, the senior editor at Compass American Guides. Also, much gratitude to the many individuals who helped me in Denali National Park—Rick McIntyre, Fred Dean, Ken Kehrer, Russ Berry, Bill McDonald, Michio Hoshino, and Ralph Cunningham. Two fishing guides were most helpful during my annual trips to the Kenai River—Robert Johnson of Ken's Bait and Tackle Shop in Soldotna and Eric Painter of American Wildland Adventures in Cooper's Landing. A special thanks to former colleagues in the English Department at the University of Alaska, Fairbanks: Eric Heyne, Roy Bird, Joe Dupras, Burns Cooper, Lillian Corti, Mark Box, Dave Stark, Mike Schuldiner, Joan Worley. All offered good company and cheer. And finally, deepest thanks to four outstanding Alaskans—Joe Firmin, Lynn Castle, Billy Campbell, and Michio Hoshino.

Bush planes are an important form of transportation in Alaska, linking otherwise inaccessible regions to the larger towns.

J. Webber, an artist with Captain Cook's expedition in 1778, created this portrait of an Aleutian Indian woman. (Bancroft Library)

H I S T O R Y

My islands, you are my islands. The sky over them in the morning today is joyous. Just so is the morning of today. If I shall live henceforth, let them be just so in memory.
—Lines from an Aleut song, 1840

IMAGINE A SUMMER DAY 40,000 YEARS AGO. You are standing on the low grassy hills north of Denali. A cold wind is blowing from the west. The sun is high in the sky. The scenery appears much as it does today. But take a closer look. What are those animals feeding along the river? Elephants? But how could there be elephants in the subarctic? You climb a knoll, close the distance. Yes, they are definitely a form of elephant, quietly browsing the fresh green willow and birch leaves. But these odd pachyderms are covered with shaggy brown fur. And their ivory tusks are different. They curve upward and then inward, and finally cross at the tips. Not too close now. The leader, the old gray female, has taken notice. Her tattered ears are flared, her flexible trunk raised warily. She is listening closely, taking your scent, assessing your intentions. Her eyes may be small but they see far. In that high-domed skull is the well-developed brain of a woolly mammoth. Don't step too close. Keep walking.

What else do you see in the McKinley Valley—itself part of a corridor leading through glaciers toward warmer land to the south? A rank-smelling steppe bison with the headgear of a Texas longhorn and a thick coat like a musk ox? A yak? A herd of wild Asiatic horses? A family of animals that resemble camels? A friendly trio of lions? A curmudgeonly cave bear? A pack of dire wolves patrolling the riverbanks? A saber-toothed tiger and her young ones devouring a ground sloth? A pair of giant condor circling curiously on a thermal? A stag-moose with vast palmate antlers? A beaver the size of a black bear?

Yes, this fantastic bestiary did exist in Alaska, and not very long ago in terms of geological time. This was the during the last ice age, the period in which human beings came out of Africa and spread through Europe and Asia to become the dominant species on Earth (at least from the human point of view). Even today, the arctic ice may preserve some of these ancient animal bodies intact. More than once in recent memory, modern scientists have had the chance to gaze upon a frozen, well-preserved mammoth.

■ HUNTERS CROSS THE LAND BRIDGE

Perhaps 10,000 years after that summer day near Denali, a small band of lean, sturdy folk walked about 60 miles from Asia into North America, over a narrow stretch of tundra. Recently, the climate had grown colder, locking up more water in ice, lowering the ocean's water level, and leaving a dry passageway between the two continents. The emigrants were Asiatic people, and they carried all they owned with them. Alert, wolfish-looking animals patrolled ahead of the clan, distant ancestors of the modern dog. The leaders were no doubt pleased with the widening valley between the glaciers that they found to the east. For one thing, the land forms, fauna, and flora were the same as those in northeastern Siberia. For another, there were no other people around to hunt the game.

These hunters were only the first of successive waves of nomadic people who came during the next 25,000 years into the new world. There were perhaps five or six great migrations of very different tribal groups, each bringing different traditions and different languages. Each new invasion of outsiders must have spurred others to move east or south. Some turned inland, crossing the broad rivers by boat in the summer, and by sleds across the ice in winter. Some no doubt used ocean-going kayaks or long boats to move south along the coast of Canada and the Pacific Northwest. They explored mountains, penetrated forests, discovered valleys, formed alliances, fought battles, settled in new homelands, celebrated marriages, had children, buried the dead, told stories, repeated histories, invented myths.

This ivory needlecase, carved in the shape of a human figure, was found near St. Michael on the Bering Sea and is thought to be about 500 years old. (Anchorage Museum of History and Art)

Much of their culture was perishable, and so we have only such artifacts as skulls, bones, flint points, arrowheads, grinding stones, and scattered ornaments to form the basis of our speculations about it. We know that those first hunters must have been infused with the bravery that was necessary to human survival during the Pleistocene: picture a group of hungry men with stone-tipped spears facing a wounded woolly mammoth on the vast rolling steppes of prehistoric Alaska. Now *that* was big game hunting. We also know that about 11,000 years ago, as glaciers retreated from North America the great mammals of the Pleistocene began to die out, to be replaced by the fauna we know now in North America. In historic times that bravery was applied to hunting whales in skin boats on the open seas, and farther south, to hunting bear with arrows and lances.

This painting of a Siberian Koryuk village, done in 1892 by artist George A. Frost, shows nomadic tribespeople and their reindeer, which are domesiticated caribou. Alaska's early inhabitants migrated from Siberia, as did the caribou Eskimos and Indians hunt today. (Anchorage Museum of History and Art)

From the first hardy pioneers, through epic migrations southward into the Americas, came such very different and vibrant cultures as the Uto-Aztecan people—town-dwellers and agriculturists who spread into the American Southwest and Mexico; the Inuit or Eskimo, who circled the Arctic and were known to the Russians in Siberia and the Norsemen in Greenland; the Algonquin people, who successfully destroyed the Norse settlements along the eastern shores of the continent only to fall prey to the English and French; the Na-Dene group—the Athabaskans—among the last to migrate from Asia, some staying in Alaska, others moving south, cultural anthropologists surmise, to become the Navajo and Apache. The last king of Aztec Mexico, Montezuma, as well as Pocahontas, Sitting Bull, and Geronimo, all probably traced their ancestry to hunters who crossed during the great migrations between Asia and Alaska.

By the year 1700, Alaska's natives had become either people of the interior or people of the coast. Some, such as the Aleuts and the Tlingit, preferred life near the Pacific, where the Japanese current warmed the maritime provinces. Most

Tlingit medicine men, here adorned with Chilkat blankets, inhabited the southeastern coast of Alaska. (Anchorage Museum of History and Art)

Eskimos stayed in the frozen north, where the Arctic Ocean provided a reliable bounty in the late summer and fall. The Athabaskan people settled among the hills, valleys, forests, and meadows that comprise the immense heart of Alaska—a state of affairs that persisted for thousands of years. Remnants of their old camps can still be found along Dry Creek just north of Denali National Park, in the foothills of the Brooks Range, and along the cutbanks of the Yukon and Tanana Rivers. For centuries they moved and breathed with the land, and their way of life changed little.

Photographer Edward S. Curtis photographed this Nunivak Eskimo mother and child in 1928. (Anchorage Museum of History and Art)

■ RUSSIAN EXPLORERS AND TRADERS

Then suddenly, about 250 years ago, the situation in Alaska was altered dramatically and forever. A group of explorers sailing east under a Russian flag headed east from Kamchatka in June 1741, seeking to fill a blank space on the map. No one knew what lay between arctic Asia and the Americas. It was one of the last unexplored corners of the Earth. Did a northern passage exist between the Pacific and the Atlantic? What sort of people inhabited the region? Could gold be found, and other treasures? Captain-Commander Vitus Bering, an ambitious Dane in the service of the Russian navy, undertook to answer these important questions. With only two small wooden vessels, the *St. Peter* and the *St. Paul,* he ventured into what for the Europeans was the unknown. The voyage of discovery was something like a "Star Trek" episode. Everything that could go wrong did. Two landing boats full of men disappeared. A storm destroyed the *St. Peter,* and left the crew stranded for the winter. Scurvy killed many of the sailors. The Captain-Commander died.

A Russian art poster depicts Vitus Bering being greeted by Alaskan natives. The map depicts the journeys of his two ships, the St. Peter *and* St. Paul.

Among the survivors of the *St. Peter* was one of the most capable scientists of his time, a sort of "Mr. Spock," to extend the "Star Trek" analogy. His name was George Wilhelm Steller, and he was a brilliant botanist, zoologist, and geologist. One of the only reasons he survived and was able to return to Russia on a makeshift craft was that he insisted on eating native plants; unknown to him they contained vitamin C, and thus prevented scurvy. It was Steller who recorded for the first time many unusual plant and animal species of Alaska, including the Steller's jay, which still may be seen in campgrounds around Homer; the sea otter, which is still plentiful in areas such as the Kenai Fjords National Park; and the now-extinct Steller's Sea Cow, which was a gentle, shallow water manatee of the North Pacific islands.

Following the ill-fated Bering reconnaissance, more Russian expeditions explored the region, as well as two historic British missions, the first led by Capt. James Cook in 1778, the second by Cook's former lieutenant George Vancouver in 1794.

French artist Louis Choris accompanied a Russian voyage of exploration in 1815 and recorded the enormous herds of seals in the Bering Sea islands. Beginning in 1834 Russian and American companies began hunting the animals for their fur and by 1911 only 110,000 out of an original population of some four million animals were left. (Anchorage Museum of History and Art)

VANCOUVER SEES PRINCE WILLIAM SOUND

Friday, May 16, 1794

The weather was delightfully serene and pleasant, and the morning of the 16th was ushered in by a sight we little expected in these seas. A numerous fleet of skin canoes [kayaks], each carrying two men only, were about the Discovery, and, with those that at the same time visited the Chatham, it was computed there could not be less than four hundred Indians present. These were almost all men grown, so that the tribe to which they belonged must consequently be a very considerable one. They instantly and very willingly entered into trade, and bartered away their hunting and fishing implements, lines and thread, extremely neat and well made from the sinews of animals; with bags ingeniously decorated with needle work, wrought on the thin membrane of the whales intestines; these articles, with some fish, constituted the articles of commerce with these people, as well as with our Indian friends in Cook's inlet. . . .These good people, like all the others we had lately seen, conducted themselves with great propriety. . . . The coast we sailed along this day is in most parts very mountainous, and descends rather quickly into the ocean. We could not avoid remarking, that the whole of this exterior coast seemed to wear a much more wintry aspect than the countries bordering on those more northern inland waters we had so recently quitted. . . . Many trees had been cut down since these regions had been first visited by Europeans; this was evident by the visible effects of the axe and saw. It was remarked that during the surveying excursions not a single sea otter, and but very few whales or seals had been seen; and that the wild fowl were not met with in that plenty during Mr. Whidbey's, as in Mr. Johnstone's [previous British explorers], expedition.

—George Vancouver, *Voyage of Discovery to the North Pacific Ocean in the Years 1790–1792*

Captain Cook conversed with Russian traders and observed Tlingit Indians along the coast. He was not enthusiastic about the latter, in whom he noted, "a dull, phlegmatic want of expression." He accurately identified the Eskimos as the same people he'd encountered sailing the coast of Greenland, recording in his logs their similar vocabularies and the facility of the Eskimo in all things technological. Cook sailed north of 63 degrees north latitude into the Bering Straits, a daring feat for the primitive vessels of that century. (Later that same year Cook was killed by Hawaiians in a dispute over stolen goods.) George Vancouver conducted an important survey of what is now Cook Inlet, the coast of the Kenai Peninsula, and

Prince William Sound. Interestingly, Vancouver noted—and this was 1794—that "the visible effects of the axe and saw" were already noticeable in the forests along the coast and that populations of sea otters, whales, and seals were rapidly being depleted by the Russians.

Indeed, during this period the Russians were obliterating the sea otters with incredible rapacity. Employing (more like coercing) the native Aleuts, who were skilled hunters and trappers, the Russians virtually laid waste to entire colonies of otters, moving southward year after year until they reached the Mendocino coast of California. As for the Aleuts, they themselves nearly disappeared due to disease.

Within 50 years of Bering's 1741 voyage, the central geographic facts about Alaska were known to the world, and one error after another was corrected. The maps began to fill with fascinating details. There were enormous rivers, like the Yukon and Copper, and towering mountain ranges, including one massif—called by the natives "Denali"—that appeared as high as the great peaks of the South American Andes. Glaciers abounded, in appearance like those of Norway only much larger. The animal life was far more abundant than in Europe—islands along the coast were populated with more brown bears than people. And there were hundreds of islands, ranging in size from a pile of rocks to something on the

A view of Prince William Sound drawn by Captain Cook's shipboard artist, J. Webber. (Anchorage Museum of History and Art)

CHURCH OF
ST. NIKOLAS
ПРАВОСЛАВНАЯ
СТАЯ НИКОЛЫ Ч.

order of Hawaii's Big Island. Along the southern coast the cedar totem poles of the Haida and Tlingit towered over deep, cold bays, and in those bays were millions of salmon. The interior—the central part of Alaska—still remained a mystery.

■ SEWARD'S FOLLY

Eventually the fur trade collapsed, and the Russians, facing hard times after the Napoleonic and Crimean wars, approached that little-known real-estate magnate Abraham Lincoln about selling what was then known as "Russian-America." Lincoln was intrigued with the idea—it would constitute the last major land purchase for the United States—but he had a Civil War to fight. Two years after Lincoln was buried back in Illinois, his former Secretary of State, William Seward, concluded the negotiations begun by his mentor. After the usual rancorous Senate debate, the territory was sold to the United States for $7.2 million. Considering that Alaskan tourism currently represents an $830 million annual business, Alaska has to be one of the best investments ever made by the people of the United States. At the time, however, it was referred to as "Seward's Folly," with the common

This mid-19th-century political cartoon (above) derides the purchase of Alaska. Secretary of State Seward is handing over American gold for a chunk of Russian ice. In the background John Bull eyes the scene suspiciously. (Library of Congress). Russian tradition lives on in the village of Nikoaevsk on the Kenai Peninsula as represented by the town church of St. Nikolas (opposite).

ALASKA HISTORY TIMELINE

30,000 yrs ago	First hunters cross an Ice Age land bridge between Asia and North America, the first of many migrations over the next 26,000 years.
4,000 yrs ago	Déne (Athabaskans) from whom Apaches are descended cross the land bridge.
2,500 yrs ago	Eskimos arrive.
1700s	Kaigani Haida Indians migrate up the coast to Prince of Wales Island, driving out the resident Tlingit.
1728	Vitus Bering explores Bering Sea for Russia and confirms that Asia and North America are separate continents.
1778	British navigator Captain Cook explores the coast of Alaska and meets with Russian fur traders.
1779	Cook's ships, loaded with sea otter furs, reach Canton. Their cargo finds eager buyers. News of this starts the Northwest Coast fur trade.
1799	Russian territorial governor Alexander Baranof buys a parcel of land from the Tlingit and founds Sitka to use as a fort.
1816	Russian navigator Otto von Kotzebue visits the Eskimo village 30 miles north of the Arctic Circle that now carries his name.
1830s	American whalers arrive in the north Pacific and sail back to New England with ships full of whale oil, baleen, and walrus ivory.
1867	U.S. Secretary of State William H. Seward buys Alaska for $7.2 million from the Russians.
1878	Salmon canneries open at Klawock and Old Sitka.
1880	Joe Juneau and Richard Harris find gold near the site of present-day Juneau.
1884	Protestants divide up Alaska for missionary purposes: Episcopalians get the Yukon; Moravians, the Kuskwim; Baptists, Kodiak Island.
1891	Rev. Sheldon Jackson introduces reindeer into Alaska.

1896–1898	Klondike Gold Strike in the Yukon. Prospectors travel to the placer districts via southeast Alaska.
1899	Union Pacific magnate Edward Harriman takes John Burroughs, John Muir, William Dall, and photographer Edward Curtis to Alaska.
1912	Katmai and Novarupta volcanos erupt, turning the Katmai region from a land of tall grasses and scattered trees into a barren waste.
1913	First successful ascent of Mount McKinley.
1917	Mount McKinley National Park (Denali) established.
1925	Diphtheria epidemic breaks out in Nome and dog sledders race over 674 miles in six days carrying anti-toxin serum to inoculate citizens. Now commemorated as the annual Iditarod dogsled race, which covers 1,100 miles from Anchorage to Nome.
1942	Japancsc bomb Dutch Harbor and occupy Attu and Kiska islands; all 42 native Aleutians are taken to Japan. Construction on the Alaska Highway begins, connecting Alaska to the Lower 48.
1957	Oil is discovered on the Kenai Peninsula.
1959	Alaska becomes 49th state.
1964	A 9.2 magnitude earthquake, the strongest ever recorded on the North American continent, hits Alaska on Good Friday.
1971	Alaska Native Claims Settlement gives Aleuts, Eskimos, and Indians title to 44 million acres of land.
1977	800-mile-long oil pipeline completed from Prudhoe Bay to Valdez. Oil begans to flow.
1988	Alaskans visit the Soviet city of Providenyia, opening up the border between the United States and the eastern Soviet Union.
1989	Exxon supertanker spills more than 240,000 barrels of Prudhoe Bay crude oil into Prince William Sound.

THE SEATTLE POST-INTELLIGENCER.

VOL. XXXII. NO. 62. SEATTLE, WASHINGTON, SATURDAY, JULY 17, 1897. EIGHT-PAGE EDITION.

LATEST NEWS FROM THE KLONDIKE.

9 O'CLOCK EDITION.

GOLD! GOLD! GOLD! GOLD!

Sixty-Eight Rich Men on the Steamer Portland.

STACKS OF YELLOW METAL!

Some Have $5,000, Many Have More, and a Few Bring Out $100,000 Each.

THE STEAMER CARRIES $700,000.

Special Tug Chartered by the Post-Intelligencer to Get the News.

The Latest Reports From the New Eldorado Arrive This Morning—Interviews With Those Who Have Come Down From the North With New-Found Fortunes—The Recent Strikes Seem to Be as Rich as Reported—There Is Plenty of Gold, But Only the Hardy and Provident Can Secure It—No Man Who Is Without a Suitable Outfit Should Tempt Fortune in That Remote Region—There Will No Doubt Be a Great Rush for the New Discoveries, and the Majority Will Outfit In and Leave From Seattle.

BRINGING BACK GOLD.

THE LAND OF GOLD.

Gold fever strikes Seattle on July 17, 1897. The city's mayor resigned to join the exodus northward.

perception being that the Russians had extracted all the valuables from the region before selling it.

Alaska's riches had not nearly been depleted, though, and in the years to come Americans learned about fur seals, whales, halibut, salmon, herring and, finally, in 1897, gold. At first it was Klondike gold, a Yukon strike reached most easily from the Alaskan coastal settlement of Skagway. A depression-weary American public leapt at this opportunity for instant wealth, and within a matter of weeks over 100,000 men (with a few women and children) rushed for their stake in America's last great frontier. Among them was the mayor of Seattle, who resigned and headed north. Indeed, the Klondike gold rush and opening of Alaska has been called North America's "Last Grand Adventure, the ultimate human saga in the conquest of North America," by author William Bronson, a chronicler of the event.

This was the momentous event that drew impressionable young writers Jack London *(The Call of the Wild)* and Robert Service *(The Cremation of Sam McGee* and *The Shooting of Dan McGrew)* into the northern light country. Eventually gold was discovered in locations across Alaska, from Birch Creek near Circle City to the interior settlement that would one day become Fairbanks to the hills above Nome on the Seward Peninsula. Gold drew prospectors, and all the detritus that follows prospectors, into nearly every corner of the territory.

Ultimately, it was big eastern mining ventures that profited the most from the Alaska-Yukon gold strikes. (Anchorage Museum of History and Art)

■ Alaska's Naturalists

Following the official expeditions of William Dall (1866) and Henry Allen (1885), a different sort of explorer, more tourist than government-sponsored geographer, began to venture north into Alaska. One of the first of these new private undertakings was led by Union Pacific magnate Edward Harriman, who in 1899 took naturalists John Muir and John Burroughs, along with photographer Edward Curtis, on a cruise trip north to Alaska. Muir had first visited the area in 1879 and was delighted for the opportunity to explore the "wonderland" of such places as Glacier Bay again. It is interesting to note that the glacial ice observed by Muir in Glacier Bay in the last century has now receded 25 miles farther up into the bay, a result, many scientists believe, of global warming.

The most significant event in the early years of this century was the formation of Mount McKinley National Park in 1917, largely as a result of the work of hunter-naturalist Charles Sheldon, author of *Wilderness of Denali.* Years later, national monument status was conferred on both Katmai (1918) and Glacier Bay (1925). These would form an important precedent, and help shape public perceptions of the territory as a nature refuge as well as a treasure trove of natural riches.

■ Japanese Invade Alaska

The United States has experienced two foreign invasions since the War of 1812. The first was Pancho Villa's raid on Columbus, New Mexico in 1916; the second was in June of 1942, when a sizable Japanese naval force overwhelmed U.S. military installations on Kiska Island in the Aleutians.

Within months the Japanese Imperial forces controlled Attu, Shemya, and Amchitka islands. The generals and admirals were interested in Alaska for several reasons. First, Admiral Yamamoto was

U.S. troops land on the west arm of Holtz Bay on Attu Island to recapture the island from the Japanese on May 11, 1943. (Underwood Archives, San Francisco)

concerned about the aircraft carriers that had escaped destruction at Pearl Harbor. He planned to lure them into the North Pacific, where they would be vulnerable to heavy land-based bombers. Second, the Japanese high command needed a North American base from which to launch attacks against strategic targets on the U.S. West Coast, especially the Boeing aircraft plant in Seattle. And finally, this invasion would be a critical diversion from the Battle of Midway.

The construction of the Alaska Highway progressed at the astonishing speed of eight miles per day in spite of all the natural obstacles in its way. It was built in order to move ground troops into Alaska in the event of a large-scale Japanese invasion.

The key battle that restored American control over Alaska was fought in May of 1943 at Attu Island, 1,700 miles west of Anchorage. Over 34,000 U.S. ground troops were involved in the operation. Enemy losses in the battle exceeded 2,000, including hundreds of young infantrymen who committed suicide in "Massacre Valley" rather than surrender. It was during the Attu battle that U.S. forces retrieved an intact Japanese Zero, designed by the skilled engineers of Mitsubishi. The study of this sophisticated aircraft helped the Allies better prosecute the air war in Asia and Europe.

During this same period the Alaska Highway was built in order to move ground troops into Alaska in the event of a large-scale Japanese invasion. The road extended 1,500 miles from Dawson Creek in Alberta to Fairbanks in central Alaska. It was opened to the public in 1948, and, primitive though it was, the Alaska Highway led to the first wave of post-war immigration into the Alaskan Territory.

Homeseekers!

Come Where Land Is Cheap and Make Your Own Property Valuable

Much of Alaska, America's last frontier, is still public domain and offers opportunities for homestead settlement—free and exempt from taxes, adjacent to The Alaska Railroad and near established markets,—to those possessing the vision, spirit and virility of our pioneer forefathers.

Of Alaska's total area of 590,884 square miles, it is estimated that approximately 32,000,000 acres are suitable for cultivation by clearing, and about the same acreage is suitable for grazing.

There are two districts adjacent to The Alaska Railroad suitable for agricultural development and settlement: The Matanuska Valley near Anchorage in south central Alaska, and the Tanana Valley in the central interior where the thriving city of Fairbanks is situated. Both are on the line of The Alaska Railroad.

The lands in the Matanuska Valley have been withdrawn from entry pending the completion of plans of the Alaska Rural Rehabilitation Corporation (a Government corporation), headquarters Palmer, Alaska, which is in charge of the colonization project in the valley.

Complete information relating to homesteads and agricultural possibilities in Alaska will be promptly and gladly supplied by

The Alaska Railroad

Transportation and Markets

The Matanuska and Tanana valleys have excellent transportation facilities — not only within themselves, but also to markets located at considerable distances from the sources of production. In addition to the railroad and river transportation, there is available from Fairbanks by automobile, nine hundred and fifty miles of road, and from Anchorage and Matanuska, two hundred and seventy-five miles of road. These roads are built and maintained by the Alaska Road Commission with funds provided by the Federal and Territorial governments. The Alaska Road Commission is engaged in an active and ever-increasing program year by year for the extension of roads already established.

Schools

The school system of Alaska consists of Municipal, District, Rural and Federal schools. The first three are under the general supervision of the Territorial Commissioner of Education, while the latter are under the supervision of the Commissioner of Indian Affairs of the U. S. Department of the Interior. The system also includes the University of Alaska, Fairbanks, Alaska, the affairs of which are administered by a Board of Trustees with the president of the University as chief executive officer.

This 1930s promotion encourages homesteaders to relocate to Alaska, preferably somewhere near the route of the Alaskan Railway, which ran this ad in one of their brochures. (Courtesy of Brad S. Lomazzi, Western Railroad Collectibles)

■ STATEHOOD

Just as their ancestors had endured the travails of the Oregon Trail to reach the West Coast, a new generation of American homesteaders put up with axle-deep mud and jarring ruts to reach the wide open country of the Last Frontier. Here they encountered challenges and opportunities. For one thing, any person living on 160 acres for five years could have the land forever. (The homesteading

This commemorative bronze medallion celebrates Alaskan statehood. (Courtesy of Ken Berger)

program no longer exists.) For another, along the Pacific Coast there were canneries hiring, and lumber mills opening up, and gold mines in need of workers. In 1954 the first pulp mills opened in Ketchikan, and in 1957 Atlantic Richfield discovered oil at Swanson River on the Kenai Peninsula.

Two years later, on January 3, 1959, Alaska was admitted to the Union as the 49th state. Almost immediately, and largely through the efforts of Supreme Court Justice William O. Douglas (a noted conservationist), the nine-million-acre Arctic National Wildlife Range was established in the extreme northeast corner of the state. This wildlife refuge is now over 19 million acres in size—larger than the state of Maine. Just as the fledgling state was preparing for a promising future, a major natural disaster struck. On March 27, 1964, Alaska was devastated by the most violent earthquake to hit North America since the New Madrid earthquake of 1812. Measuring 9.2 on the Richter Scale, the earthquake leveled parts of Anchorage and generated killer tidal waves that nearly destroyed the coastal towns of Kodiak, Valdez, and Seward. To this day survivors recount stories of great holes opening up in the earth and swallowing houses, and ten-story waves thundering in from the sea to drown seaside villages.

The central business district of Anchorage was devastated by the 1964 earthquake. (Anchorage Museum of History and Art)

■ MODERN ALASKA

The 1970s got off to a strange start when, in 1971, President Nixon ordered the detonation of an atomic bomb on the island of Amchitka, destroying a sea otter colony in the process. A more positive development was passage of the Alaska Native Claims Settlement Act, which allowed Native Alaskans to select over 40 million acres of federal lands for village, tribal, and individual ownership. For the first time in U.S. history, native populations were given a settlement that recognized their long (thousands of years) tenure on the land.

In 1974, construction began on a pipeline designed to carry oil 800 miles from Prudhoe Bay on the Arctic Ocean south to Valdez in Prince William Sound. In order to send hot oil over the Arctic permafrost without melting it, the three-foot-wide pipe had to be insulated and elevated above the ground. Construction crews scaled mountain ranges, crossed rivers, and battled the elements, until in August of 1977 the first oil was sent down the pipeline to Prince William Sound, completing one of the most impressive engineering feats in history.

Three historic events marked the eighties. The first was the Alaska National Interest Lands Conservation Act, signed into law by President Jimmy Carter on December 2, 1980. This bill—passed over the vehement protestations of the Alaskan congressional delegation—effectively doubled the lands administered by the National Park Service and tripled the size of the wilderness system. Many new parks—Gates of the Arctic, Kenai Fjords, and Wrangell-St. Elias (biggest park in the world)—came into being at this time. The second development was the boom and bust of oil revenues, from an astonishing flood of money in the early 1980s to a crash in oil prices in 1985 that sent Alaska's economy reeling. The third development was an unmitigated disaster—the grounding of the Exxon *Valdez* near Valdez on March 24, 1989. This was the worst oil spill in U.S. history and dumped over 11 million gallons of crude oil into the same Prince William Sound. The once-rich fisheries of Prince William Sound still have not fully recovered from the effects of this catastrophe.

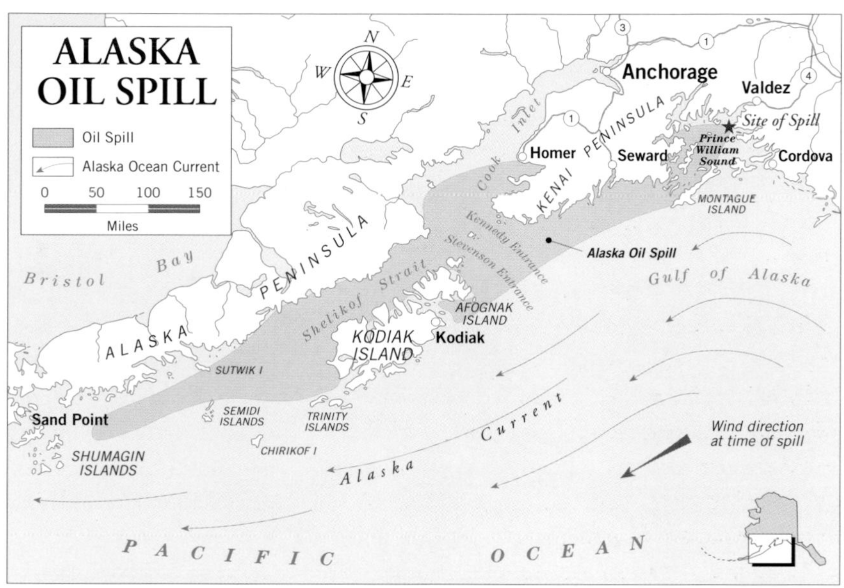

The dawn of the 21st century has brought new variations on the old theme of boom and bust, new voices arguing for development and new voices making the case for conservation. The biggest problems faced by Alaska continue to be in the area of natural resources—overfishing of the north Pacific, particularly by Asian factory fleets; overharvesting of timber in Southeast Alaska, which threatens to destroy historic salmon fisheries; the steady loss of oil in the once-immense Prudhoe Bay field; and continued contentious debate about whether to open up the Arctic Refuge to oil drilling. A century from now, this will all be history. One hopes that the fisheries will still be there, and the forests, and all else that, since the beginning of time, have helped to define this remarkable place the natives proudly called Alyeska, the Great Land.

Chief Ano-Tlosh of the Taku Tlingit tribe. (Bancroft Library, U.C. Berkeley)

P E O P L E

AS A UNIVERSITY TEACHER IN NORTHERN ALASKA for half a dozen years, I came to know the people of the state. They were my students, my colleagues, the folks I saw in the stores and about town and in the bush every day. Alaskans are an incredibly diverse group, I came to learn, among them Yupik and Inupiaq Eskimos, Aleuts, Athabaskans, Tlingit, Tsimshian, and Haida, as well as those of European, Asian, and African descent. In Fairbanks, as with the rest of the state, the bulk of the people were of European descent, individuals whose reasons for living in Alaska were as diverse as their personal histories. We also had a sizable Korean-American community, many the children and grandchildren of pioneers who had originally come to work in coastal canneries. Near Fort Wainwright there was a large African-American community, consisting of military dependents, as well as those who came to Alaska as active-duty personnel and liked it so much they stayed. The town supported Native Alaskans from all parts of the state, who came to the university to further their education and then return to home villages.

An Inupiat girl in traditional garb. (Photo by Nick Jans)

■ PERSONALITY AND SPIRIT

The chief quality of Alaskans is independence of spirit. They are a tough and self-reliant people, and freedom is in abundance here, as on any frontier. One of the state's political parties is the Alaska Independence Party, whose expressed purpose is to secede from the Union.

The long, cold, and sunless winters create a variety of problems for Alaska's people. Many people living in the higher latitudes are effected by Seasonal Affective Disorder, which results from the body being denied a proper amount of sunlight. The light of the sun stimulates melatonin production in the pineal gland, and melatonin is essential to the circadian rhythms that control sleeping, eating, and cognition. When there is a paucity of sunlight—in Fairbanks there are only three hours of "twilight" at the winter solstice (in Barrow there is no light)—melatonin production falls off precipitously. The results range from the nearly universal symptoms of insomnia, and carbohydrate craving, to chronic "blues."

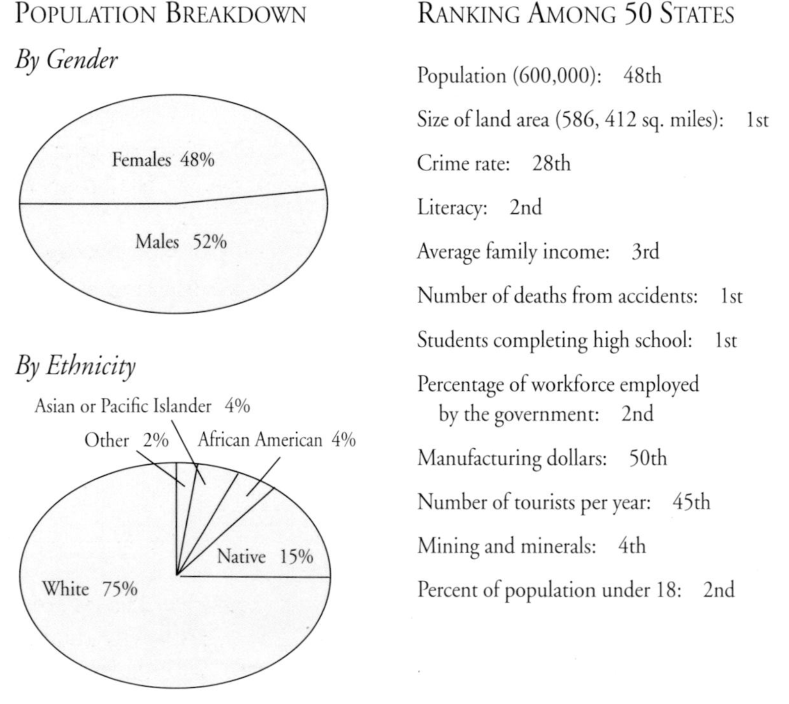

RANKING AMONG 50 STATES

Population (600,000): 48th

Size of land area (586, 412 sq. miles): 1st

Crime rate: 28th

Literacy: 2nd

Average family income: 3rd

Number of deaths from accidents: 1st

Students completing high school: 1st

Percentage of workforce employed by the government: 2nd

Manufacturing dollars: 50th

Number of tourists per year: 45th

Mining and minerals: 4th

Percent of population under 18: 2nd

Trying to make the best of their close quarters, these cabin-bound miners enjoy a New Year's dinner. (Anchorage Museum of History and Art)

Cabin fever is a related affliction familiar to all long-term denizens of the Far North. During prolonged periods of cold, people are trapped inside homes and offices for days, weeks, and months. Alcohol consumption is high.

And yet Alaska is a good place to live, particularly around Anchorage where the warmer ocean waters moderate the effects of winter, and direct flights to places like Honolulu and Cabo San Lucas are readily available. One distinct advantage of living in the state is that there is no state income tax. As a result of the Alaska Permanent Fund—state oil revenues invested in stocks, bonds, and real estate—each Alaskan resident, regardless of age, receives an annual check. In recent years the dividend has ranged between $900 and nearly $2,000. Many parents use this to establish college educational funds for their children. Currently, the value of the Alaska Permanent Fund exceeds $30 billion and represents one of the largest investment portfolios in the world.

At their best, the people of Alaska are optimistic and innovative. They approach hardship and adversity with humor and resourcefulness. To my way of thinking, the greatest resource of the state is not its fisheries, lumber, and minerals, but its people.

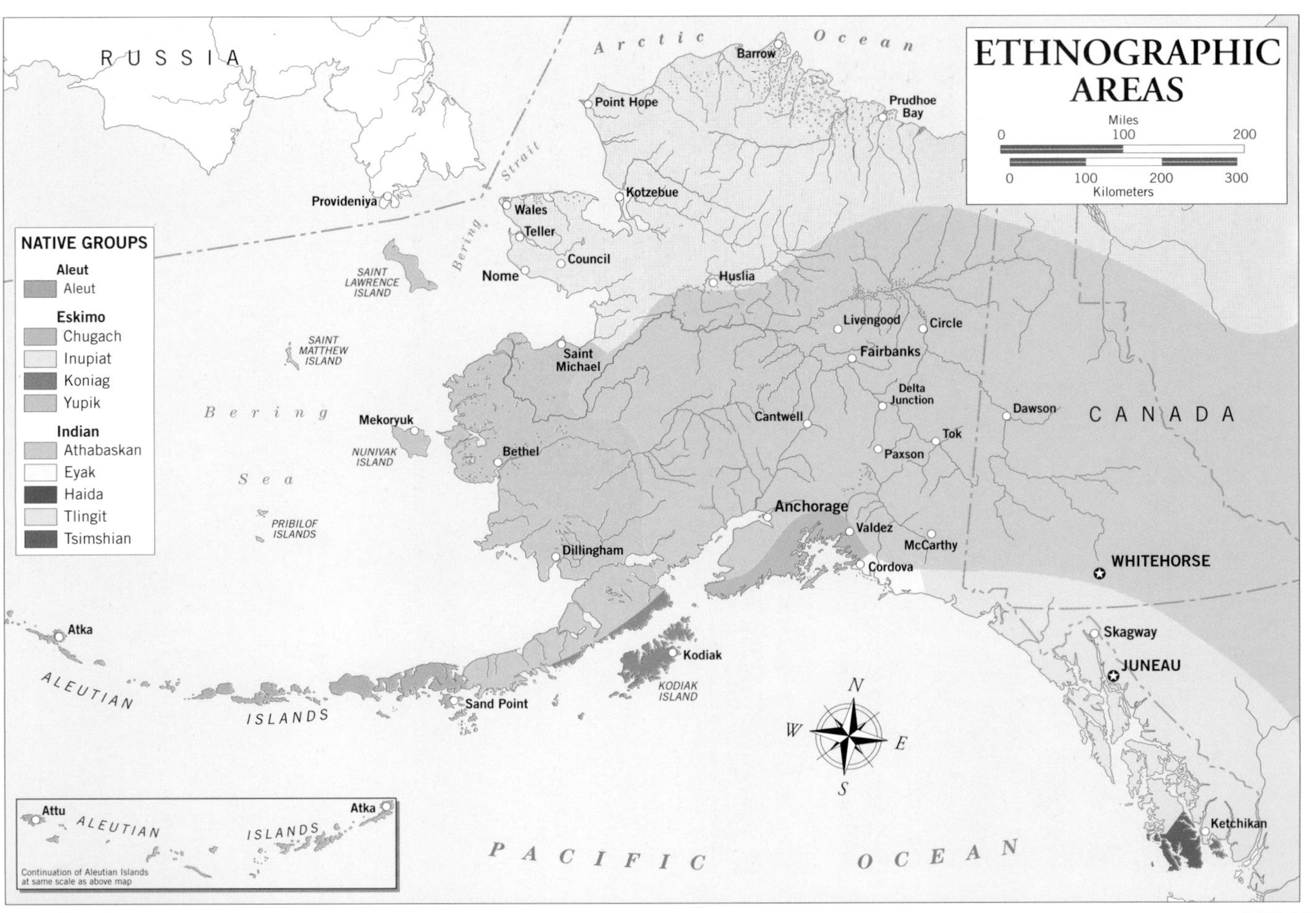
ETHNOGRAPHIC AREAS
Miles
0
100
200
0
100
200
300
Kilometers
NATIVE GROUPS
Aleut
Aleut
Eskimo
Chugach
Inupiat
Koniag
Yupik
Indian
Athabaskan
Eyak
Haida
Tlingit
Tsimshian
RUSSIA
Arctic Ocean
Barrow
Point Hope
Prudhoe Bay
Bering Strait
Providenya
Kotzebue
Wales
Teller
Council
Nome
Huslia
SAINT LAWRENCE ISLAND
SAINT MATTHEW ISLAND
Livengood
Circle
Fairbanks
Saint Michael
Delta Junction
Dawson
CANADA
Bering Sea
Mekoryuk
NUNIVAK ISLAND
Cantwell
Tok
Bethel
Paxson
Anchorage
Valdez
McCarthy
PRIBILOF ISLANDS
Dillingham
Cordova
WHITEHORSE
Skagway
JUNEAU
Atka
Kodiak
KODIAK ISLAND
ALEUTIAN ISLANDS
Sand Point
N
W
E
S
Ketchikan
Attu
Atka
ALEUTIAN ISLANDS
Continuation of Aleutian Islands at same scale as above map
PACIFIC OCEAN

NATIVE ALASKANS

Native Alaskans fall into one of two groups—those who live by the sea and those who inhabit inland areas. Those who live by the sea include the Inupiat Eskimo, who reside along the northern and northwestern coasts; the Yupik Eskimo, who make their home along the Bering Sea coast and along the lower stretches of the major rivers (Yukon, Kuskokwim); the Aleut, who are found in places like Kodiak Island; and the Tlingit, Chugach, Eyak, Haida, and Tsimshian, who inhabit the forested coastline from Prince William Sound to the Alaska Panhandle. These people traditionally had economies that were based on hunting and fishing for marine mammals, salmon, and waterfowl. The world of Native Alaskans has been dramatically changed by the arrival of modern culture. In 1971, the Alaska Native Claims Settlement Act provided Alaska's tribes with large land settlements, now owned and managed by Native corporations.

INUPIAT AND YUPIK ESKIMO

The 40,000 Eskimo people of Alaska are related to the larger Eskimo populations of northern Canada, Siberia, and Greenland (collectively known as *Inuit).* In Alaska they have settled along the Bering Sea, the Arctic Ocean, and on remote islands such as St. Lawrence and Nunivak. In 1778, Captain Cook noted in his log:

> I have frequently mentioned how remarkably the natives of this northwest side of America resemble the Greenlanders and Eskimo in various particulars of person, dress, weapons, canoes, and the like. I was struck by the affinity which we found subsisting between the dialects of the Greenlander and Eskimo and those of Norton Sound and Unalaska. . . .

A Louis Choris portrait of Eskimo residents from the Kotzebue Sound area. (Anchorage Museum of History and Art)

The two linguistic groups of the Eskimo language are the Inupiat of the Far North and the Yupik on the Bering Sea coast. Long known to outsiders as Eskimo—an Athabaskan term that means "raw meat eater"—many now proudly identify themselves by that name once given in ridicule; others prefer to be called by the more proper name, which for both Inupiat and Yupik translates as "The Real People." No offense is likely to be taken unless you commit the ultimate faux pas of calling an Eskimo an Indian, or vice versa—like calling an Irishman a Brit. Physically, Eskimos have an Asiatic look but are of a unique physical type; they are unrelated to American Indians or to any other race.

Eskimos hunting seals. (Anchorage Museum of History and Art)

Eskimo culture changed dramatically in the last century, especially in the 1980s and '90s. No longer will you find people living in traditional dome- or Quonset-shaped sod homes—roofs supported by driftwood or whale bones and covered with insulating sod. (Igloos, or ice dwellings, were not used as regular dwellings by Alaska's Eskimos, but were built as temporary trail shelters.) Eskimos now live in prefabricated housing, and are centrally gathered in various communities and towns, some of which are quite large. Rarely will you find dogsleds used for anything other than racing—snowmobiles are the primary means of off-road transportation in winter.

Traditionally, the Eskimo pursued a semi-nomadic existence, moving with the caribou, fish, whale, and ringed-seal populations that provided much of their food. Today, in many cases, their income largely derives from oil and gas leasing, outfitting and guiding hunters and fishermen, commercial fishing, and activities related to the summer tourist season. Despite many changes, the northern Eskimo still seasonally hunt various marine mammals such as seals and whales (and polar bears through special provisions in international endangered species accords). As a group they are among the world's toughest people, having lived successfully in the harshest environment of North America for at least 2,500 years.

◆ Aleut

Racially related to the Eskimo, the Aleut historically lived on the barren Aleutian Islands, on the southwest coast of Alaska, and on Kodiak Island. They were among the first Native Alaskans to have contact with European civilization. All through the last 50 years of the 18th century, a variety of Russian and English explorers and traders encountered the Aleut during expeditions along Alaska's southern coastline. Often these contacts were not friendly, and sometimes they degenerated into outright violence.

The natural world in which these people lived, though severe to the eye of the outsider, was rich in animal life that permitted their culture to thrive. Historically, the Aleut harvested the salmon and the marine mammals that provided them with food and clothing, and they fashioned grass baskets so finely woven they hold water. When the Russians appeared on the scene, as indicated earlier, they employed the Aleuts—usually in a nonvoluntary fashion—as hunters for their otter fur industry.

Today, about 7,000 Aleuts live in Alaska, most on Kodiak Island, some on the Aleutian and Pribilof islands. In the mid-1990s, the Aleut people of Kodiak sold the U.S. Department of Interior a large tract of critical wildlife habitat on Kodiak Island, which the Aleut had planned to commercially develop. In this way, everyone came out a winner—the Aleut, the American people, and the last of the great coastal brown bears.

Aleutian kayakers drawn by Choris, ca. 1825. (Anchorage Museum of History and Art)

◆ ATHABASKAN

Life for the Athabaskans has always been a difficult proposition. Living as they do in the vast, austere wilderness between the Brooks Range on the north and the coastal mountain ranges on the south, they were always only a few weeks or months from starvation. A late winter, an early spring, a short summer—any of these minor climatic variations could spell death for an entire family, clan, or valley tribe. Anthropologists generally agree that sometime in the 16th century a large scale migration of Athabaskans—perhaps prompted by environmental changes or wars with the Cree—took them south into Arizona and New Mexico, where they became known as the Navajo and Apache. Alaskan Athabaskans survived their harsh yearly cycle by hunting geese, cranes, and ducks that returned to lakes and ponds in spring. By late June and early July the sea-run salmon had begun to reach their headwater streams, and the Athabaskan caught and dried large numbers of these fish. August was a good time to begin gathering wood. September through early winter found men out in the marshes hunting moose and small game with bows and arrows. Women and children gathered forest and tundra berries, especially blueberries. Winter was spent fur-trapping and living more quietly indoors, particularly during the brutal cold spells of January. March was traditionally a time for visiting relatives in the region, before the snow began to melt and travel became quite difficult for several weeks.

Athabaskans are a diverse group, primarily united by language. This group includes the Kutchin of the upper Yukon Valley, the Koyukon of the Koyukuk River Country, the Tanana of the Tanana Valley, and the Tanacross of the Upper Tanana Valley. And this is only a partial list. Most live in small villages found near rivers, where they are readily accessible by boat in summer and dog sled or snowmobiles in winter. In many parts of Alaska—Huslia, Arctic Village—these villages can be visited by outsiders in the summer, a trip I would highly encourage.

Today, Athabaskans live in Fairbanks, as well as in more remote bush locations such as Fort Yukon. Others live near Cook Inlet and along the Cooper River near Cordova.

◆ TLINGIT

The Tlingit [pronounced KLINK'-IT] have long inhabited Southeast Alaska, and fought fiercely against incursions by the Russians in the 18th century. Tlingits are known for their carved and painted "totem" poles, which record clan figures and histories on cedar logs. Like the Aleut, the Tlingit have been historically a seafaring people who traveled through the coastal waters in kayaks and huge ocean-going canoes carved from tree trunks. They built large houses near good fishing grounds and fished for salmon, hunted deer, and trapped important fur-bearers such as the sea otter. Traditionally a slave-holding people, they established social status by sponsoring enormous feasts, called potlatches, during which the host family gave away everything it owned, setting up an obligation of reciprocity.

Today, the Tlingit still live in the small villages of the Southeast. At such places as Sitka, the Tlingit still perform their traditional dances, and their artifacts can be viewed at the museums in Sitka and Juneau.

Tlingit Indians in dance costumes pose outside of Chief Klart-Reech's house in Chilkat. (Underwood Photo Archives, San Francisco)

Eskimo Artistry

Mask, Northwest-Coast

For the Inupiat Eskimo in northwest Alaska, masks represented the spirits of animals and deities. They were made by shamans or carvers working under their direction, and usually used for ceremonial dances. The shaman also wore the mask while working his power for good hunting, weather, or health.

Eskimo Parka

Patterned after the traditional Inupiat style, this Eskimo parka is made of muskrat, wolverine, beaver, and wolf furs, with the calfskin trim representing three mountains. Typically, parkas were worn by women in the village and considered among their most elegant articles of clothing. This parka was made by Esther Norton of Kotzebue.

Coiled Grass Basket

Eskimo grass baskets are made mainly in southwest Alaska and are woven from very fine grass harvested in fall. Traditionally, seal gut colored with the dye of berries is interwoven into the baskets. The basket pictured here was woven by Lucy Post, a Yupik Eskimo weaver from Tununk village.

INK ON SEAL SKIN

Walrus on Ice Floe by Florence Malekwotkuk tells the story of her people and the animals on whom the Eskimos of Saint Lawrence Island depended on for subsistence. Malekwotkuk is presently one of the most notable artists in the Bering Sea region and her work is widely available throughout the state.

IVORY GOOSE

Walrus ivory has always been the primary material used by Eskimo carvers, and Alaska seabirds a typical subject for coastal and island artists. This carving was done by Ted Mayac, Sr., from King Island Village. He is especially noted for his attention to detail and his careful coloring.

SEA MONSTER BOWL

This wooden bowl from Nunivak Island features a mythological creature, a favorite motif of Bering Sea artists. Yupik Eskimos painted bowls and other wooden objects for ceremonials such as the bladder festival, messenger feast, and the launching of a new kayak. Circa 1945; artist unknown.

(All photos courtesy of Anchorage Museum of History and Art)

W I L D L I F E

ALASKA OFFERS SOME OF THE FINEST wildlife viewing opportunities in the world. Following is basic information about some of Alaska's more impressive animals and tips to increase your chances of observing them. It is always prudent to check with the State of Alaska Department of Fish & Game, *907-344-0541*, as local conditions and game populations vary both seasonally and annually. Alaska Division of Tourism will send you the beautiful and helpful "Wildlife Viewing in Alaska" map and brochure; *907-465-2010.*

■ BLACK BEARS

Black bears are forest-dwelling animals. Largely vegetarian, they are more retiring than grizzly bears, which prefer more open country. Black bears also exploit more habitats than grizzlies, and they have a higher reproductive rate. For these reasons, they are more plentiful. In fact, black bears outnumber all other types of bears found in Alaska, and there are more here than anywhere else in the United States. Areas of greatest black bear density in Alaska include the Kenai Peninsula, the perimeter of Prince William Sound, and Prince of Wales Island. In these areas there can be as many as 70 black bears per 100 square miles. The overall black bear population in Alaska exceeds 50,000.

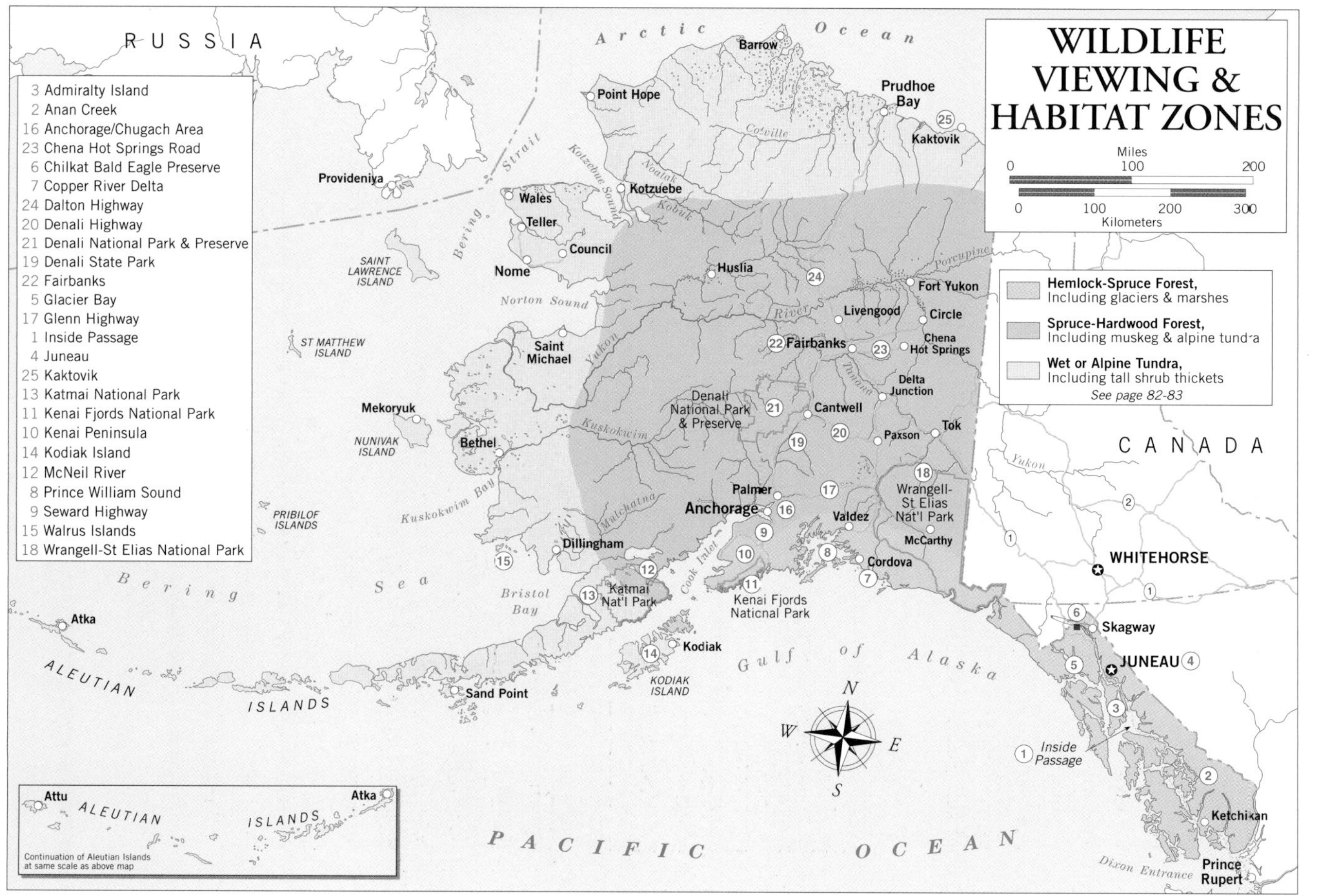
WILDLIFE VIEWING & HABITAT ZONES
Miles 0 100 200
0 100 200 300 Kilometers
Hemlock-Spruce Forest, Including glaciers & marshes
Spruce-Hardwood Forest, Including muskeg & alpine tundra
Wet or Alpine Tundra, Including tall shrub thickets
See page 82-83
3 Admiralty Island
2 Anan Creek
16 Anchorage/Chugach Area
23 Chena Hot Springs Road
6 Chilkat Bald Eagle Preserve
7 Copper River Delta
24 Dalton Highway
20 Denali Highway
21 Denali National Park & Preserve
19 Denali State Park
22 Fairbanks
5 Glacier Bay
17 Glenn Highway
1 Inside Passage
4 Juneau
25 Kaktovik
13 Katmai National Park
11 Kenai Fjords National Park
10 Kenai Peninsula
14 Kodiak Island
12 McNeil River
8 Prince William Sound
9 Seward Highway
15 Walrus Islands
18 Wrangell-St Elias National Park
RUSSIA
CANADA
Arctic Ocean
PACIFIC OCEAN
Gulf of Alaska
Bering Sea
Bering Strait
Norton Sound
Kotzebue Sound
Bristol Bay
Kuskokwim Bay
Cook Inlet
Dixon Entrance
Inside Passage
ALEUTIAN ISLANDS
PRIBILOF ISLANDS
ST MATTHEW ISLAND
SAINT LAWRENCE ISLAND
NUNIVAK ISLAND
KODIAK ISLAND
Barrow
Point Hope
Prudhoe Bay
Kaktovik
Kotzebue
Fort Yukon
Circle
Chena Hot Springs
Livengood
Fairbanks
Delta Junction
Tok
Paxson
Cantwell
Huslia
Denali National Park & Preserve
Wrangell-St Elias Nat'l Park
McCarthy
Valdez
Cordova
Palmer
Anchorage
Kenai Fjords National Park
Kodiak
Katmai Nat'l Park
Dillingham
Council
Teller
Wales
Nome
Saint Michael
Bethel
Mekoryuk
Provideniya
Sand Point
Atka
Attu
WHITEHORSE
Skagway
JUNEAU
Ketchikan
Prince Rupert
Yukon
River
Tanana
Kuskokwim
Colville
Noatak
Kobuk
Porcupine
Mulchatna
Continuation of Aleutian Islands at same scale as above map
N E S W

Anan Creek Bear Observatory, Tongass Forest

Map site: **2**

Black bears, and occasionally brown bears, fish for salmon in Anan Creek and can be observed at close range from the viewing platform and along a maintained trail. *35 miles southeast of Wrangell in Tongass National Forest, accessible only by boat or floatplane from Ketchikan or Wrangell. For more information contact the ranger district office, 907-874-2323. "SOUTHEAST" chapter.*

Chena State Park

Map site: **23**

Bear sign is often encountered along the Chena River. Probably your best bet for viewing black bears is to hike the Chena Dome Trail into the uplands north of the river, find a good vantage point and use binoculars. This is a particularly effective technique from early August until the snows fall, as black bears feed on the blueberries widely available across the tundra. *A short drive northeast of Fairbanks on Chena Hot Springs Road. "ARCTIC" chapter.*

Chugach State Park

Map site: **16**

Black bears can be seen along most of the major drainages in early spring, foraging for grass and horsetail. Later in the season they migrate into the uplands, where grizzly bears can also be observed. Access to the park is via the Eklutna Lake Road and the Eagle River Road. There is also a good trail from the Ski Bowl Road. This trail provides access to Ship Creek. *This large state park is found due east and south of Anchorage. "SOUTH-CENTRAL" chapter.*

Prince William Sound Area

Map site: **8**

If you take a boat charter in the Sound, study snowslide areas for bears, as well as beaches and intertidal areas. Because of their striking color, black bears often are visible at great distance in the green vegetation of summer, or in the golds and reds of autumn foliage. *From Valdez board boat or ferry. "SOUTH-CENTRAL" chapter.*

■ BROWN AND GRIZZLY BEARS

No other animals as powerfully evoke the North American wilderness as do the grizzly and brown bears of Alaska. The sight of a heavy silvertip grizzly lumbering over the tundra, or of a brown bear fishing for salmon in the rapids of a coastal river, will be one of your greatest memories of Alaska.

In Alaska, the interior brown bear *(Ursus arctos horribilis)* is known as the grizzly bear, and is distinguished by its silver-tipped coat, massive shoulder hump, and dished face. A large adult can be eight feet long and weigh 900 pounds and will

Kodiak brown bears looking for lunch on the island's wildlife refuge.

live 15 to 30 years. The coastal brown bear is an even larger bear than the grizzly, both because of genetics and because of the rich diet of sea-run salmon, coastal berries, and succulent vegetation. Bears can easily outrun humans. Strong swimmers as adults, their cubs can drown while following their mothers in swift glacial streams and rivers (especially in their first spring when they are so tiny).

A grizzly in a given range visually recognizes every other adult grizzly, and instantly knows where it fits in its respective social hierarchy. Social position determines order of access to prime feeding sites such as berry patches, salmon streams, or wolf kills. Fights in the wild are rare—most often bears communicate through body posturing and vocalization so as to avoid conflict. In June, during the breeding season, aggressive interactions increase between males. Body language is very important, as are facial expressions.

Most often you will see bears at a great distance. Look for a somewhat circular form that moves ponderously and low to the ground over the landscape—not at all in the long-legged manner of animals such as moose and caribou. Bear sign includes digging sites (where the bears have torn up the tundra to get at plant roots), day beds (excavated sleeping pits in the tundra or forest floor), trails (look for snagged hair on tree branches), kill sites (always avoid these), and winter dens (very hard to find in the subarctic and arctic). Often you will see sows and cubs—avoid them! Generally, grizzlies and brown bears are visible in Alaska from May through September, after which they retire to winter dens.

Authorities estimate there are about 30,000 brown bears and grizzlies in Alaska. On Kodiak Island southwest of Anchorage there are several thousand brown bears, and in years past, the bears outnumbered the people. In other parts of Alaska the bears have low-density populations; in the arctic a grizzly may have a home range of 1,800 square miles.

Brooks Falls, Katmai National Park
Map site: **13**

Brown bears catch and feed on salmon in the Brooks River and at Brooks Falls. *Commercial jets fly into King Salmon and from there you'll need to take a floatplane. Reservations are required and must be made months in advance. Call Katmai National Park, 907-246-3305. Visitors who cannot get into Brooks Camp can contact commercial air charters in Anchorage, Soldotna, and Homer. These outfits fly to lesser-known regions of Katmai Park and also to Hallo Bay, a private reserve. "SOUTHWEST" chapter.*

Dalton Highway
Map site: **24**

Grizzly bears often are seen in the vicinity of the Chandalar Shelf and Atigun Pass. In early summer they hunt Dall sheep lambs on Atigun Pass. Later they move about in the greenery eating shrubs. In the autumn, look for reddish-colored blueberry patches. Grizzlies can often be seen gorging themselves on the abundant berries in these distinctive areas. *About 300 miles north of Fairbanks. "ARCTIC" chapter.*

Denali National Park
Map site: **21**

Best viewing begins just past Mile 32 on the national park road, in what is known as Igloo Canyon. Sable Pass, at the head of the canyon, as well as all of the country from the Toklat River to the Eielson visitors center at about Mile 66 are also good places to find bears. *Entrance 237 miles north of Anchorage on the George Parks Highway. "INTERIOR" chapter.*

Kodiak Island
Map site: **14**

Access is via the town of Kodiak by floatplane to Fraser River. Brown bears gather in this area during salmon runs from early July through early August. Registration is required. The O'Malley River is another popular viewing point. *Contact Kodiak National Wildlife Refuge Headquarters just south of the town of Kodiak for information. 907-487-2600. "SOUTHWEST" chapter.*

McNeil River State Game Sanctuary
Map site: **12**

The falls on McNeil River, in the northeast corner of Katmai Park, are known for their concentrations of brown bears; up to 50 bears can be seen at one time as they feed on the salmon. *Alaskan Peninsula southwest of Anchorage, with access primarily by floatplane. Application deadline is April 1 for lottery permits issued for June, July, and August. Contact the State of Alaska Department of Fish & Game, for applications and additional information. "SOUTHWEST" chapter.*

Stan Price State Wildlife Sanctuary, Admiralty Island
Map site: **3**

Bears feed here on salmon from mid-July through mid-August. *Pack Creek, Admiralty Island. Access from Juneau via floatplane or boat. Hotels and cabins available inside and outside the park. Registration is recommended and information can be obtained from the State of Alaska Department of Fish & Game in Anchorage, 907-344-0541, or the Admiralty Island National Monument in Juneau, 907-586-8790. "SOUTHEAST" chapter.*

The arctic tundra is home to migrating herds of caribou from mid-August through September. Many ford the Kobuk River near Onion Portage (right); exact timing and crossing places vary from year to year. (Photos by Nick Jans)

■ Caribou

The sudden, unexpected migrations and equally sudden disappearances of caribou baffle wildlife biologists. Alaska has a number of large "herds" (more regional population than herds), including the Mulchatna Herd, the Porcupine Herd, and the Central Arctic Herd. Their annual migrations can easily cover over 1,000 miles.

The 800,000 caribou in Alaska prefer wet tundra and mountains during the summer and are sometimes seen near roads. In the winter caribou descend to valleys where snow level is lower and forage is easier to reach. Caribou are social animals. Herds may range in size from a few dozen to several thousand.

Denali National Park

Map site: **21**

Caribou can be encountered anywhere in the park. Often seen by Primrose Ridge just above the Savage River turnout at Mile 14, the Toklat River gravel bar, Highway Pass, Thorofare Pass, and the highlands around Wonder Lake. *Entrance is 237 miles north of Anchorage. "INTERIOR" chapter.*

Dalton Highway

Map site: **24**

Seen north of Atigun Pass between late July and early September. As the days shorten the main caribou herd moves south from its summering area on the coastal plain near the Arctic Ocean. At times you will see caribou in every direction—more than 100,000 animals on the arctic coastal plain. *Dalton Highway runs north of Fairbanks to the Arctic Ocean. "ARCTIC" chapter.*

Denali Highway

Map site: **20**

Caribou are seen throughout the summer here, especially near Tangle Lakes. *Denali Highway runs between Richardson Highway to the east and George Parks Highway on the west. Try pullouts at miles 13, 50, 117. "INTERIOR" chapter.*

■ DALL SHEEP

Dall sheep navigate treacherous sheer rock cliffs, and nimbly run, jump, and gallop across rock pinnacles with thousands of feet of vertical relief below. The lambs are especially vulnerable to predation in May, shortly after birth, and are a favored delicacy of the Alaskan wolf. About half of them do not survive the winter.

Yellowish white in color, the Dall sheep of Alaska appear almost as dots of snow on the tundra and rocks. The areas they inhabit—the rugged mountains of the subarctic and arctic—offer some of the most spectacular scenery on the continent. Despite their preference for the wildest mountains, Dall sheep can be seen at a number of points from gravel or paved roads.

Anchorage Area/Seward Highway
Map site: **16**

Just southeast of the city on the Seward Highway, Dall sheep step down off the cliffs and graze along the side of the roads. *"SOUTH-CENTRAL" chapter.*

Dalton Highway
Map site: **24**

A small herd of Dall sheep grazes on or near the top of Atigun Pass, which is the place where the Dalton Highway crosses the Arctic Divide in the Brooks Range. Sometimes these Dall sheep are literally in the road. *Dalton Highway runs north of Fairbanks to the Arctic Ocean. "ARCTIC" chapter.*

Denali National Park
Map site: **21**

A hike up Primrose Ridge from the Savage River turnout will normally reward you with a sight of the sheep. From the road itself they can be seen in Igloo Canyon, Sable Pass, and Polychrome Pass. The big rams are in the area before Memorial Day and after Labor Day—they spend the summer in the higher mountains to the west. *Entrance 237 miles north of Anchorage on the George Parks Highway. "INTERIOR" chapter.*

Glenn Highway
Map site: **17**

Look for Dall sheep in the Eklutna/Twin Peaks area (access via the Glenn Highway Mile 26.3 exit), and in the Sheep Mountain Closed Area near Mile 106 and Mile 116. *Glenn Highway (Alaska Route 1) runs from Anchorage east to Tok where it connects to the Alaska Highway. "INTERIOR" chapter.*

Kenai Peninsula
Map site: **10**

Dall sheep are seen often from the Sterling Highway at the Cooper Landing Closed Area at Mile 41.1. They are also sometimes spotted along miles 104 through 106 along the Seward Highway. Hiking further increases your chances to see the Dall sheep, but be careful, as brown and black bears are numerous here. *Southwest of Anchorage and accessible by highway. "SOUTH-CENTRAL" chapter.*

PHOTO BY NICK JANS

Always there are many rams in these lofty pastures, many old veterans with long, gracefully curved horns. There is something entrancing about a mountain-sheep horn, something about its sweep that satisfies our sense of smoothness while the ruggedness of its surface gives its character. The horns of these white sheep are especially free in their sweep, are relatively slender, and often have a pleasing amber hue.

—Adolph Murie, *A Naturalist in Alaska,* 1961

EAGLES

Four eagle species make their home in Alaska: bald eagle, golden eagle, white-tailed eagle, and the rare Steller's sea eagle. These are among the most magnificent birds in the world. The migratory eagles (bald, golden) travel from several hundred to several thousand miles to reach Alaska, attracted to the state for two reasons: fish and rodents. Eagles are monogamous, mate for life, and return to the same natal site each year, as long as the site is not disturbed by humans. They nest in steep cliff-faces and also in tall trees, including dead trees. Immature bald eagles have a dark head with some white mottling for the first couple of years, before they get the distinctive pure white hood of maturity. In Denali and in the interior, eagles subsist primarily on ptarmigan, arctic ground squirrels, and predator or road-killed animals such as Dall sheep, caribou, and moose. Along the coast, eagles prey primarily on fish. Visitors will see them stationary on tree perches, in flight at both low and high altitudes, and actively killing prey such as salmon, trout, and Dolly Varden. The wingspan of a mature bald eagle can range from six to eight feet, and the birds can fly with a salmon that weighs as much as they do.

A bald eagle scouts for prey in Homer, Alaska

Salmon Traps Eagle

The heaviest load a mature eagle can carry is ten pounds. Occasionally, it will misjudge a salmon's size and hook into a twelve- or fifteen-pounder. While out in the kayak, I once spotted an eagle down on the water, bobbing over low waves. As I drew closer, I saw a flashing metallic shape underneath—a large salmon hooked to talons. The eagle was gasping for breath, wings spread limply over the pierced salmon. I then burst out laughing as the eagle spun around, then was zipped from side to side by the running fish. Putting comedy aside, I reached down and flopped both eagle and big catch into the boat. The spent bird lay over on its side, unable to release the fish because its talons were sunk in up to the hilt. However, it wasn't a good set: the sharp curves, missing the spinal cord, were buried into side meat. When the salmon flopped, the eagle squawked as it was thrown about. I quieted both by clubbing the fish over the head, and then pushed victor and vanquished overboard onto the nearest beach.

—Michael Modzelewski, *Inside Passage,* 1991

Only in recent years has the bald eagle, national symbol of the United States, finally been removed from the endangered species list in the Lower 48 states.

Chilkat Bald Eagle Preserve

Map site: 6

The largest concentration of bald eagles in the world is found at the Chilkat Preserve. Up to 3,000 eagles flock here every autumn and can be observed into the winter, feeding on salmon and carrion. *North of Haines on the upper arm of the Lynn Canal, 80 air miles from Juneau. "SOUTHEAST" chapter.*

Inside Passage, aboard ship or ferry

Map site: 1

Visitors who travel to Alaska via the Inside Passage of Southeast Alaska will see bald eagles on a daily basis in the saltwater bays and channels. *There is no road access to this area, but a variety of cruises to choose from, see page 124. "SOUTHEAST" chapter.*

Juneau

Map site: 4

When salmon are spawning in the streams and rivers around Juneau, bald eagles can be seen. Good viewing can be found on Douglas Island as well as on Eagle River north of town in summer and autumn. *Alaska's state capital can be reached by marine ferry or by plane, but it cannot be accessed by road. "SOUTHEAST" chapter.*

Kenai Peninsula
Map site: 10

Bald eagles are quite common along the sea coast and on major streams and rivers, especially on the Kenai River. Park at one of the campgrounds near Cooper Landing and walk down to the river to look for eagles. Another possibility is to drive up to Captain Cook State Recreation Area north of Kenai where bald eagles often fish in the intertidal areas. *"SOUTH-CENTRAL" chapter.*

Prince William Sound
Map site: 8

Any of the boat charters that leave daily in the summer from Seward should lead you into prime bald eagle habitat. *Reached by boat from Valdez; or drive from Anchorage to Portage (one hour south) and take the Alaska Railroad to Whittier, then board boat or ferry (reservations necessary) for Prince William Sound.* "SOUTH-CENTRAL" chapter.

■ MOOSE

The largest member of the deer family, moose stand up to six and a half feet tall at the shoulder and weigh up to 1,800 pounds. Because they feed on submerged aquatic plants, they wade at the edge of streams, rivers, lakes, beaver ponds, and muskeg, dipping their muzzles down into the water, then raising their heads to chew and look around. Though shy and solitary, they assemble in small bands in winter and tramp the snow firm in a small area to form a "moose yard."

Moose are among the most easily seen large animals in Alaska and are found from the coastal regions to the highest mountains, from the forested interior to the Arctic Slope. Even at a distance they are easily recognized, with their stiff-legged, shuffling gait. In the winter they often amble down into cities, sometimes climbing up on rooftops to nibble at tree branches appearing above the snow.

Moose sign to look for in the wild includes the large cloven tracks (especially in soft substrates such as mud, sand, and snow), day beds in swampy areas and out on the wet tundra, shed winter hair, shed antler velvet, shed antlers, and old bones and skulls from wolf or grizzly kill sites. Moose calves are especially vulnerable to wolf and grizzly predation in the first week following birth, which normally occurs in May. This is the time of year when you are most likely to see grizzlies and wolves in hot pursuit of a young calf. Cow moose will aggressively attack predators threatening their young, and are a force to be reckoned with. Breeding season occurs in September and October, when the bulls assemble harems and challenge each other—often violently—for the right to breed the cows.

During the fall rut, bull moose are especially dangerous, and cow moose accompanied by calves should always be considered dangerous.

Chena Hot Springs Road
Map site: 23

The 56-mile Chena Hot Springs Road offers some of the best moose viewing possibilities in Alaska. Mornings and evenings are always a good time to look for moose along this road, part of the immense Chena State Park. *North of Fairbanks and off the Steese Highway at Milepost 4.9. "INTERIOR" chapter.*

Chugach State Park
Map site: 16

Moose are frequently seen throughout Chugach State Park, which is located in the eastern suburbs of Anchorage. Virtually any trail into the park will lead you into prime Alaskan moose habitat. *From downtown Anchorage follow the Glenn Highway and exit at Eklutna Road (Milepost A 26.3) Continue 10 miles to reach the park's largest lake or exit Glenn Highway at Arctic Valley Road (Milepost A 6.1) and continue 7.5 miles to enter the park. Chugach State Park office: 907-345-5014. "SOUTH-CENTRAL" chapter.*

Dalton Highway
Map site: 24

Moose are found along the length of the Dalton Highway and are almost always seen in the vicinity of Coldfoot and in the region around the Yukon River. *North of Fairbanks. "ARCTIC" chapter.*

Denali National Park
Map site: 21

Moose are widespread in Denali National Park. Especially good spots include: the timberline forest around Riley Creek Park Headquarters, the area around the bridge over the Teklanika River, Sable Pass, and all of the country from the Eielson Visitor Center west to Wonder Lake. The shores of Wonder Lake offer some the finest viewing opportunities, as the moose are seen feeding around a large picturesque lake with Denali in the background. These sites are on the park bus route. *Entrance 237 miles north of Anchorage on the George Parks Highway. "INTERIOR" chapter.*

Denali State Park
Map site: 19

Moose can frequently be seen along the George Parks Highway, which passes through Denali State Park. Other good spots accessible by trail include Troublesome Creek and Byers Lake. *Adjacent to the southern border of the national park, Denali State Park may be approached via the George Parks Highway or the Alaska Railroad. For information call Alaska State Parks, 907-745-3975. "SOUTH-CENTRAL" chapter.*

Wrangell-St. Elias National Park
Map site: 18

Moose are visible along the McCarthy Road, which runs east from Chitina at the end of the Edgerton Highway. Be especially alert along Sculpin Lake, Moose Lake, and Long Lake. *Located in Southeast Alaska, the national park is reached via the Richardson Highway, which runs from Valdez to Delta Junction. "SOUTH-CENTRAL" chapter.*

■ MUSK OX

Musk ox were eradicated in Alaska early in the 20th century, but have now been restored to several locations such as the Arctic National Wildlife Refuge and sites in western Alaska including Nunivak Island in the Bering Sea. They have flourished in their natural habitat since the Pleistocene era when they shared the tundra with woolly mammoths and saber-toothed cats. With fur 15 to 20 inches long that is reinforced by a dense undercoat, thick skin, and a layer of insulating fat, the musk ox can live comfortably with a wind chill factor of 80 degrees F below zero and colder. The animal, with its peculiarly downsloped horns and long shaggy coat of silken hairs, can weigh 500 to 900 pounds. Despite its name, the musk ox has no musk gland.

Musk ox are social animals that live in small herds and form a highly effective protective circle around their young when attacked by arctic wolves.

Gift shops at the University of Alaska, Fairbanks, and elsewhere sell small packets of the unusual soft hair, called qiviut, from which the Eskimo make yarn for woven and knitted clothing.

Large Animal Research Station, University of Alaska, Fairbanks Map site: 22

A small herd of musk ox are housed here along with caribou and reindeer. *Off Yankovich Road, off Ballaine Lake Road. Contact the Office of University Relations, 907-474-7581. "INTERIOR" chapter.*

Musk Ox Development Corporation, Palmer Map site: 16

The cooperative maintains a small herd and collects the qiviut for village artisans who weave it into garments. Each village has a distinctive decorative pattern.Guided tours daily from May to September. *East of Palmer on the Glenn Highway at Milepost 50.1. "SOUTH-CENTRAL" chapter.*

Musk ox, once rare, are now farmed in Palmer, Alaska.

Polar bears are the largest species of bear in the world and may be found wandering the arctic shores of Canada and Alaska. (Photo by Barbara Cushman Rowell)

■ Polar Bears

Standing up to 10 feet tall and weighing in excess of 1,200 pounds, the polar bear is an awesome predator. Semi-aquatic, it lives on drifting oceanic ice floes, and unlike the brown bear and black bear, it is almost exclusively carnivorous, eating seals, whales, walruses, and other marine mammals. The soles of its feet are hairy, both insulating it from cold and facilitating movement across ice. Like most bears, polar bears only tolerate the presence of other bears near an abundant food source, such as a whale carcass. For most of the year, polar bears actually live on the ice and snow, far from the shore, hunting for marine mammals.

One to four two-pound cubs are born in winter in a den of ice or snow, often inland in caves excavated from snow drifts or in soft earthen banks. In the Arctic National Wildlife Refuge, these natal den sites can be located as far as 30 miles from the nearest salt water (one of the reasons for concern about coastal oil drilling). Cubs remain with their mother for several years, but other than that polar bears remain solitary animals. Under the terms of various treaties and laws, some Alaskan native groups are permitted to seasonally hunt this rare animal.

Kaktovik
Map site: 25
Polar bears can be observed in this Eskimo community on the Arctic Ocean in the fall, when whales are killed and butchered. Access is via commercial airline to Kaktovik, and there is lodging available in town. The polar bear viewing season runs from mid-September through mid-October. Also seen in Barrow along the beach, but be certain to keep your distance—polar bears are extremeley dangerous. *"Arctic" chapter.*

■ SEA LIONS

The Steller sea lion, named for the naturalist who first wrote about the northern sea lion when he explored Alaska with Vitus Bering in 1742, is the largest of the eared seals. On average, it grows to 11 feet and weighs 2,200 pounds, but bulls can reach 13 feet and 2,400 pounds. They inhabit the coastal waters from the southern end of the southeast panhandle to the Bering Sea and live in large colonies on rocky points and capes. Like seals, sea lions are protected from indiscriminate hunting and can be hunted only by Native Alaskans. Pups of sea lions and other sea mammals are raised at the face of two glaciers in Glacier Bay.

Steller sea lions sunbathe near Cape Insurrection on the Kenai Peninsula. In 1950 105,000 of these northern sea lions were counted between the Kenai Peninsula and the Aleutian Islands. By 1990 the population dropped to under 25,000 and they were classified as a threatened species under the Endangered Species Act. Females can live up to 30 years, and males to 20.

Glacier Bay National Park
Map site: 5

Sea lions can be seen in the Inland Passage at the foot of glaciers in Glacier Bay. *Approximately 100 miles northeast of Juneau by boat or plane. Permits for pleasure boats are required. Inquire with the Glacier Bay National Park Headquarters, 907-697-2230.* *"SOUTHEAST" chapter.*

Kenai Fjords National Park
Map site: 11

Charter boats based in Seward will take you into Resurrection Bay, where sea lions are readily seen. Because Seward is a three-hour drive from Anchorage, this is probably the best opportunity for visitors to see the sea lion in Alaska. *A number of charter boats operate out of the Seward Small Boat Harbor.* *"SOUTH-CENTRAL" chapter.*

Prince William Sound Area
Map site: 8

If you take a boat charter in the Sound, you will see sea lions along rocky islands and shoreline. *From Valdez board boat or ferry.* *"SOUTH-CENTRAL" chapter.*

■ Sea Otters

A sea otter wallows in a bed of kelp. (Photo by Galen Rowell)

The sea otters' playfulness indicates a highly developed brain, especially in the frontal lobes that are associated with cognition, or thought. Though trapped to extinction in other parts of North America, they maintained a stronghold in the Far North, where they now thrive, protected by tough federal laws. They are also coming back strongly all along the Pacific Coast of Canada and the Lower 48. Currently, there are in excess of 150,000 sea otters in Alaska. They are most often seen along the shore in giant sea kelp beds, where they fish and hunt for shellfish.

Sea otters are continually grooming themselves, rubbing water-resistant oil from subcutaneous glands onto their fur to make a more effective barrier to water. They are a wonderful animal to watch, as they float in huge groups in kelp beds, nursing pups, occasionally diving for shellfish, or peacefully napping in the rolling swells. Sea otters employ a rudimentary form of tool technology, using rocks to crack open shellfish, which are placed on their chests for the opening process.

Inside Passage, aboard ship or ferry
Map site: 1

Visitors who travel to Alaska via the Inside Passage often will see otters in the saltwater bays and channels. *There are a variety of cruises to choose from, as well as the Alaska state ferries. "SOUTHEAST" chapter.*

Kenai Fjords National Park
Map site: 11

From Seward (just a three-hour drive from Anchorage) take a charter boat into Resurrection Bay, where both sea lions and sea otters crowd the waters. *A number of charter boats operate out of the Seward Small Boat Harbor. "SOUTH-CENTRAL" chapter.*

Prince William Sound
Map site: 8

Sea otters can sometimes be seen in the vicinity of the Valdez docks. It was in this area that the *Exxon Valdez* grounded on Bligh Reef in 1989, causing the worst oil spill disaster in U.S. maritime history. Many sea otters and other wild animals perished as a result. *At northern extent of Gulf of Alaska. From Valdez board boat or ferry. "SOUTH-CENTRAL" chapter.*

■ WALRUS

Walruses live in groups of up to one hundred and frequent relatively shallow water, beaches, and ice floes. Occasionally, they feed on seals and other marine animals, but their diet consists mainly of clams, which they dig for with their long tusks and shovel into their mouths with stiff whiskers. Their tusks, which both sexes possess, are also used for hauling themselves onto the ice, and rarely for fighting. The male walrus is much larger than the female and can reach a maximum length and weight of about 12 feet and 2,770 pounds.

Walrus Islands State Game Sanctuary
Map site: 15

About 10,000 walruses summer at the Walrus Islands, as well as up to 1,000 Steller sea lions and hundreds of thousands of puffins, auklets, gulls, cormorants, kittiwakes, and murres. There is also a small population of red foxes. *Located on Round Island, a windy, remote island about 70 miles southwest of Dillingham. Reached by charter from Dillingham via the Eskimo village of Togiak.* *"SOUTHWEST" chapter.*

Walruses on Round Island in Walrus Islands State Game Sanctuary. (Photo by Robert Holmes)

Harlequin ducks on Kodiak Island.

■ WATERFOWL

The migratory waterfowl and shorebirds of Alaska are a miracle of nature. The **golden plover,** for example, migrates south to Antarctica each year and then returns to Alaska in the summer. Other migrations—ducks, geese, cranes—are no less amazing, and involve the mass movement of large bird populations across thousands of miles of open sea, coastal mountains, and vast interior regions. Alaskans always hopefully await the arrival of the first birds in May, and sadly note the departure of the great flocks each August. In many ways, summer can be defined by the presence of the migratory birds. One of my favorites is the **common loon**, which nests on inland lakes and ponds. This loon is strikingly beautiful, and its black-and-white checkered plumage is best described as surreal. The bird has a haunting, yodeling song that echoes forlornly over the subarctic waters in the twilight hours. Once mated, the male and female loon construct a nest of twigs and feathers in the reeds and share nesting responsibilities—one adult feeding while the other warms the eggs or hatchlings. It's always wonderful to see the parents and young birds paddling around the lake. One of the best places to look for loons is Wonder Lake in Denali National Park.

Colorful **tufted puffins** are found in great abundance along the Pacific coast of Alaska. Puffins have thick dark bodies, distinctive white-feathered faces, and bright orange beaks that resemble those found on parrots. Puffins are social birds and their extensive nesting colonies—built into rocky ledges overlooking the sea—are widespread, particularly in the Southeast in such areas as Glacier Bay National Park. Puffins feed widely on the food resources of the open sea and coastal bays and estuaries, eating everything from crabs to young salmon. Puffin facsimiles are a favorite at gift shops in places like Homer and Kenai—kids love them.

Copper River Delta
Map site: 7

A vast, 400-square-mile river delta, where each spring millions of migratory birds stop on their way north. Snow geese, sandhill cranes, arctic terns, jaegers, great blue herons, and bald eagles are only a few of the bird species that come here. The Copper River Delta hosts an annual shorebird festival in May. *Located west of Cordova. Access by Copper River Highway, boat, or floatplane. Cordova Ranger District, 907-424-7661. "SOUTH-CENTRAL" chapter.*

Creamer's Field, Fairbanks
Map site: 22

One of the best places to observe migratory waterfowl such as ducks, geese, and cranes. Each May and September these planted fields are aswarm with tired, hungry birds either just arriving or preparing to leave. *Located on College Road near the offices of the the State of Alaska Department of Fish & Game. "INTERIOR" chapter.*

Kenai Fjords National Park
Map site: 11

A tour boat from Seward will take you through Resurrection Bay, where tens of thousands of colorful seabirds can be observed. *Seward is a three-hour drive south from Anchorage. Tours depart from the Seward Small Boat Harbor. "SOUTH-CENTRAL" chapter.*

Potter's Marsh, Anchorage Area
Map site: 16

Geese, ducks, trumpeter swans, and other waterfowl can sometimes be seen here. The best time of year to visit is between the first week of April and mid-September. Noise from the freeway running along one side of the marsh and gun-fire from the rifle range across the road make this place less than tranquil. *Located on the Seward Highway just east of town, turnoffs at mile 117.4 and 116 Seward Highway. "SOUTH-CENTRAL" chapter.*

A tufted puffin perches along the rocky coast of one of the Pribilof Islands. (Photo by Robert Holmes)

WHALES AND ORCAS

Humpback whales winter in the warm waters around Baja, Mexico and Maui, Hawaii, where visitors sometimes observe them giving birth. As spring advances over the northern hemisphere the whales respond to an ancient migratory urge and swim north. By mid-June they arrive in their rich summer feeding grounds in Alaska. At this time they are often seen by summer visitors traveling at sea. If there are humpback whales in the vicinity of your fishing boat or cruise ship you will know about it! First, whales sometimes breach—rocket out of the water and crash on to their sides with a resonant splash. Second, you will see their spray spouts as they come up to breathe. Third, you may see their flukes just before they slide beneath the surface. There are few experiences in this world as magnificent as seeing a whale at sea.

Humpbacks are not toothed whales, like sperm whales or orcas, but rather have fringed baleen plates set in their jaws. By straining water through these extensive natural filters, the humpbacks are able to feed on swimming crustaceans and small fish. Humpbacks have been observed schooling and moving through water in such a way as to concentrate their food sources, and then taking turns diving through the concentrated krill. Marine biologists operating in the north Pacific waters and utilizing hydrophones suspended from research boats have recorded the beautiful songs of humpbacks. These songs have not yet been deciphered, but the fact that many of these long compositions are repeated, virtually note for note, year after year, is intriguing. There are perhaps 2,000 humpback whales in the north Pacific, with several hundred migrating to southeastern Alaska every summer.

Orcas, or killer whales, can grow to 30 feet long. They are easy to identify when they surface because of the prominent dorsal fin. On males, the dorsal fin may be as high as six feet. Biologists use the distinctive black-and-white marking on the dorsal fin to identify particular orcas in their field study areas. Orcas have large teeth that resemble sharpened ceramic coffee mugs in size and surface appearance.

These large ocean-going predators travel in "pods," which are small groups roughly conforming to an extended family. They communicate acoustically under water. These whales are expert hunters—the wolves of the open sea. Their prey includes everything from salmon to whales (but never humans). The orca is actually, from a taxonomic standpoint, a gigantic dolphin (in much the same way that a wolverine is a giant weasel). It is thought that at least 300 to 400 killer whales live along the Pacific Coast of Alaska, although these numbers fluctuate considerably.

Glacier Bay National Park and Juneau Area

Map site: 5

Whales can be seen in Glacier Bay and the areas around the park, including Icy Strait, Chatham Strait, and Lynn Canal from early July through September. Whale watching cruises are available in Juneau. A researcher claims to have observed the same whale returning to Glacier Bay for 12 consecutive years. *Southeast Alaska at northern end of Inside Passage. Inquire at the Glacier Bay National Park headquarters* (907-697-2230) *or book a tour out of Juneau.* (See SOUTHEAST" chapter).

Inside Passage

Map site: 1

Whales are seen along the Marine Highway most often in the spring and fall, when they are migrating either north or south. *"SOUTHEAST" chapter.*

Prince William Sound

Map site: 8

Whales are sometimes observed in the southwestern part of Prince William Sound, near Montague Strait and the Gulf of Alaska. *South-central Alaska. Reached from Valdez at northern extent of Gulf of Alaska.* *"SOUTH-CENTRAL" chapter.*

Humpback whales may be seen breaching the waters of Prince William Sound every summer. (Photo by Paul Chesley)

■ WOLVES

Adult Alaskan wolves range in size from 90 to 140 pounds. Signs most often encountered in the wild include the five-toed (dog-like) tracks, kill sites (which will not be covered with ground debris as with a bear kill site), natal den sites (often old fox dens that have been enlarged), summer rendezvous sites (a day bed area for the pack), and scent marking sites (which have a pungent smell and are often located near or on prominent rocks or trees). Pups are born in the late spring. For the first few weeks, the mother remains with the cubs, while the rest of the extended family, which may include non-blood-related members, hunts. When they return, the adult wolves regurgitate, thus feeding both the mother and the cubs as they are weaned from the mother's milk. Eventually, the mother resumes hunting, and in mid-summer the pack abandons the natal den site for the summer rendezvous site, from which they hunt.

Dalton Highway
Map site: 24

Wolves are sometimes seen on Atigun Pass, where they hunt Dall sheep, and on the coastal plain, where they hunt barren-ground caribou. Wolves are trapped and hunted in this area, so they are not as easily seen as in the national parks. The caribou migration on the coastal plain begins in early August; at that time the Central Arctic Herd of around 120,000 animals moves south toward the foothills of the Brooks Range. Wolves, closely following the herd as it moves south, can be seen along the Dalton Highway in this region at that time. *Dalton Highway runs north of Fairbanks to the Arctic Ocean. For a more specific location of the herd, check with the BLM office in Fairbanks or with the State of Alaska Department of Fish & Game in Fairbanks 907-459-7200. "ARCTIC" chapter.*

Denali National Park and Preserve
Map site: 21

The best place to look for wolves is the open country that ranges from Sable Pass on the east to Thorofare Pass on the west. In the past several years, wolves have been seen on the road to Wonder Lake, but normally the sightings are at distances of 200 or more yards. Wolves are most active at night and in the twilight hours. A good place to sit and watch for them is near the bridge over the East Fork of the Toklat River, as well as near the bridge on the Toklat River. There is an active wolf den about a mile upstream from the East Fork bridge; this entire area is off limits to cross-country hiking, but with good binoculars the wolves can often be seen at dawn or dusk. There is also an active wolf den downstream of the bridge over the Toklat River. This is also an excellent area for wolf viewing. *"INTERIOR" chapter.*

Wolves are Listening

The wolves must have seen me first. In the slanted sunlight of late evening, they couldn't miss a bright orange tent, a snowmachine, and a man on the valley floor. I looked up, wondering what had spooked the sheep, and saw them: ten wolves, strung out along the ridge, silhouetted against the snow. They worked across the snowfield, down into a draw, and out of sight.

I went back to camp chores, feeling lucky. Even far back in the western Brooks Range, most packs have learned the hard way about men. But these wolves didn't run, though they paused and stared toward me. Maybe there was something about the way I stood or even what I thought that reassured them. If wolves are experts at anything, it's reading intentions.

I cooked dinner and watched the upper Noatak Valley slide into the twilight that, in late April, passes for night. As I sat alone, a chorus of howls rose from the mountain, then faded into the wind.

I awoke the next morning to more howls, much closer now. Stumbling from the tent into the bright blue day, I scanned the ridge behind me. There, a head on the skyline, five hundred yards above me in the rocks. I was being watched, and no doubt discussed. Scanning, I found other wolves as they crested the ridge. They apparently wanted to move downhill, on a course that would take them right through camp.

Slowly, one at a time, in almost imperceptible movements, they made their way down, one here, two there. If I sat and watched, they moved little or not at all, feigning indifference, plopping down and curling up as if for a quick nap. When I ducked into the tent and checked five minutes later, they'd shifted closer.

After a half hour of this, I'll admit I was getting edgy. The wide sweep of the Noatak Valley echoed with silence. I didn't exactly feel threatened, but how many people have sat calmly, alone, as a dozen wolves worked their way into camp?

All the warnings I'd heard from older Eskimos swirled back. Clarence, the master wolf hunter, had admonished me to be careful around large packs. When I replied that I wasn't afraid of wolves, and tried to counter with my white-guy-feel-good-about-wolves-they-are-our-brothers statistics, Clarence grew suddenly irritated. "Quiet! Wolves are listening right now!" His tone of voice was the same as when he'd warned me I'd unknowingly crossed some dangerous ice.

I suppose I should have waited. But what if I just sat here and they passed just on the other side of that knoll? I shouldered my camera tripod and hustled to intercept them.

continues

From the crest I spotted one gray loping off, pausing to look back. The others seemed to have evaporated. This was wolf behavior I understood. I watched and waited, was about to give up, when I spotted another lying in the brush, close enough to make me start. But though I was in plain sight a few dozen yards away, the young male ignored me, gazing off down the slope. When I moved closer, he rose, stretched, and regarded me with casual interest. When I inched closer, he moved off an equal distance. After a few minutes of this inter-species two-step, he trotted off, apparently bored by my company.

Suddenly he stopped, intent on something. He gathered himself, pounced, and came up with an ordinary-looking stick. Shaking his head like an overgrown puppy, he paraded away.

When I looked back up the hill, the rest of the pack was retreating, circling west. One big black and a limping gray seemed especially wary; they stood on the skyline, looking down. Then they were gone.

As I trudged back to camp, I kicked myself for not staying put. Then again, maybe the pack wouldn't have come any closer. I'd never know, but this much was true: we'd each taken steps toward the other, and something like peace had passed between us.

Back in Ambler, old Nelson Greist would shake his head and laugh at my earnest explanation. "Maybe they try to eat you," he said. "You just never know it."

—Nick Jans, *A Place Beyond,* 1996

PHOTO BY NICK JANS

■ Safety and Regulations

Remember it is illegal to possess migratory bird feathers and to collect antlers and skulls from national parks. The body parts of endangered marine mammals (and most marine mammals are endangered) are also protected by federal law. These laws are designed to protect wildlife from illegal activities, such as poaching, which are unfortunately a significant problem in Alaska. If you have any questions regarding souvenirs found in the field, feel free to inquire with state or federal agencies or local law enforcement officials. Hikers should understand that it is a federal crime to be in possession of an eagle feather. Authorities trying to protect wildlife have no way of knowing whether a person in the backcountry found the feather on the ground or killed a bird to get it.

◆ Words of Caution

Make noise while hiking: sing, carry a whistle, or converse loudly.
Keep food and garbage properly stored and away from your sleeping area.
If you encounter a bear, don't run. Back away slowly with eyes averted.
If you encounter a moose, don't crowd it.

A Story in the Snow

To one who lives in the snow and watches it day by day, it is a book to be read. The pages turn as the wind blows; the characters shift and the images formed by their combinations change in meaning, but the language remains the same. It is a shadow language, spoken by things that have gone by and will come again. The same text has been written there for thousands of years, though I was not here, and will not be here in winters to come, to read it. These seemingly random ways, these paths, these beds, these footprints, these hard, round pellets in the snow: they all have meaning. Dark things may be written there, news of other lives, their sorties and excursions, their terrors and deaths. The tiny feet of a shrew or a vole make a brief, erratic pattern across the snow, and here is a hole down which the animal goes. And now the track of an ermine comes this way, swift and searching, and he too goes down that white shadow of a hole. . . .

—John Haines, *The Stars, The Snow, The Fire,* 1977

HABITAT ZONES

RAIN FOREST OF THE SOUTHEAST

The Panhandle's rain forest of evergreen hemlock and Sitka spruce is the habitat of the forest-dwelling black bear, deer, flying squirrels, owls, woodpeckers, and songbirds. Millions of salmon return from the ocean to spawn in freshwater creeks, and bald eagles wait to snatch them from the water. Along the edge of the rain forest, in the waterways of the Inside Passage, live whales, porpoises, seals, and sea lions.

Sitka spruce forest

SPRUCE-HARDWOOD FOREST OF THE INTERIOR

White spruce forest

Between the coastal rain forest and the treeless tundra of Alaska's north and west is a low forest of birch, white spruce, aspen, fir, pine, and poplar trees. The forested lowlands are home to bears, moose, and wolves. On the mountain peaks and treeless tundra of higher elevations, Dall sheep and golden eagles are found.

Wet Tundra of the Arctic

Wet tundra

Dwarf shrubs and a variety of grasses and mosses grow on soggy tundra. Legumes are common near streams and lakes. Vast herds of migratory caribou, grizzlies, swans, ducks, geese, loons, jaegers, and snowy owls can be found here. Millions of mosquitoes breed in the swampy muskegs of these areas, providing food for hungry migratory birds that fly thousands of miles to summer here. On the icy sea of the far north, polar bears feed on seals and walrus.

Dry tundra

Dry Tundra

Higher elevations in the arctic and subarctic regions support dry alpine tundra, which is characterized by barren ground and rock as well as by such vegetation as lichens, grasses, sedges, berries, and some herbs. Willows grow along the streams. Feeding on these shrubs and grass are caribou herds, wolves, grizzlies, ptarmigan, and plovers.

SOUTHEAST
AND THE INSIDE PASSAGE

■ HIGHLIGHTS

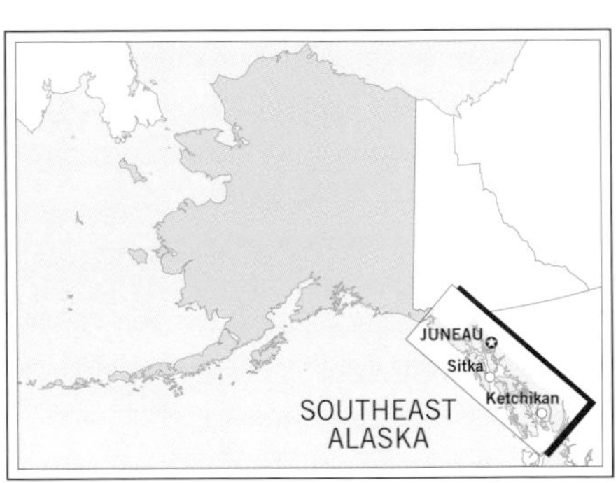

◆ MAPS

◆ PRACTICAL INFORMATION

■ LANDSCAPE AND TRAVEL

Alaska's long and narrow southeastern panhandle is made up of myriad islands, of quiet deep bays with breaching whales and of ancient forests thick with moss, where great bears lumber silently. Skies are forever lowering under some new Pacific squall, then rising unexpectedly to reveal great snowcapped mountains. Seal pups are born at the edge of glaciers that themselves "calve" into the sea. Here, too, lies the most beautiful state capital site in the United States, Juneau, which remains, even at the end of the 20th century, unconnected by road to the rest of the continent.

The best way to travel in Southeast Alaska is by ferry or cruise ship up the Inside Passage. Most leave from Bellingham, Washington (one and a half hours north of Seattle, and one hour south of Vancouver) and travel north to Ketchikan, Petersburg, Juneau, Skagway, and Haines.

You Can't Make Hay While It Rains

I never saw a richer bog and meadow growth anywhere. The principal forest-trees are hemlock, spruce and Nootka cypress, with a few pines. . . . I have found southeastern Alaska a good, healthy country to live in. The climate of the islands and shores of the mainland is remarkably temperate and free from extremes of either heat or cold throughout the year. It is rainy, however,—so much so that hay-making will hardly ever be extensively engaged in here. . . . The most remarkable characteristic of this summer weather is the velvet softness of the atmosphere. . . . I never saw summer days so white and so full of subdued lustre.

—John Muir, *Travels in Alaska,* 1879

After Fishing *by C. (Rusty) Heurlin, 1960. (Anchorage Museum of History and Art)*

The Inside Passage *maps pages 86, 87, 124 & 125*

The Alaskan Marine Highway System begins in Bellingham, Washington, plowing through the picturesque green islands of Puget Sound and up the incised coast of British Columbia. The coast becomes increasingly rugged after you pass Prince Rupert and re-enter American waters south of Ketchikan. For the next couple of

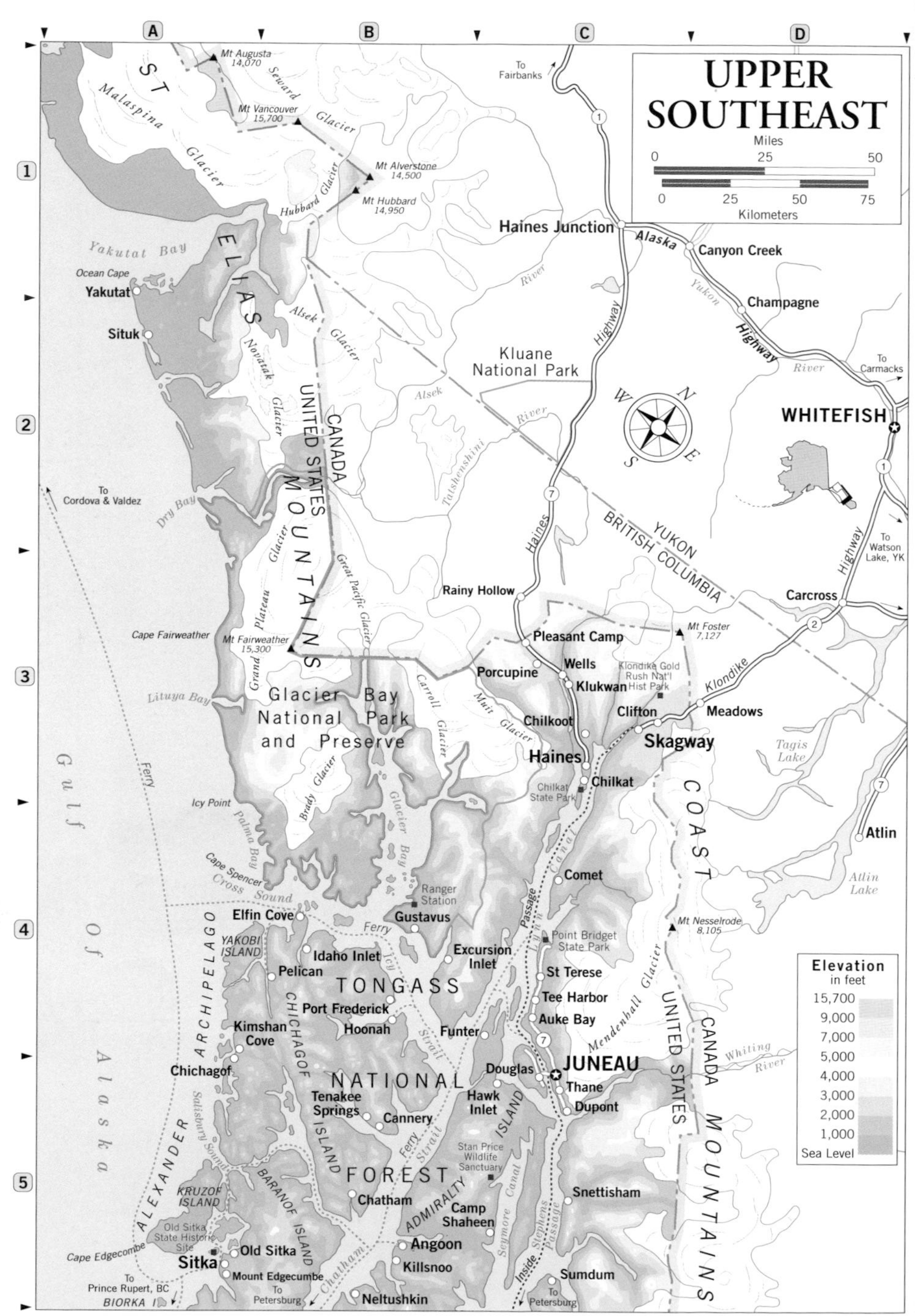

UPPER SOUTHEAST
Miles
0 25 50
0 25 50 75
Kilometers
Elevation in feet
15,700
9,000
7,000
5,000
4,000
3,000
2,000
1,000
Sea Level
A
B
C
D
1
2
3
4
5
Mt Augusta 14,070
Mt Vancouver 15,700
Mt Alverstone 14,500
Mt Hubbard 14,950
Mt Fairweather 15,300
Mt Foster 7,127
Mt Nesselrode 8,105
Seward Glacier
Malaspina Glacier
Hubbard Glacier
ST ELIAS MOUNTAINS
COAST MOUNTAINS
To Fairbanks
Haines Junction
Alaska Highway
Canyon Creek
Champagne
Yukon River
To Carmacks
Kluane National Park
Alsek River
Alsek Glacier
Tatshenshini River
WHITEFISH
To Watson Lake, YK
Carcross
Klondike Highway
Meadows
Tagis Lake
Atlin
Atlin Lake
YUKON
BRITISH COLUMBIA
CANADA
UNITED STATES
Yakutat Bay
Ocean Cape
Yakutat
Situk
Novatak Glacier
To Cordova & Valdez
Dry Bay
Glacier
Plateau Glacier
Grand Plateau
Great Pacific Glacier
Cape Fairweather
Lituya Bay
Glacier Bay National Park and Preserve
Carroll Glacier
Muir Glacier
Brady Glacier
Glacier Bay
Haines Highway
Rainy Hollow
Pleasant Camp
Porcupine
Wells
Klukwan
Klondike Gold Rush Nat'l Hist Park
Clifton
Skagway
Chilkoot
Haines
Chilkat
Chilkat State Park
Gulf of Alaska
Ferry
Icy Point
Palma Bay
Cape Spencer
Cross Sound
Ranger Station
Elfin Cove
Gustavus
YAKOBI ISLAND
Idaho Inlet
Icy Strait
Pelican
Excursion Inlet
TONGASS NATIONAL FOREST
Port Frederick
Hoonah
CHICHAGOF ISLAND
Kimshan Cove
Chichagof
Funter
ALEXANDER ARCHIPELAGO
Comet
Passage
Lynn Canal
Point Bridget State Park
St Terese
Tee Harbor
Auke Bay
Mendenhall Glacier
JUNEAU
Douglas
Thane
Dupont
Whiting River
Hawk Inlet
Tenakee Springs
Cannery
Salisbury Sound
Ferry Strait
Stan Price Wildlife Sanctuary
ADMIRALTY ISLAND
Seymore Canal
KRUZOF ISLAND
BARANOF ISLAND
Chatham
Camp Shaheen
Snettisham
Old Sitka State Historic Site
Cape Edgecombe
Old Sitka
Angoon
Killsnoo
Sitka
Mount Edgecumbe
To Prince Rupert, BC
BIORKA I
To Petersburg
Chatham
Neltushkin
Inside Stephens Passage
Sumdum
To Petersburg

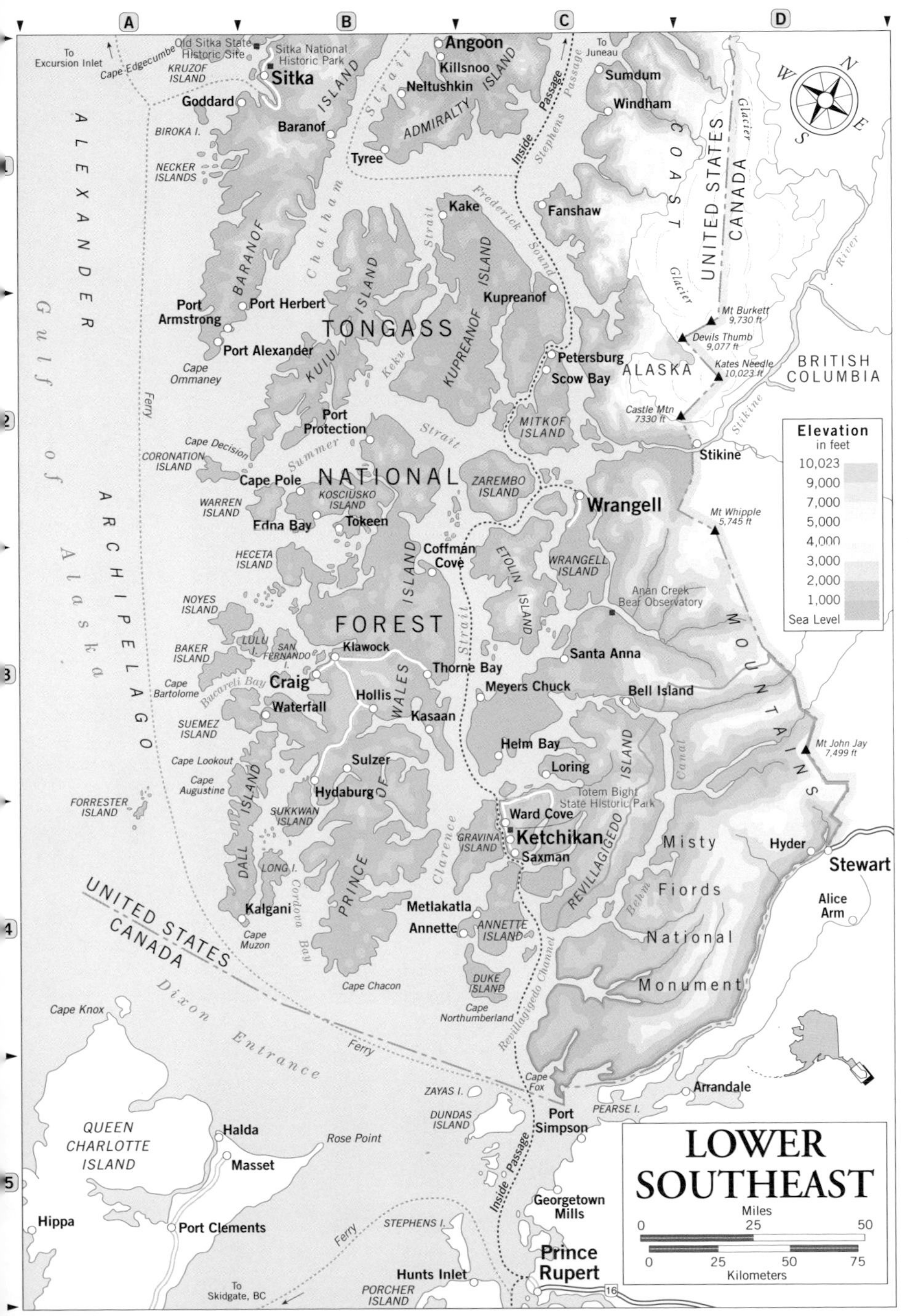
LOWER SOUTHEAST
Angoon
Killisnoo
Sitka
Sitka National Historic Park
Old Sitka State Historic Site
Goddard
Baranof
Tyree
Neltushkin
ADMIRALTY ISLAND
Sumdum
Windham
Kake
Fanshaw
Kupreanof
TONGASS NATIONAL FOREST
Port Herbert
Port Armstrong
Port Alexander
Petersburg
Scow Bay
ALASKA
BRITISH COLUMBIA
UNITED STATES
CANADA
COAST MOUNTAINS
Port Protection
Cape Pole
Edna Bay
Tokeen
Wrangell
Stikine
Coffman Cove
Anan Creek Bear Observatory
Klawock
Craig
Thorne Bay
Hollis
Waterfall
Kasaan
Santa Anna
Meyers Chuck
Bell Island
Helm Bay
Loring
Sulzer
Hydaburg
Totem Bight State Historic Park
Ward Cove
Ketchikan
Saxman
Hyder
Stewart
Alice Arm
Misty Fiords National Monument
Kalgani
Metlakatla
Annette
Port Simpson
Arrandale
Halda
Masset
Hippa
Port Clements
Georgetown Mills
Hunts Inlet
Prince Rupert
QUEEN CHARLOTTE ISLAND
ALEXANDER ARCHIPELAGO
Gulf of Alaska
Dixon Entrance
Mt Burkett 9,730 ft
Devils Thumb 9,077 ft
Kates Needle 10,023 ft
Castle Mtn 7330 ft
Mt Whipple 5,745 ft
Mt John Jay 7,499 ft
Elevation in feet
10,023
9,000
7,000
5,000
4,000
3,000
2,000
1,000
Sea Level
Miles
0 25 50
0 25 50 75
Kilometers

days you will travel through a wonderland of islands both large and small, expansive bays and inlets, massive glaciers, towering mountains. Everywhere the northern coastal forests will amaze you—lush and green as a tropical rain forest. Sometimes you will spot wildlife—moose, bears, deer—going about their affairs along the beaches and coves. Out on the water you will often see sea otters, sea lions, killer and humpback whales, sea gulls, and bald eagles in primordial abundance.

There will be stops, of course, and time to explore the crowded waterfronts that smell of fish, salt air, brewing coffee, diesel engines, and wood-burning cabin stoves. But then you will be back on the water—in a world too vast to be captured on a photograph or scribbled about on a postcard. North of Ketchikan, turning west into Clarence Strait, you will enter one of the last great wilderness areas on earth. Prince of Wales Island will be on the west—third largest island in the United States—and on the east there will be a rich profusion of smaller islands, all part of the immense Tongass National Forest. Farther north you will pass Admiralty Island, where most valleys have more bears than people. Approaching Juneau through spectacular Stephens Passage, on a clear day, you'll spot to the east the forbidding peaks and glaciers of the Tracy Arm-Fords Terror Wilderness.

Much of this area is included in the Tongass National Forest. About one-third of the Tongass has been designated "commercial forest lands," which means it is slated to be clear-cut sooner or later, but there are a dozen wilderness areas in the area, including much of Admiralty Island, small portions of Baranof Island and Prince of Wales Island, and Misty Fiords National Monument.

One of the chief attractions of the Tongass is the 150 public recreational cabins maintained by the U.S. Forest Service, which are reached only by floatplane or boat.

The towns of Southeast Alaska partake of two worlds—the sea and the land. They are surrounded by glaciers and mountains and forests, and yet they are as much a part of the salt water as the herring gulls and the hermit crabs. The people who live in them work in the forests, on the sea, or in commerce, including tourism. They must contend with being isolated from the mainland highways,

A calm summer night in Glacier Bay. The peaks of Mount Crillon, over 12,000 feet high, and Mount Bertha, 10,000 feet high, are visible in the background. (following pages) A spectacular vista appears as the clouds part over the Inside Passage near Petersburg.

MARTINA

connected to the rest of the country only by satellite dishes, telephones, and computers. The towns of the Panhandle are different from all other island and coastal towns in the United States. Because they are on the busy Marine Highway, and are also easily accessed from the air, visitors will not find the xenophobia—the distrust of outsiders—that sometimes exists in isolated rural or bush communities. There is a worldliness about these Southeast towns, a tolerance of differences, a warm friendliness, and a natural generosity.

■ KETCHIKAN *map page 87, C-4*

SOUTHEAST

Ketchikan's economy is based on three industries: salmon fishing, logging, and tourism. The town has found itself in the national news frequently in the past decade at the center of an intense debate over clear-cutting old-growth forest. Recent federal legislation has restricted harvests and forced large multi-national companies to shut down pulp mills in Ketchikan and Sitka. This is good news for

John Neary harvests bears' bread, a wild fungus, from the forest near Stink Creek.

Clear-cutting, such as this on Admiralty Island, has been a controversial issue in this region. Recent legislation has restricted this sort of logging.

salmon (whose spawning streams were being destroyed because of siltation), but bad news for people working in the timber industry.

The population of Ketchikan Gateway Borough and city is 14,275 (making it the fourth largest city in Alaska), but that may decrease if present trends continue. The town rambles along the coast for quite a distance, never more than a dozen blocks wide, and climbs the hills on wooden stairways that offer pretty views over the neighboring islands.

Ketchikan began as a Tlingit salmon fishing camp, called *Kitschk-Hin,* or "The Creek of the Thundering Wings of an Eagle." It subsequently became a center for salmon canneries (the industry collapsed as the fisheries were depleted). Today, you'll find the remnants of wilder days, including a red-light district (Creek Street), a bordello turned into a museum (Dolly's House), and a lively local bar, the Sourdough. The **Totem Heritage Cultural Center** at 601 Deermount Street displays 33 totem poles, the largest exhibit of original totems in the United States. The city walking tour map is available at the visitors center on Front Street. A

Deer Mountain rises above Bar Harbor in Ketchikan

short walk from the Totem Heritage Cultural Center is the **Deer Mountain Hatchery,** always an interesting and educational stop. If you have time, a number of local tour operators can transport you by boat or floatplane to the spectacular **Misty Fiords National Monument,** which is only 30 miles east of Ketchikan. As with Petersburg, Sitka, and Juneau, Ketchikan has daily jet service from Seattle and Anchorage via Alaska Airlines.

■ MISTY FIORDS *map page 87, C&D-3&4*

At the southern end of the Tongass National Forest, directly beside the Canadian border, is a magnificent wilderness of some 2.3 million acres known as Misty Fiords National Monument. The name powerfully evokes the place—perpetually misty and characterized by a multitude of deep fjords. Thundering waterfalls drop hundreds of feet from sheer rock cliffs. Mountains rise vertically from the cold salt water to the snowfields. Everywhere the northern rain forest vegetation is lush and green.

Reached from Ketchikan, this area is a favorite for boating and for fishing. Camping can be tough because the tides range upwards of 20 feet, and dry flat areas are often a challenge to find. One of the most popular ways of visiting Misty Fiords is on a larger-sized boat, where passengers can sleep comfortably on board—somewhat similar to touring Lake Powell in Arizona on a houseboat. Wildlife ranges from black and brown bears to moose and mountain goats, with the waters offering the normal Pacific complement of whales, seals, and sea lions. The area is also known for its bald eagle population.

The Totem Heritage Cultural Center has the largest exhibit of totem poles in the United States.

■ Prince of Wales Island *map page 87, B-2, 3&4*

At 2,231 square miles, Prince of Wales Island is easily the largest island in Southeast Alaska. In fact, it is the third largest island in the United States—the first being the big island of Hawai'i and the second Kodiak Island. Because of the wet maritime climate, much of Prince of Wales Island is heavily forested. In recent decades up to a dozen active logging camps operated on the island. More recently, though, timber harvesting has declined for several reasons: available allotments have been clear-cut, public sentiment has turned against harvesting wood at a loss for export to Japan, and Congress in response has begun to rein in the industry. As a result of the logging industry, there is a gravel road system that connects the three primary towns—Craig, Klawock, and Thorne Bay—as well as other areas where both logging and mining have taken place. Alaska state ferries serve Hollis on the east side of the island. Although the timber and mining industries historically go from boom to bust and back again, the salmon industry has provided a renewable natural resource that faithfully supports many of the permanent residents on Prince of Wales Island. The island is a favorite with sport fisherman, big-game hunters, and sea kayakers.

Craig is located on the west side of Prince of Wales Island about 60 miles west of Ketchikan. Like many of the smaller villages in the region, Craig began its life as a Tlingit fishing camp in the years before the Russian empire arrived. Today, Craig is an important regional center for the logging and fishing industries. Visitors use the town as a base of operation for fishing and hunting expeditions into the backcountry. There is a lodge in Craig *(see page 130)*, as well as restaurants and a store.

The lush forests of Prince of Wales, Admiralty, and Chichagof Islands receive in some locations over 150 inches of rain a year.

■ WRANGELL *map page 87, C-2*

A good-sized town of about 2,500 inhabitants, Wrangell is located in close proximity to the Stikine River, which drains from British Columbia to the sea. The Stikine is one of the most famous fishing rivers in the Pacific Northwest. Like many of the towns in the region, Wrangell owes its existence to the expansive Russian fur empire of the 18th and 19th centuries. Upon arriving on the ferry, you'll find the **visitors center** on Outer Drive right along the waterfront. At the corner of Outer Drive and Front Street, only two hundred yards away, is **Kiksadi Totem Park,** which pays homage to the rich Indian cultures of the region. There are three hotels, several bed and breakfasts, and a number of gift shops in Wrangell. As with other Southeastern towns on the state ferry system, Wrangell can be used as a jump-off point for a number of outdoor activities, including sport fishing, sea kayaking, camping, hiking, and wildlife photography. There are about a dozen Forest Service cabins available for renting in the Wrangell area *(see page 140).*

A Wrangell Indian village painted by Theodore J. Richardson around 1900. (Anchorage Museum of History and Art)

Petersburg is often described as the "Norway of Alaska" because of its fjord-like setting and Norwegian immigrant heritage.

Famous **Anan Creek Bear Observatory** is only 28 miles by plane or hired boat from Wrangell. During the salmon runs, you can observe blacks bears and a few brown bears. *(For more information see page 56.)*

■ PETERSBURG *map page 87, C-2*

Petersburg, on Mitkof Island south of Juneau, is a picturesque little town and is often referred to by Alaskans as "Little Norway" for its beautiful fjord-like setting and neat, white, Scandanavian-style homes and storefronts. Magnificent views open to the eye in every direction: to the east across Fredrick Sound to Horn Mountain and the Horn Cliffs on the mainland; to the north and west, mountainous Kupreanof Island. In the six-block downtown area, you'll find a **Tongass National Forest office**, the **Sons of Norway Hall, Clausen Memorial Museum** (corner of Second Street and Fram Street), and the **Harbor Bar** (at the corner of Dolphin Street and Nordic Drive). The main attraction is the **Frederick Point Boardwalk,** which leads from the Sandy Beach Recreation Area through classic southeastern hemlock forest and moose muskeg, to a salmon stream where you can watch the fish spawn, in season. Visitors can use Petersburg as a base of operations for sport fishing, camping, sea kayaking (Le Conte Glacier is a popular destination), photography, or hunting trips.

■ SITKA *map page 87, B-1*

Sitka (pop. 9,200) has a mild, damp climate moderated by the sea. Even in the short dark days of January the average daily temperate in Sitka is a balmy (by Alaskan standards) 33 degrees Fahrenheit. This contrasts markedly with Fairbanks, where the average daily temperature in January is between 2 and 18 degrees below zero. Like other Southeast towns, Sitka is often drenched in rain, receiving more than 100 inches a year. This site historically was used by Tlingit Indians, and in 1799 Russian fur baron Alexander Baranof (for whom Baranof Island itself is named) built a fort here to anchor his trade in sea otter pelts.

A view of Sitka painted in 1885 by Cleveland S. Rockwell. Baranof Castle is visible on the rock in the middle of the bay. (Anchorage Museum of History and Art)

The interior of a Tlingit house in 1787 as depicted by J. Webber, Captain Cook's shipboard artist. (Bancroft Library)

SITKA JACK'S HOUSE

We visited "Sitka Jack," an arrant old scoundrel, but one of the wealthiest men of the Sitka tribe. Of course his house stood among the largest, at the fashionable end of the town. These houses were built of planks, three or four inches thick, each one having been hewed from a log, with an adze formed by lashing a metal blade to the short prong of a forked stick. In constructing the native cabin, the planks are set on edge and so nicely fitted that they need no chinking. The shape of the house is square; a bark roof is laid on, with a central aperture for chimney. The door is a circular opening about two feet in diameter. It is closed with a sheet of bark or a bear-skin or seal-skin. On arriving at Sitka Jack's hut we crawled through the door, and found ourselves in the presence of Jack's wives, children, and slaves, who were lounging on robes and blankets laid on a board flooring which extended along each side of the room. A dirt floor about seven feet square was left in the center, and on this the fire burned and the pot of halibut boiled merrily. Our arrival was hailed with stolid indifference. The family circle reclined and squatted as usual, and went on with the apparently enjoyable occupation of scooping up handfuls of raw herring-roe, which they munched with great gusto.

—[Author unknown], "Among the Thlinkits in Alaska,"
The Century Magazine, July 1882

Today, a large part of the attraction of Sitka is its Russian and Tlingit past. Visitors can see a relic of the old **Russian Blockhouse** and of **St. Michael's Cathedral,** at the center of Lincoln Street downtown. The cathedral was built between 1844 and 1848 by Bishop Innocent Veniaminov of the Russian Orthodox Church. **Sitka National Historical Park,** located at the end of Lincoln Street within easy walking distance of the downtown area, preserves both Sitka's Tlingit and Russian past. There is a totem pole assemblage, as well as the Russian bishop's house and a monument marking the site of the Tlingit fort destroyed in 1804 by the Russians (the Tlingits had destroyed the Russian fort here in 1802). Also, in the downtown area (downtown here denoting an area a few hundred yards long and about the same wide) you will find a **Tongass National Forest office,** the well-known **Pioneer Bar** on the waterfront (Katlian Street), **Sheldon Jackson College and Museum,** and the **Isabel Miller Museum,** which focuses on the history of Sitka and its people.

Sitka's two harbors are filled with brightly painted fishing boats and face toward numerous pine-covered islands. Above them to the west rises Mount Edgecumbe, an extinct volcano with a pyramid shape. To the east are rugged snowcapped peaks, often shrouded in clouds.

The area around Sitka is famous for its sport fishing. Rangers at the Forest Service office will acquaint you with a number of recreational resources including the names of local boat operators who can you guide you to some great fishing spots (or remote hiking/camping locations). Rangers can also tell you about the developed hiking trails that are accessible from Sitka's road system, as well as the local public campgrounds. Drop by their office at 201 Katlian, Suite 109, to pick up maps and information sheets.

■ JUNEAU AND VICINITY *maps pages 86, C-5 and 106*

> The calm bay was full of the fantastic, beautiful harlequin ducks, geese were returning from their feeding-grounds near the shore, and on the land itself, varied thrushes and sparrows were singing in the trees. We dodged among the reefs, slipped through great quantities of sea-weed, everywhere abundant. . . . It had cleared and the day was beautiful and sunny.
>
> —Charles Sheldon, *Wilderness of the North Pacific,* 1909

A city of 28,800 people (a state capital smaller than 17th-century Boston), Juneau is a cosmopolitan community, with highrise buildings, cultural facilities, legislative assembly chambers, and shopping malls, yet Mother Nature is everywhere—a sprawling glacier, the cold blue northern sea, mysterious dark spruce and hemlock forests, soaring snowcapped peaks, and abundant wildlife. Part of the reason Juneau remains beautiful is the seamless way wild nature and human culture blend into an integrated whole in which neither is diminished.

All of this is particularly remarkable when you consider that Juneau, like so many other Alaskan towns from Fairbanks to Nome, began as a disorganized mining camp. The historians tell us that in 1880 a couple of misfit miners named Dick Harris and Joe Juneau discovered gold in the stream that now runs through the center of town, rushing past Tenth Street and Ninth Street on its way to the Gastineau Channel. They were directed to the area by none other than John Muir, who noticed the local rocks' similarity to those in California's gold-bearing areas.

For a time the state capital was located in Sitka, but in 1906 common sense dictated the capital be moved to Juneau, where all the action was. Nearly $100 million worth of gold was extracted from Juneau before the mines closed in 1944.

Juneau in 1900, six years prior to being designated the capital of Alaska, following the decline of Sitka and the Klondike Gold Rush. (Bancroft Library)

Juneau is a compact, friendly town to walk around in. It is also the only state capital in the country where the governor's mansion is only nine blocks from prime bear habitat. The downtown streets, surrounding a creek that annually hosts spawning salmon, are laid out in a grid. In the residential areas on the slopes above, the streets bend with the steep contours, conforming to the vagaries and vicissitudes of the rather jumbled landscape. The local air is heavy and moist, and it smells of seashore and spruce forest. In summer, the flower gardens are spectacular, and the scent of blossoms tinges the air.

◆ Downtown Juneau Walking Tour

Visitor Information *map page 106, C-2*
If you arrive by sea, your boat will dock by Marine Park. Here at the visitor's kiosk you can pick up a map illustrating a downtown walking tour. Maps are also available at the **Davis Log Cabin Information Center** at 134 Third Street. Before you set out on your tour, be certain you have your umbrella or a raincoat—rain can occur without notice in this temperate, maritime climate.

Red Dog Saloon
You might want to start your tour at the popular **Red Dog Saloon**, just across the street from Marine Park.

State Capitol Building *map page 106, C-2*
The capitol building is on Fourth Street

During the summer months downtown Juneau is enlivened by some 200,000 visitors, many of whom end up retiring to the infamous Red Dog Saloon.

between Seward and Main Streets. Behind it stands one of Juneau's finest totem poles, the five-story totem.

The Governor's Mansion

map page 106, B/C-1/2

The mansion, at Fourth and Calhoun Streets, is open for viewing only in December.

St. Nicholas Russian Orthodox Church *map page 106, C-1*

The small, onion-domed church on Fifth Street at Gold is the oldest original Russian Orthodox church in Southeast Alaska.

Wickersham House

map page 106, C-1

At the top of the hill on Seventh and Main streets is the once home of pioneer judge and legislator James Wickersham. The main floors are open to the public.

Aerial tram over Gastineau Channel and Juneau.

Alaska State Museum

map page 106, B/C-2

Here, at one of the state's most impressive museums, you can see a 40-foot walrus-hide umiak used by Eskimos to hunt whales and a recreated Tlingit tribal house.

Gold Mining

The **Juneau–Douglas City Museum** across from the capitol features gold mining history and a hands-on history museum, especially interesting for kids. If you become fascinated with the city's gold-mining past, walk up to see the ruins of the old **Alaska-Juneau Mine** at the end of Basin Road (the north end of Cope Park), or to the nearby **Glory Hole** accessed by the Perseverance Trail (*see page 107*). Another possibility, across the Gastineau Channel is the **Treadwell Mine** on Douglas Island. You can reach the island by taxi or city bus if you don't have a rental car. Other people try their hand at gold-panning in one of the public creeks (Forest Service officials will provide directions and guidance or you can arrange to take one of the commercial tours. *For more details, see pages 134 & 135.*)

◆ Fishing Industry Sights

Gastineau Salmon Hatchery

This privately run, modern facility has a glass-sided fish ladder, saltwater acquariums, and informational displays. It's a very popular place to visit, and highly recommended. *Located on Channel Drive, about three miles north of town via Egan Drive.*

Auke Bay Marine Lab

The Marine lab, 12 miles further down Egan Drive, is associated with the University of Alaska, Juneau. Daily tours show visitors the laboratory's saltwater aquarium and fishery displays.

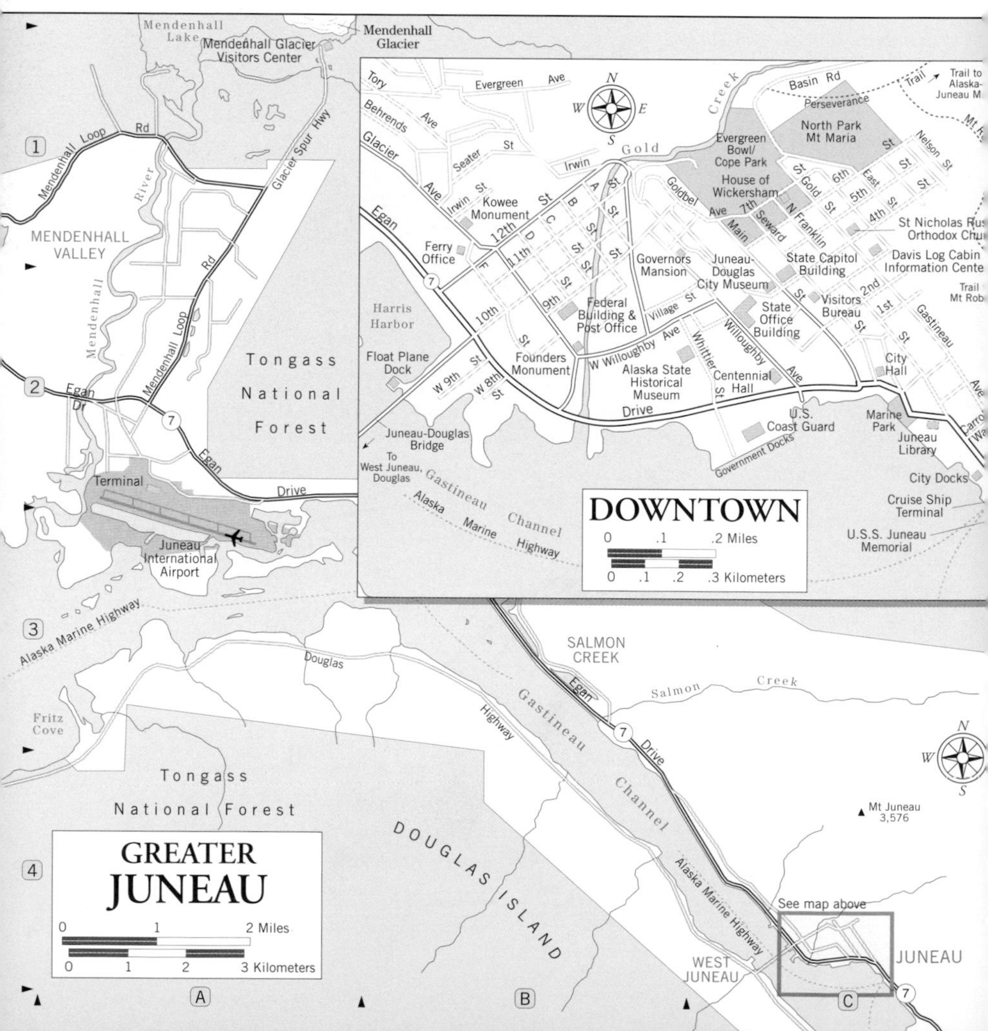

◆ Hiking around Juneau

Information *map page 106, C-2*
The **Davis Log Cabin Visitor Center** offers general information on hiking in the Juneau area. Detailed U.S. Geographical Survey topographical sheets are available in local stores and are highly recommended for any backcountry excursions.

Bears
Even in Juneau you need to keep an eye out for black and grizzly bears. Always wear bells or make a lot of noise while hiking in bear country. And never hike at night; you should even avoid hiking at dawn or dusk.

The Perseverance Trail *map page 106, C-1*
Reached by walking up Basin Road from the center of town, this trail leads you into typical coastal rain forest habitat: towering spruce and hemlock trees overhung with moss rise from a lush understory—a thick carpet of wild blueberries, devil's club (a native shrub with painfully sharp thorns), and innumerable wildflowers. Those with enough hiking experience and physical fortitude can continue up the Perserverance trail to 3,576-foot **Mount Juneau.**

Douglas Island
Douglas Island, across Gastineau Channel, has developed hiking and cross-country skiing trails. The more remote trails require overnight trips into the wilderness; they can be accessed by sea kayak, chartered boat, or air charter.

Farther Afield
You can go by boat or plane to Glacier Bay National Park and Preserve *(page 110)*, landing in the quaint community of Gustavus, or head to Admiralty National Monument *(page 108)*, or to a remote sport fishing camp or wilderness cabin in Tongass National Forest. Numerous charter boat companies can take you fishing, whale watching, or sightseeing.

SOUTHEAST

◆ Mendenhall Valley *map page 106, A-1&2*

About 15 miles west of town on Egan Drive lies the lovely Mendenhall Valley. The valley is dominated by the immense Mendenhall Glacier, which drains south from the interior peaks of the Coastal Mountains. Not only is this a region of geological importance, it is also an important wildlife habitat area; spawning salmon, black bear, beaver, and mountain goats are commonly seen (the latter at a distance). A beautiful visitors center is maintained near the base of the glacier, and there is a top-notch Forest Service campground on the west shore of the lake. The nearby 3,789-acre Mendenhall Wetlands State Game Refuge protects one of the few large salt marshes between the Fraser River in British Columbia and the Gulf of Alaska. It is an important resting area for migratory waterfowl. Mendenhall Refuge also provides habitat for bald eagles, herons, and a variety of smaller birds. Guided raft or kayak trips down the river afford fine views of the glacer and brief stretches of whitewater.

■ Admiralty Island *maps pages 86 & 87*

Mention Admiralty Island to anyone in Alaska and the first association is the great brown bear, *ursus arctos middendorfi,* an animal that grows to mind-boggling proportions on the extravagant diet of sea-run salmon, berries, and vegetation, and scavenged marine mammal carcasses. Ninety percent of Admiralty Island is managed as the Admiralty Island National Monument and is home to hundreds of brown bears, making it one of the famous spots in Alaska for those interested in observing wildlife.

◆ Stan Price Wildlife Sanctuary *map page 86, C-5*

Admiralty Island is easily reached by air or by sea from Juneau, which is only 15 miles away. By far, most visitors interested in seeing the big bears head for the **Stan Price State Wildlife Sanctuary at Pack Creek.** This sanctuary is located about 28 miles south of Juneau, making for a short air flight. Like much of the Alexander Archipelago of the Alaska Panhandle, the Pack Creek area is a dense, jungle-like

Angoon residents Annie and George Turnmir dry salmon in their smokehouse.

A Tlingit war canoe as depicted in Harpers Weekly *in the 1880s.*

forest of spruce and hemlock with clear-running streams that support annual runs of pink and chum salmon. The estuary and tidal flats are also good places to look for bears out in the open. Primitive camping is permitted in the sanctuary in various designated areas.

◆ ANGOON *map page 86, B-5*

Set on a peninsula on the west side of Admiralty Island, about midway between Juneau and Sitka, you will find the village of Angoon. It is one of the major Tlingit Indian communities in the Southeast (around 640 inhabitants), and the only permanent community on the island, and yet it is a very small village, with only three miles of roadway. Informal dress and manners prevail among the local residents, who pursue a traditional lifestyle that utilizes such resources as salmon, shellfish, deer, bear, and berries. There is a Tongass National Forest office in Angoon, and rangers will be happy to offer advice to those interested in kayaking, canoeing, fishing, or hunting in the area. Visitors will find two lodges and a bed and breakfast in Angoon.

■ CHICHAGOF ISLAND *map page 86, B-4&5*

◆ TENAKEE SPRINGS *map page 86, B-5*

Located on the east side of Chichagof Island, **Tenakee Springs** is best known for its natural hot springs. Accommodations are available at the Tenakee Inn. Campers could head for the nearby Tongass National Forest. The area is popular with sport fishermen, big-game hunters, and sea kayakers. With only around 200 residents, Tenakee Springs is representative of the truly small villages in southeastern Alaska.

◆ HOONAH *map page 86, B-4*

Across Icy Strait from Glacier Bay National Park, and on the northern shore of Chichagof Island, you will find the predominantly Tlingit village of Hoonah, population 1,200, which features an airstrip, several lodging options, a restaurant or two, and well-stocked stores. Hoonah is often used as a jumping-off point for big-game hunters and sport fishermen. A small seining and trolling fleet is based in Hoonah, plying the shallow coastal waters for salmon and halibut. Sportfishing and sightseeing charter boats are locally available.

■ GLACIER BAY NATIONAL PARK AND PRESERVE

map page 86, A—C-3

The friendly little village of **Gustavus** *(map page 86, B-4)* serves as the gateway community to Glacier Bay National Park. Visitors arriving by air or boat from Juneau will no doubt have the chance to see Gustavus. There are several good lodges in the area, a grocery store in the village, and public campgrounds at nearby Bartlett Cove. Everything from sea kayaks to bicycles, boats to airplanes can be chartered in Gustavus. Sea kayaks provide an excellent means of accessing the roadless national park. Gustavus is without a doubt one of the friendliest small villages (less than 300 souls year-round) in Alaska. And what a location!

Surrounded by towering mountains (including 15,320-foot Mount Fairweather), Glacier Bay is a magnificent spectacle. Although the park is about the same size as Yellowstone National Park—3.3 million acres—unlike its southern cousin, it cannot be reached by road. Visitors reach Glacier Bay, which is 50 miles west of Juneau, either by airplane or by boat. Accommodations are in public campgrounds near Gustavus, or at the rustic lodge. By far the most popular way to visit Glacier Bay is by cruise ship or by smaller day-tour craft.

> When the sunshine is shifting through the midst of the multitude of the icebergs that fill the fiord and through the jets of radiant spray ever rising from the tremendous dashing and splashing of the falling and up-springing bergs, the effect is indescribably glorious. Glorious, too, are the shows they make in the night when the moon and stars are shining. The berg-thunder seems far louder than by day. . . . But it is in the darkest nights when storms are blowing and the waves are phosphorescent that the most impressive displays are made.
>
> —John Muir, *The Trip of 1880*

As the epigraph from Muir indicates, the chief attraction of this national park is the magnificent bay surrounded by active glaciers. In fact, the first scientist to seriously study the glaciers was John Muir, who made a number of trips to the area beginning in 1879. Muir had first studied glaciers in the Sierra Nevadas, particularly in what has become Yosemite National Park, and was astounded by the beauty

Muir Glacier was named after the famous conservationist following his visit to Glacier Bay in 1880. Painting by Thomas Hill, 1889. (Anchorage Museum of History and Art)

and diversity of the glaciers in this particular bay. Interestingly enough, the glaciers have retreated far up the bay since Muir's time, an effect noticed elsewhere in the northern hemisphere.

As impressive as the geology of Glacier Bay is the wildlife, which ranges from northern Pacific marine mammals—orcas, humpback whales, sea otters, seals, and minke whales—to the host of subarctic terrestrial mammals, including moose, wolves, grizzly and black bears, coastal blacktail deer, lynx, mink, and beaver. More than 200 bird species are found in the bay, and fishing (halibut, Dolly Varden, salmon) is considered excellent. And just as interesting as the wildlife is the plant life. Because of the rapid glacial retreat, it is possible to observe the dynamics of plant succession firsthand and up close, as lichens, moss, and grasses work to create soils suitable for primitive grasses and eventually more complicated vascular plants such as fireweed, alder, and wild blueberries.

SWEET AIR OF THE GLACIER

There is no air so indescribably, thrillingly sweet as the air of a glacier on a fair day. It seems to palpitate with a fragrance that ravishes the senses. I saw a great, recently captured bear, chained on the hurricane deck of a steamer, stand with his nose stretched out toward the glacier, his nostrils quivering and a look of almost human longing and rebellion in his small eyes. The feeling of pain and pity with which a humane person always beholds a chained wild animal is accented in these wide and noble spaces swimming from snow mountain to snow mountain, where the very watchword of the silence seems to be "Freedom." The chained bear recognized the scent of the glacier and remembered that he had once been free.

In front of the glacier stretched miles of sapphire, sun-lit sea, set with sparkling, opaline-tinted icebergs. Now and then one broke and fell apart before our eyes, sending up a funnel-shaped spray of color—rose, pale green, or azure.

At every blast of the steamer's whistle great masses of ice came thundering headlong into the sea—to emerge presently, icebergs. Canoeists approach glaciers closely at their peril, never knowing when an iceberg may shoot to the surface and wreck their boat. Even larger craft are by no means safe, and tourists desiring a close approach should voyage with intrepid captains who sail safely through everything.

—Ella Higginson, *Alaska, the Great Country,* 1908

An aerial view of Norris Glacier (just east of Juneau) shows how the region's glaciers have been retreating, exposing a bedrock surface previously engulfed by the ice.

The largest sea wave ever to hit shore occurred in Glacier National Park, which is located over the tectonically active point where the Pacific and North American plates converge and create enormous friction. In 1958, an earthquake sent a colossal sea wave into Lituya Bay, which is on the other side of the Brady Icefield from Glacier Bay, sloshing 1,740 feet (the height of a 140-story building) over Cenotaph Island and up over the north side of the bay. The killer wave literally took everything back into the sea as it retreated—trees, plants, animals, and soil. Only the sheer, slick bedrock on the mountainside remained—a truly awesome example of the power of nature.

There are many activities that can be pursued in Glacier Bay National Park, including sea kayaking, boat or aerial touring, sport fishing, hiking, camping, and landscape or wildlife photography. Visitor numbers to most park areas are regulated by permit, so inquire ahead.

Following a massive landslide in Lituya Bay in July of 1958, the largest wave in recorded history (over 1,700 feet high) washed over the opposite shoreline stripping it to the bedrock. (U.S. Coast and Geodetic Survey)

GLACIER BAY
NATIONAL PARK
0 5 10 Miles
0 5 10 15 Kilometers
1794 Historical extent of glaciation
CANADA
UNITED STATES
Muir Glacier
Riggs Glacier
Carroll Glacier
Rendu Glacier
Casement Glacier
1976
1972
1960
1948
1966
Rendu Inlet
Queen Inlet
1892
1929
Wachusett
1907
1949
Muir Inlet
RUSSELL ISLAND
1880
Adams Inlet
Reid Glacier
Tidal Inlet
Glacier Bay
1879
1919
1860
1857
1845
DRAKE ISLAND
Beartrack River
Icefield
Beartrack Cove
WILLOUGHBY ISLAND
BEARDSLEE ISLANDS
Wood Lake
Brady Glacier
Abyss Lake
Dundas
Berg Bay
River
Visitor Center
Glacier Bay Lodge
Park Headquarters
1794
Airport
Gustavus
1961
1750-80
PLEASANT ISLAND
Dundas Bay
North Passage
Icy Strait
Taylor Bay
Graves Bay
LEMESURIER ISLAND
INIAN ISLANDS
South Passage
Cape Spencer
N
W
E
S

HAINES *map page 86, C-3*

Many—perhaps most—who take the ferry from Bellingham, Washington, eventually ride it all the way to Haines, which sits at the head of Lynn Canal about 70 miles north of Juneau.

Haines entered modern history in World War II, when engineers built a road from the sleepy little port to the Alaska Highway. In Haines you will find a **visitors center** at the corner of Second Avenue and Willard Street, as well as the usual assemblage of hotels, restaurants, and stores nearby. Fishermen will find abundant opportunities to pursue their sport around Haines (information available at the visitors center). Although there is much to see in the way of culture—the **Sheldon Museum** at the corner of Front Street and Main Street, the many art galleries near the visitors center—the star attraction of Haines is the **Chilkat Bald Eagle Preserve.** Each winter thousands of bald eagles flock to this area in order to feed on salmon. Some of the best views are around Mile 20 on the Haines Highway. The season peaks from October through January.

About 120 miles north of Haines is **Kluane National Park**—the Denali of the Canadian subarctic. Dall sheep, moose, and grizzlies are observed here regularly.

SKAGWAY *map page 86, C-3*

Skagway is located in the immediate vicinity of Haines at the head of Lynn Canal, about 90 miles north of Juneau. If you take a cruise ship to Alaska, you will most likely stop in Skagway, one of the most popular and interesting ports. Like many towns in Alaska, Skagway owes its existence to the gold rush days. It was here that Jack London began his famous trek into the Yukon gold mines, an adventure that resulted in his world-famous works, *The Call of the Wild* and "To Build a Fire." Be sure to take in the town's colorful history at the visitor center in the old railway depot, followed by a walking tour of the downtown streets. Within the six-block downtown area you will find many restored turn-of-the-century buildings, Klondike Gold Rush Historical Park gift and crafts shops, and the **Trail of 98 Museum,** where mining artifacts, exhibits, and videos tell the history of Skagway. During the evening, the liveliest show in town is **"The Days of '98,"** which for more than 70 years has been dramatizing the life and death of Soapy Smith, the scoundrel boss of early Skagway. Before leaving town, you can visit the gold rush cemetery where Soapy is buried. (Note that Frank Reid, the vigilante who was

Johns Hopkins Glacier empties into Glacier Bay under a towering mountain spire some 8,000 feet above.

Skagway prospers as the summer of 1898 approaches and the Klondike gold rush begins to peak. (Bancroft Library)

killed while dispatching the scoundrel, rates by far the handsomer monument.) Some of the locals enjoy impersonating historical figures, so don't be surprised if you run into Soapy above ground, too. You might even meet Robert Service, who will be happy to oblige you with a recitation of one of his poems.

In curious contrast to its wild and woolly past, the town is rather neatly laid out in orderly blocks, with wide streets that are largely empty; empty, that is, until a cruise ship or busload of tourists arrive, instantly filling the curio shops and small art galleries. Yukon moose wander into town from time to time from the surrounding mountains.

In the 1890s humanity streamed into this town on its way to the gold fields of the Yukon. Most came aboard steamers from Seattle, disembarked along the Alaska coast, and followed trails inland over the coast range.

Nine miles north of Skagway, along an old Indian route, runs one of the most famous and historic trails in Alaska, the **Chilkoot Trail.** Originating near the water's edge at what is now Dyea and climbing over the 3,246-foot Chilkoot Pass

Slippery Soapy Smith

Alaska's most notorious outlaw, and "America's last frontier badman of legend" according to chronicler William Bronson, was a confidence man by the name of Jefferson Randolph Smith, popularly known as "Soapy" Smith. He got his name as a result of a trick he used in Colorado mining towns where he sold bars of soap by convincing dupes that $20 bills were concealed in the wrappers.

The facts surrounding his sojourn in Alaska appear to be as slippery as the man himself. According to pioneer Judge James Wickersham, Soapy settled in the Skagway and Dyea region in 1897. He quickly assembled a confederacy of crooks, strong-arm men, and tricksters, and began robbing the miners flooding the region on their way to the Klondike gold rush. Soapy and his men virtually took over Skagway and were on "friendly" terms with the town's only lawman, a U.S. marshall. Soapy's henchmen began systematically bilking money from the transient population through scams, fraud, highway robbery, and murder.

Paradoxically, Soapy gave away as much money as he made and was considered a philanthropist by some residents (he was careful not to rob the locals). But when Klondikers returning from the mines began avoiding Skagway because of its reputation, local business owners decided Soapy was more of a liability than an asset. In July of 1898, a vigilante group had a showdown with Soapy and his men. Most were rounded up and booted out of town (including the crooked marshall). Three ringleaders were tried and sentenced to many years in the Washington State Penitentiary and Soapy was shot to death on Skagway Pier by citizen/vigilante Frank Reid. Reid also died in the shootout and remains the town's greatest hero—his gravestone reads, "He gave his life for the honor of Skagway."

The notorious Soapy Smith sashays up to the bar of his saloon in Skagway in the company of his minders, just months before his death at the hands of vigilantes. (Library of Congresss)

Alaska and the Yukon
WHITE PASS and YUKON ROUTE

before it drops down to the Yukon River, it is an arduous 32-mile trek that takes three days to complete. Despite the difficulties of this hike, thousands of miners and entrepreneurs made the trip, hoping to reach the gold fields of the Yukon. It's an exposed route, which should be followed with caution, but it's followed by thousands of hikers every summer.

From Skagway itself runs an old trail over White Pass. The suffering endured by hopeful prospectors and their 3,000-odd horses and dogs (many of whom died) on the trail was horrendous: the trail was renamed **Dead Horse Trail** in 1897.

Unlike all other towns of the Southeast except Haines, Skagway is connected to the mainland by a road. The Klondike Highway is a spectacular route that closely follows the old Dead Horse Trail to the picturesque gold rush town of Carcross (98 miles) and to Whitehorse (183 miles).

The cover of an old railroad brochure promotes the White Pass and Yukon Route Railway (left), which was constructed in 1900 to obviate the incredibly arduous climb over Chilkoot Pass (above) most miners had to endure in order to reach the gold fields of the interior. (Brochure courtesy of Brad S. Lomazzi, Western Railroad Collectibles; photo above from Bancroft Library Collection)

Gazing from the Deck

No other excursion that I know of may be made into any other American wilderness where so marvelous an abundance of noble, newborn scenery is so charmingly brought to view as on the trip through the Alexander Archipelago to Fort Wrangell and Sitka. Gazing from the deck of the steamer, one is borne smoothly over calm blue waters, through the midst of countless forest-clad islands. . . . We seemed to float in true fairyland, each succeeding view seeming more and more beautiful. . . . Never before this had I been embosomed in scenery so hopelessly beyond description.

— John Muir, *The Alexander Archipelago,* 1880

The easiest way to catch a glimpse of the old Dead Horse Trail without having to break a sweat (or a leg), or to crane your neck from the driver's seat of a car, is to take a ride on the old **White Pass and Yukon Route Railway**. Completed in 1900, the spectacular narrow-gauge railway almost single-handedly kept Skagway from turning into a ghost town after the Klondike gold rush ended. For more than eight decades, it transported goods and travelers from Skagway's port up the Skagway River Gorge, with a lunch stop (often including moose steaks) midway, near the ghost town of Bennett. Although the completion of the highway temporarily halted the run of this glorious little railway, the old train now makes daily tourist excursions up the pass, and even to Whitehorse. *(See page 140, following).*

■ Yakutat *map page 86, A-1*

Yakutat is located far up the Gulf of Alaska along the wave-swept outer coast of the Southeast's uppermost panhandle, where rugged peaks rise from sea level, and there are few sheltering bays. Most people see the region from the airplane as the pilot wings westward from Juneau toward Anchorage and points to the Malaspina glacier around Mount St. Elias, informing you the glacier is larger than the state of Rhode Island. In Yakutat you will find a few lodges, cafes, bars, and stores. The area is well known for its big-game hunting and for its sport fishing, especially for steelhead and salmon. The Yakutat Forelands area is ranked as one of the finest bird-watching areas (cranes, geese, ducks, trumpeter swans) on the whole coast, especially during peak migration times in the spring and fall. Later salmon runs attract bald eagles and brown bears. *(Best visited by plane; see pages 125 and 141.)*

TRAVEL INFORMATION

◆ GETTING THERE AND GETTING AROUND

Much of Southeast Alaska consists of islands and inlets which are only accessible by water or air. The Southeast's major city (and state's capital), Juneau, is served by only one major carrier, Alaska Airlines. The Alaska state **ferry system, cruise ships, and tour boats** originating in Bellingham, Washington, and Prince Rupert, Canada, also serve the area. The total length of the Canadian–U.S. Inside Passage is over 1,000 miles. The Alaskan part of the Passage is 550 miles. **By car**, the Panhandle's northernmost towns of Haines and Skagway can be reached by driving north from the U.S. border on the eastern side of the coastal mountain range through British Columbia and part of the Yukon via the Alaska Highway.

The S.S. Princess *may have been taking the "marine-bus" concept a step too far when it ran aground on Sentinel Island north of Juneau in 1910. (Underwood Photo Archives, San Francisco)*

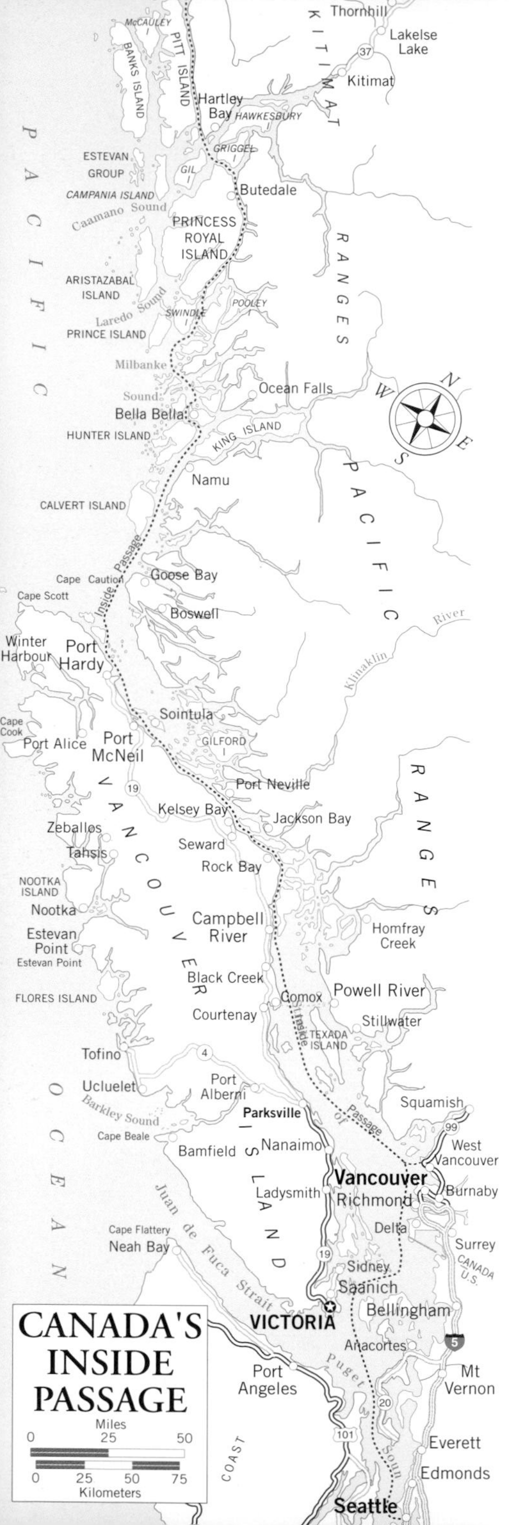

By Ferry

Alaska has an excellent ferry public-transportation system akin to a marine-bus service. The ferries connect Bellingham, Washington, and Prince Rupert, British Columbia, with many of the major towns along Alaska's Inside Passage. A peak-season one-way trip (May through September) from Bellingham, Washington, to Skagway, the Southeast's northernmost town, will take three days and will cost around $250 per person one way, and an additional $294 for a three-person cabin (one-way). With a car, add $581, and for a bicycle or kayak, add $40. Leaving from Prince Rupert, Canada, will reduce your fares by almost half.

In summer the cabins and car decks are usually full, so make your reservations at least six months in advance—or allow for plenty of flexibility in your schedule. Generally, stops in ports do not allow enough time for shore excursions, so you may want to customize your trip by adding stop-overs (a port-to-port rate may increase your fare, but it may be worth the extra expense). The Alaska ferry terminals will provide a computer printout describing the sights and accommodations of all the towns en route.

Alaska Marine Highway. *Juneau; 800-642-0066 or 907-465-3941*
B.C. Ferries. *B.C. 250- 386-3431.*

Cruise Ships and Ocean Liners

Cruises provide spacious, often luxurious accommodations on their tour of the Inside Passage. Fares for a cabin on an ocean liner range from $250–$500 per person, per day, based on double occupancy, in high season (May through September); early reservations (made by February 14) can save you from 10–45%. Ocean liner and cruise ships provide entertainment, activities, and formal and informal dining. Smaller cruise ships and specialty vessels are able to traverse the shallow coves and narrow waters where the big ships can't go. Many of these have a staff of naturalists onboard who give informal lectures on natural history along the way. Because of the great variety in cruise options, you may need to work with a travel agent or contact individual companies for details on itineraries, tours, and add-ons.

By Charter Boat

Tour boat companies are designed to connect passengers with the Southeast's smaller towns and remote villages. Arrangements often may be made upon arrival in these towns. To plan in advance contact local visitors bureaus for information; these are listed by town. Also see information numbers listed by town under "Food, Lodging, & Tours" on page 129. *In Juneau call 907-586-2201.*

By Plane

From Juneau it is possible to travel to Haines, Skagway, Angoon, Hoonah, Glacier Bay National Park, and other Southeast islands by commuter carriers offering intrastate scheduled air service. The airlines sometimes offer packages in conjunction with the ferry service, allowing travelers to

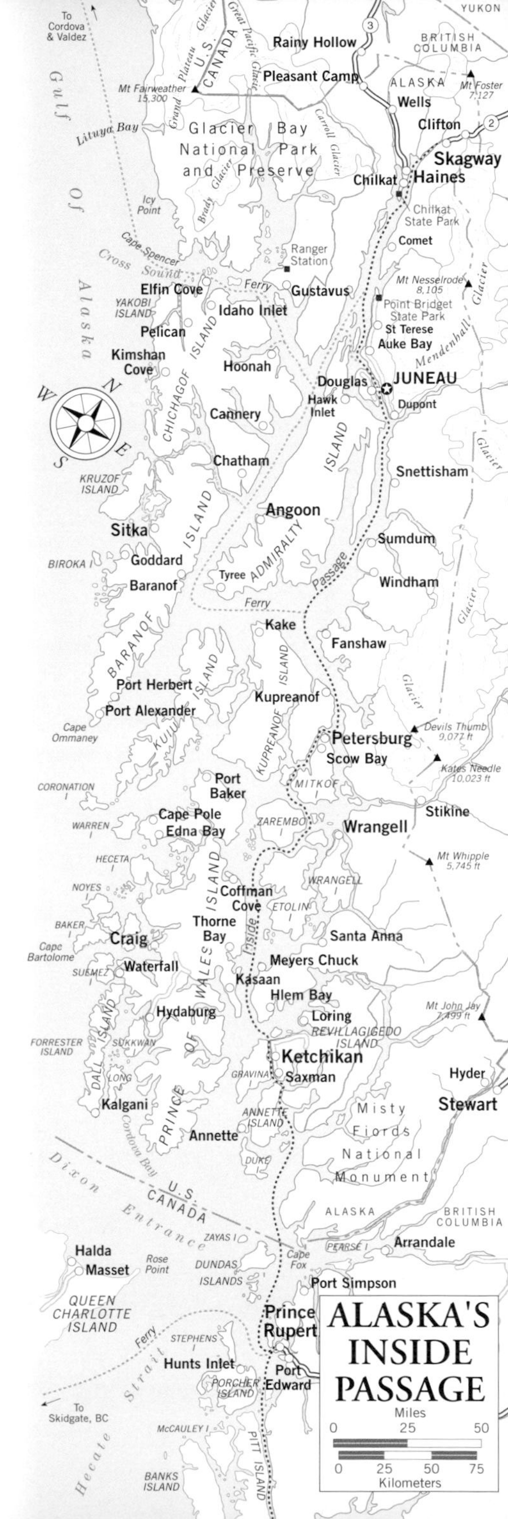

(top) Floatplanes on the Taku River at Taku Glacier Lodge. (bottom) A cruise ship meets the White Pass & Yukon Route Railroad at Skagway. (opposite) Wanda Culp enjoys the scenery from the back of a Glacier Bay ferry.

fly in and ferry back. Inquire at **Alaska Airlines,** *206-439-4539,* for chartered flights from Juneau or at the **Federal Aviation Administration** in Anchorage, *907-271-2000,* which also has a list of certified air taxi operations throughout Alaska including the following: **L.A.B. Flying Service** (Alaska Airlines mileage partner), *800-426-0543;* **Loken Aviation,** 907-*789-3331;* **Wings of Alaska,** *907-789-0790.*

By Car

When traveling around the Southeast there is no need for a car. If you're planning to visit the region en route to Anchorage or Fairbanks via the Alaska Highway, consider taking your car on a ferry from Seattle or Bellingham and transporting it to Skagway at the end of the Panhandle. From there it is a day's drive to Fairbanks, where you can turn north to the Arctic or south toward Anchorage.

Charges for cars brought aboard the ferry are based on the number of passengers and the size of the vehicle. Although it may cost as much as $600 to take a car the 1,000 miles of the Inside Passage, travelers must also calculate how long, as an alternative, it would take to drive the Alaska Highway, as well as the cost and wear and tear on the vehicle. Many travelers determine that, despite its high cost, it is actually cheaper—in terms of time and traveling costs—to take the ferry. Make reservations for the busy summer traveling season as far in advance as possible—I recommend six months.

■ CLIMATE

The defining characteristic of Alaska's Panhandle is rain. Near the coast, especially along the southernmost islands, annual rainfall can exceed 15 feet, with the bulk of it falling in the fall and winter months. Temperatures are cool in the summer, and chilly but not frigid in the winter. Rain falls year round. The three stations below are all at sea level and represent the southern end of the Panhandle (Ketchikan), central portion (Juneau), and northern end (Glacier Bay National Park).

SUNLIGHT

SUMMER MAXIMUM	SUNRISE	SUNSET	# OF HOURS
Juneau	3:51 AM	10:09 PM	18:18
Ketchikan	4:04 AM	9:32 PM	17:28
WINTER MINIMUM	SUNRISE	SUNSET	# OF HOURS
Juneau	8:46 AM	3:07 PM	6:21
Ketchikan	8:12 AM	3:18 PM	7:05

TEMPS (F°)	AVG. JAN. HIGH	AVG. JAN. LOW	AVG. APRIL HIGH	AVG. APRIL LOW	AVG. JULY HIGH	AVG. JULY LOW	AVG. OCT. HIGH	AVG. OCT. LOW	RECORD HIGH	RECORD LOW
Juneau	28	16	48	30	65	48	48	36	90	-22
Ketchikan	40	30	51	36	65	51	53	42	95	-8
Glacier Bay	26	16	45	33	62	48	46	37	76	-4

PRECIPITATION (INCHES)	AVG. JAN.	AVG. APRIL	AVG. JULY	AVG. OCT.	ANNUAL RAIN	ANNUAL SNOW
Juneau	3.7"	2.9"	4.1"	7.7"	53"	99"
Ketchikan	13.9"	12.1"	8.1"	22.3"	154"	20"
Glacier Bay	3.9"	3.5"	5.5"	8.9"	71"	145"

■ FOOD, LODGING, & TOURS

◆ REGIONAL INFORMATION

Alaska Bed and Breakfast Association. 369 S. Franklin, Suite 200, Juneau, AK 99801; 907-586-2959

Southeast Alaska Discovery Center. 907-228-6214

U.S. Forest Service Information Center. 101 Egan Dr., Juneau, AK 99801; 907-586-8751

For information on public cabins, camping and hiking in Alaska.

Restaurant Prices

Per person, without drinks, tax, or tip:

$ = under $12; $$ = $12–$20; $$$ = over $20

❖

Room Rates

Per night, per room, double occupancy:

$ = under $70; $$ = $70–$100; $$$ = over $100

[lodging symbol] = lodging
[restaurant symbol] = restaurant
[campground symbol] = campground
[wilderness lodge symbol] = wilderness lodge

ANGOON *map page 86, B-5*

population 700
visitors information 907-788-3653

Admiralty Island Cabins. Contact U.S. Forest Service, Juneau, 907-586-8751

Twelve public-use cabins in Admiralty Island National Monument; first-come first-served, $25.00/night permit required; apply by mail or in person 180 days in advance; no bedding, wood, or cookware supplied.

BIG SHAEEN CABIN AT HASSELBORG LAKE

Favorite Bay Inn Bed & Breakfast. Next to the sea plane float in the harbor; 907-788-3123 or 800-423-3123 $$$

Once a general store, this 1930s-era home now offers lodging; canoes and kayaks are available. Fully guided and self-guided fishing packages are offered; $4,000 per person, per week.

Kootznahoo Lodge. 911 Kilisnoo Rd., 2 1/2 miles east of ferry terminal; 907-788-3501 $$

Overlooking the Kootznahoo Inlet, the lodge has 11 units, with bathrooms and cable television. Some units have kitchenettes. Restaurant offers standard fare.

Thayer Lake Lodge. Reservations Summer: P.O. Box 211614, Auke Bay, AK 99821; 907-788-3203, summer only. Winter: P.O. Box 5416, Ketchikan AK 99901; 907-225-3343 $$$

Remote lodge on the shores of a freshwater lake in the Admiralty Island Nat. Wilderness; accessible only by plane (or by boat and then a hike). Main lodge and two independent lakefront cabins.

THAYER LAKE LODGE

CRAIG *map page 87, B-3*

population 1,600
visitors information 907-826-3870

Haida Way Lodge. On an island connected by short causeway to the west side of Prince of Wales Island; 907-826-3268 $$

A rustic lodge with 25 rooms.

GUSTAVUS *map page 86, B-4*

population 370
visitors information 907-697-2285

Strawberry Point. On the Dock Rd.; 907-697-2227 $-$$
Cafe decorated with Alaskan artifacts and serving wholesome, homemade pastries and breads, and deli items.

Aimee's B&B. 907-697-2330 $-$$
Centrally located, on the river. Two apartments. Attached to co-op gallery that features local artists.

Glacier Bay Lodge. At Bartlett Cove; 907-697-2225 $$$
In town, close to the beach and the boat dock; beautiful rain forest views when it's not raining.

Glacier Bay Country Inn. Between the airport and Bartlett Cove; 907-697-2288 (summer) or 800-673-8480 (winter) $$$
Built from hand-logged timber, this lodge has a modern mountain ambiance and a gourmet restaurant that culls from its own kitchen garden. The lodge also can arrange flightseeing tours and charter-boat service into Glacier Bay.

Good River Bed and Breakfast. Between airport and Bartlett Cove; 907-697-2241 $
Elegant log home with beautiful garden, tasty breakfasts, and free bicycle rentals.

Gustavus Inn. On the main road; 800-649-5220 or 907-697-2254 $$$
Eight miles from Glacier Bay National Park and Preserve, this romantic old inn has a picturesque garden and an excellent restaurant.

GUSTAVUS INN

Puffin Bed & Breakfast. Central Gustavus; 800-478-2258 or 907-697-2260 $$
Five attractive cabins located in a wooded homestead and decorated with Alaskan crafts. Full breakfast included and airport transfers available.

◆ TOURS

Spirit Walker Expeditions. 907-697-2266
Day and overnight kayak trips.

Equinox Wilderness Expeditions. 907-274-9087
Day and overnight kayak trips. Extended kayak expeditions

HAINES *map page 86, C-3*

population 1,360
visitors information 907-766-2234 or 800-458-3579

Bamboo Room. Second Ave., near Main St.; 907-766-2800 $
Coffee shop serving breakfast, burgers, sandwiches, and seafood.

Fireweed Bakery. In the old historic fort. *907-766-3838* $
Mediterranean cuisine, pizza, great breakfast, and fresh baked goods.

Lighthouse Restaurant. Front St. on the harbor; 907-766-2442 $$
Restaurant with a view of Lynn Canal and a colorful bar where the local commercial fishermen gather.

Port Chilkoot Potlatch. On the parade grounds of Fort Seward at Hotel Hälsingland (see below); 907-766-2000 $$$
An all-you-can-eat salmon bake in a replica of a Tlingit tribal house.

Captain's Choice Motel. Second and Dalton Sts.; 907-766-3111 $$
In town, overlooking Portage Cove.

Hotel Hälsingland. On the parade grounds, Ft. Seward 907-766-2000 or 800-542-6363 $-$$
The Victorian-style hotel, popular with European tourists, once housed the officers of old Fort Seward.

◆ TOURS

Chilkat Guides. Beach Rd. at Portage Rd.; 907-766-2491
Knowledgeable guides host a four-hour float trip through the Chilkat Bald Eagle Preserve indicating wildlife and landscape features; picnic lunch included.

Sockeye Cycle. Portage St., Fort Seward; 907-766-2869
Bike rentals and three-hour mountain-bike tours through scenic (and hilly) Haines.

JUNEAU *map page 86, C-3/4*

population 29,230
visitors information 907-586-2201, or 907-586-JUNO for the weekly info-line

Armadillo Tex-Mex Cafe. 431 S. Franklin St.; 907-586-1880 $–$$
Popular with locals and travelers alike; Mexican fare, Texas chili, and BBQ.

The Breakwater Inn. 117 Glacier Ave.; 907-586-1045; $$–$$$
Well-prepared prime rib and Alaskan seafood, overlooking Aurora Boat Harbor.

The Cookhouse. 200 Admiral Way; 907-463-3658 $
Casual dining in the heart of town. Seafood, steaks, Alaska's largest hamburger.

The Fiddlehead Restaurant & Bakery. 429 Willoughby Ave.; 907-586-3150 $$–$$$
Eclectic, creative coastal cuisine; homebaked desserts and vegetarian entrees.

✕ **Mike's Place.** Across the bridge from Juneau in Douglas, 1102 Second St.; 907-364-3271 $–$$
In the former mining community of Douglas; looks out towards Juneau and offers an extensive menu and salad bar.

✕ **The Second Course.** 213 Front St.; 907-463-5533 $$
Thai and Pacific Rim cuisine, featuring fresh vegetables, herbs, and seafood prepared with a light touch.

✕ **The Silverbow Inn and Restaurant.** 120 Second St.; 907-586-4146 $$–$$$
Casual homestyle dining featuring full breakfasts and fresh local seafood. Also a comfortable hotel.

✕ **El Sombrero.** 157 S. Franklin; 907-586-6770 $$
Mexican food in large portions, friendly ambience. A local favorite.

✕ **Thane Ore House Salmon Bake.** Four miles south of town; 907-586-3442 $$
An all-you-can-eat salmon bake and the "Gold Nugget Review" musical comedy.

Best Western Country Lane Inn. 9300 Glacier Hwy.; 907-789-5005 or 800-528-1234 $$$
Just a few blocks from the airport, with easy access to town; complimentary continental breakfasts.

Blueberry Lodge Bed and Breakfast. 9436 North Douglas Hwy.; 907-463-5886 $$
Located on scenic Douglas Island, across the channel from downtown; quiet area, with views of the water and wildlife.

The Cove Lodge. Reservation address: P.O. Box 17, Elfin Cove, AK 99825; 907-239-2221 or 800-382-3847 $$$
Remote lodge on Chichagof Island accessible from Juneau by plane or private boat. Offers B&B accommodations or full fishing packages.

Glacier Trail Bed and Breakfast. For reservations: 1081 Arctic Circle, 99801; 907-789-5646 $$
Lovely home situated only 100 feet from Mendenhall Lake and with spectacular views of Mendenhall Glacier. Three guest rooms, including one apartment suitable for a family. The innkeepers are quite knowledgeable about natural history and wilderness excursions.

THE VIEW FROM GLACIER TRAIL B&B

Grandma's Feather Bed. 4398 Mendenhall Loop Rd.; 907-789-5566 $$$
A unique country inn with a restaurant on premises that serves breakfast and dinner.

JUNEAU *continued*

Alaska Wolf House. 1900 Wickersham Ave.; 907-586-2422 $$–$$$
Beautiful cedar home on hillside overlooking Gastineau Channel. Sumptuous breakfasts, gracious hosts.

Goldbelt Hotel. 51 W. Egan Dr.; 907-586-6900 or 800-544-0970 $$$
Modern hotel with deluxe rooms; distinguished by its wood-mural carvings. 106 rooms, dining room, lounge.

Juneau International Hostel. For reservations mail request plus $10 per person deposit to: 614 Harris St., Juneau, AK 99801; 907-586-9559 $
One of the finest youth hostels in Alaska, offering dorm space for 48 people, a comfortable community room, kitchen and laundry facilities. Open year-round, with maximum stay of three nights.

Prospector Hotel. 375 Whittier St.; 800-331-2711 $$–$$$
Modern hotel near museum with large rooms, great views, and popular bar and restaurant.

Pybus Point Lodge. Reservations address: 1873 Shell Simmons Rd., Juneau, AK 99801; 907-790-4866 $$$
On the southeast tip of Admiralty Island is this family-oriented lodge with guided fishing and hunting expeditions. Accessible by plane or private boat.

Westmark Baranof Hotel. 127 N. Franklin St.; 907-586-2660 or 800-544-0970 $$$
The hotel's lobby is know for its art-deco style and original artwork by Sydney Lawrence and other Alaskan artists. Each floor has unique decor; 194 rooms; fine dining restaurant.

◆ TOURS

Alaska Discovery. 5310 Glacier Hwy.; 800-586-1911 or 907-780-6226
One of Alaska's oldest and most respected wilderness-expedition companies. Provides kayaking, rafting, camping, and bear-watching tours. Reservations recommended.

Alaska Rainforest Tours. 1873 Shell Simmons Dr.; 907-463-3466, or fax requests to 800-493-4453
Small groups on three-day personalized trips aboard a 32-foot boat to Tracy Arm Fjord and glaciers.

Alaska Sightseeing/CruiseWest. Juneau; 907-586-6064 or 800-426-7702, or (206) 441-8687 in Seattle.
Four- to seven-day cruises to see the wildlife and the bird sanctuaries of the Glacier Bay National Park and Preserve in the west arm of the bay. May through September.

Alaska State Parks. 400 Willoughby Ave.; 907-465-4563
Public trails. Wickersham House tours.

Alaska Travel Adventures. 9085 Glacier Hwy. #204; 907-789-0052
Scenic rafting on the Mendenhall River; gold panning, sea kayak tours, sportfishing, and all-you-can-eat salmon bake.

Auk Nu Tours. Glacier Hwy.; 907-586-8687
Daily Tracy Arm cruises, Icy Straits wildlife tours, and ferry service to Gustavus; naturalists on board.

Coastal Helicopters. 2355 Ka-See-An Dr.; 907-789-5600
Available for charter, contract, heli-fishing, heli-skiing, and photography tours.

Wings of Alaska. 1873 Shell Simmons Dr., Juneau; 907-789-0790
Year-round scheduled or charter airline servicing Southeast.

KETCHIKAN

map page 87, C-4

population 15,000
visitors information 907-225-6166 or 800-770-2200

Annabell's Keg & Chowder House. 326 Front St.; 907-225-9423 $
Local seafood in the historic Gilmore Hotel; features Alaskan seafood and homemade cannery bread. Features a collection of '20s memorabilia from Ketchikan's red-light district.

Five Star Cafe. 5 Cook St.; 907-247-7827 $
Homemade soups, vegetarian fare, and desserts.

Kay's Kitchen. 2813 Tongass Ave.; 907-225-5860 $
Homemade soups and sandwiches.

Salmon Falls Resort. Mile 17, N. Tongass Hwy.; 907-225-2752 $$
Serving fresh seafood caught in local waters; octagonal dining room supported by a piece of pipe originally intended for the Alaska pipeline.

American Youth Hostel. First Methodist Church at Grant and Main sts.; 907-225-3319 $
Summer only (June through August); bring your sleeping bag. Showers and kitchen facilities; reservations (in writing only) recommended.

Best Western Landing. 3434 Tongass Ave.; 907-225-5166 or 800-428-8304 $$–$$$
Right in the heart of town, across from the Marine Ferry Terminal, with a restaurant in the building.

Campgrounds. U.S. Forest Service; 907-225-2148 or Southeast Alaska Visitor Center 907-228-6214

Six to be found north of town on North Tongass Highway and Ward Lake Road; cabins are also available.

Gilmore Hotel. 326 Front St.; 907-225-9423 $$
On the National Historic Register; 38 rooms; city-center waterfront views.

Ingersoll Hotel. 303 Mission St.; 907-225-2124 $$
Built in the '20s; 58 rooms; homey old-fashioned atmosphere. Located across the street from the cruise ship docks.

KETCHIKAN *continued*

Ketchikan Reservation Service. 412 D-1 Loop Rd.; 907-247-5337 or 800-987-5337
Information on bed and breakfasts.

Mink Bay Lodge. Misty Fiords National Monument. Reservations address: P.O. Box 8660, Ketchikan , AK 99901; 800-999-0784 or 907-225-3875 $$$

Located 50 miles south of Ketchikan; excellent freshwater and saltwater fishing. Accessible by plane or private boat.

Waterfall Resort. Prince of Wales Island. Reservations address: P.O. Box 6440, Ketchikan, AK 99901; 907-225-9461 $$$

Coastal fishing resort with luxurious accommodations 62 miles west of Ketchikan. Full bath, wet bar, refrigerator, and television and billiards. Accessible by plane or private boat.

Westmark Cape Fox Lodge. 800 Venetia Way; 907-225-8001 or 800-544-0970 $$$

Above Ketchikan and Tongass Narrows; 72 spacious rooms with views; restaurant and lounge.

Yes Bay Lodge. 50 miles northwest of Ketchikan; Reservations address: P.O. Box 8660, Ketchikan, AK 99901; 907-225-3875 or 800-999-0784 $$$

Offers saltwater and freshwater fishing, family-style meals. Accessible by plane or private boat.

◆ TOURS

Outdoor Alaska. 907-225-6044
Air-taxi service providing tours into Misty Fiords and kayak drop-offs.

Southeast Exposure.
507 Stedman St.; 907-225-8829

Provides four- to eight-day kayaking trips into the Misty Fiords, coordinated with Outdoor Alaska's drop-off runs.

PETERSBURG

map page 87, C-2

population 3,350
visitors information 907-772-4636

The Broom Hus. 411 S. Nordic Dr.; 907-772-3459 $$
Offers a homemade continental breakfast; located between the ferry building and downtown.

✕ **Helse.** Sing Lee Alley and Harbor Way; 907-772-3444 $
The menu features wholesome natural foods served in generous vegetable-laden portions.

✕ **Northern Lights.** Sing Lee Alley; *907-772-2900* $$
Serving breakfast, lunch, and dinner. Standard fare, family atmosphere.

✕ **Pellerito's Pizzaria.** Across from the ferry terminal; 907-772-3727 $$
The pizzas here are made from scratch; good microbrewery beer selection.

✕ **Studabaker.** 907-772-5000 $$
Good take-out pizza, free delivery.

Campgrounds. U.S. Forest Service office; 907-772-3871
Provides 20 remote public-use cabins around the Petersburg area. Ninety percent of the island offers free camping in national forests. "Tent City" houses young cannery workers in summer.

Scandia House. 110 Nordic Dr.; 907-772-4281 or 800-722-5006 $–$$
Petersburg's early Norwegian influences are evident in this rebuilt early 20th-century hotel. Thirty-three rooms in modern, Euro-influenced building. One block from boat harbor. Car and boat rentals.

Tides Inn. First and Dolphin sts.; 907-772-4288 or 800-665-8433 $$
Largest hotel in town; modern rooms; complimentary breakfast.

◆ Tours

Seclusion Harbor Charters. 907-772-2121
A floating vacation cabin/fishing lodge with most of the conveniences of home; guests can fish, whale watch and sightsee from two skiffs with outboards.

Tongass Kayak Adventures. 907-772-4600
No-experience-needed paddle trips around the harbor and extended trips.

SITKA *map page 86, A-5*

population 9,190
visitors information 907-747-5940

TOWN OF SITKA

✕ **Backdoor Cafe.** Lincoln St.; 907-747-8856 $
A small espresso shop behind Old Harbor Books that also serves homemade baked goods.

SOUTHEAST

SITKA *continued*

Bayview Restaurant. 407 Lincoln St.; 907-747-5440 $
Specializing in Russian foods, such as piroshki or Russian-style halibut, deli sandwiches, hamburgers, and fresh seafood. Outdoor deck overs the harbor. Also open for breakfast.

Channel Club. Mile 3.5, 2906, Halibut Point Rd.; 907-747-9916 $$–$$$
The steaks here are legendary, but if you don't have an appetite for red meat you'll be delighted by the large salad bar.

Highliner Coffee. Seward Square, No. 5; 907-747-4924 $–$$
Cybercafé with internet access, historical nautical décor. Roasts own beans on premises.

Van Winkle and Sons. 205 Harbor Dr.; 907-747-3396 $–$$
Specializing in fresh Alaskan seafood and pizza.

Alaska Ocean View Bed and Breakfast. 1101 Edgecumbe Dr.; 907-747-8310 $$–$$$
Ocean view, delicious breakfasts, and smoke-free rooms.

Camping. U.S. Forest Service; 800-280-camp or 907-747-4220 $
Four campgrounds: Starrigavan Campground at Milepost 7.8 on Halibut Point Road; Sitka Sportsman's Assoc. RV Park, one block south of ferry terminal on Halibut Point Road; Sealing Cove adjacent to Sealing Cove Boat Harbor on Japonski Island; and Sawmill Creek Campground at Milepost 5.4 on Sawmill Creek Road.

Cascade Inn. On the waterfront; 907-747-6804 $$
Beautiful views of Mt. Edgecumbe, individual patios.

International Youth Hostel. Located at the corner of 6th Street and Harris Street near Cope Park. Reservations: PO Box 2645, Sitka, AK 99835; 907-747-8661 $
Twenty beds. Open June–August only.

Rainforest Retreat. Reservations: P.O. Box 8005, Port Alexander, AK 99836; 907-568-2229 $$$
Modern cabins situated in an old-growth forest; guests can relax, hike, and enjoy health-consciously prepared meals, or for half price of normal rate, guests can cook for themselves in the light-cooking kitchen. Accessible by plane or private boat.

Westmark Shee Atika. 330 Seward St.; 907-747-6241 or 800-544-0970 $$$
The artwork displayed throughout the hotel is a tribute to the history, legends, and talent of the Tlingit people. Many of the rooms overlook Crescent Harbor; the restaurant looks out over the Sitka Sound and the local fishing fleets.

◆ TOURS

Sea Otter & Wildlife Quest. 907-747-7474
A half-day wildlife cruise to Salisbury Island, viewing sea otters, whales, bears, and sea birds. Evening harbor cruises are also available. Open May through September.

SKAGWAY *map page 86, C-3*

population 810
visitors information 907-983-2854

✕ **Northern Lights Café.** 907-983-2225 $–$$
Standard Italian, Mexican, and American fare. Generous portions at reasonable prices.

✕ **Red Onion Saloon.** 2nd Ave. at Broadway; 907-983-2222 $
Pizza, beer, and live rock music in what was once a bordello.

✕ **Stowaway Café.** A mile north of town on State St.; 907-983-3463 $$$
Fine dining, featuring local fish entrees served Alaskan and Cajun style.

✕ **Sweet Tooth Cafe.** Broadway St. at 3rd Ave.; 907-983-2405 $
This tiny cafe/saloon is a Skagway favorite, providing pastries and eggs from as early as 6:00 A.M. Don't miss the cinammon rolls.

Gold Rush Lodge. Sixth and Alaska St.; 907-983-2831 $$
Clean, comfortable rooms, all no smoking. Courtesy van. Recommended.

Golden North Hotel. Third Ave. and Broadway; 907-983-2544 or 888-222-1898 $$
Alaska's oldest operating hotel and brewery. Authentic 1898 decor with restaurant, microbrewery, and sushi bar.

GOLDEN NORTH HOTEL

Skagway Inn Bed & Breakfast. Broadway and Seventh St.; 907-983-2289 or 800-478-2290 in Alaska $$
This Victorian inn, in the Klondike Gold Rush National Historical Park, was originally established as a brothel in 1897; rooms are named after notable women from the gold rush era.

Westmark Inn. Third St. at Spring; 907-983-2291 or 800-544-0970 $$–$$$
Features period furniture, brass trim, and historical photos. The hotel restaurant has extensive wine list and diverse menu.

WESTMARK INN

SKAGWAY *continued*

Wind Valley Lodge. A mile north of town on State St.; 907-983-2236 $$
Modern hotel providing convenient shuttles to the downtown area; 30 rooms.

◆ TOURS

TEMSCO **Helicopters.** 907-983-2900.
Helicopter flightseeing tours of nearby sights; includes landing on a glacier, and a guided tour on the "river of ice," where a guide will walk you through the interesting features of the glacial terrain. Dog sled rides.

Packer Expeditions. 907-983-2544.

Guided hiking trips long and short, using helicopter and train for bush country access. Locally owned and operated.

White Pass and Yukon Route Railway. 800-343-7373
Historical train route established in the Gold Rush era; three-hour excursion from Skagway (from May through September) to 2,900-foot White Pass summit. For the best view, sit on the left when leaving Skagway.

WRANGELL *map page 87, C-2*

population 2,760
visitors information 907-874-3901
or 800-367-9745

Diamond C Cafe. 215 Front St.; 907-874-3677 $
Inexpensive food in a diner atmosphere.

Roadhouse Lodge. Mile 4, Zimovia Hwy.; 907-874-2335 $–$$
Wholesome fare; could double as a museum of early Alaska.

Harding's Old Sourdough Lodge. 1104 Peninsula St.; 907-874-3613 or 800-874-3613 $$
Situated on the docks, family-run, homey rustic rooms, and open living room/dining room.

Roadhouse Lodge. 4 Mile Zimovia Hwy.; 907-874-2335 $
Filled with Alaskan artifacts and antiques. Rooms have private baths. Downstairs are a restaurant and bar. Wholesome fare and very friendly atmosphere.

Stikine Inn. One block from ferry terminal, Stikine Ave.; 907-874-3388 $$
Standard rooms but convenient location and great harbor views. Coffee shop, restaurant, and gift shop.

Tongass National Forest Cabins. Wrangell Ranger District; 907-874-2323
A dozen cabins in the Wrangell area, over 150 in all of Tongass Nat. Forest. Rustic, but comfortable. Accessible by boat, floatplane, helicopter, or hiking trail.

◆ TOURS

Stikine Wilderness Adventures. 907-874-2085 $$
Guided jet boat tours and transport to Anan Creek bear observatory. Local expert guides.

SOUTHEAST

YAKUTAT *map page 86, A-1*

population 700
visitors information at city hall: 907-784-3323

✕ **Yakutat Lodge.**
By airport; 907-784-3232 $$
Inexpensive food in a diner atmosphere.

✕ **Glacier Bear Lodge.** Two miles from airport; 907-784-3287 $$
A lounge and restaurant with rooms in a forest setting.

Bayview Lodge. In town overlooking the bay; 907-784-3341 $$
Conveniently located in the middle of town; great views. Individual kitchens available. Also full meal service.

Blue Heron Inn. On Yakutat Bay in town; 907-784-3287 $$
Stay with a local sport fishing guide and his family. Guiding service and vacation rentals.

Leonard's Landing. Five miles from the airport; 907-784-3245 $$
Cabins and restaurant on water by the boat harbor.

The Tlingit tribal meeting house in Saxman.

Festivals and Events

February

Ketchikan: Festival of the North. A month-long arts, music, and drama festival to cheer winter-weary locals. 907-225-6166

Wrangell: Tent City Winter Festival. Held on the first weekend in February to celebrate the role Wrangell played in the Gold Rush; food, crafts, and beard-growing and tall-tales contests. *907-874-3901*

April

Juneau: Alaska Folk Festival. A mix of music, food, and handmade crafts. *907-789-0292*

May

Juneau: Jazz and Classics Festival. Performances by nationally known musicians. *907-364-2801*

Petersburg: Little Norway Festival. In celebration of Petersburg's Norwegian heritage; features folk dancing, folk food, costumes, halibut filleting contests, and Viking raids. *907-772-3646*

June

Juneau: Gold Rush Days. A two-day celebration including logging competitions between miners and loggers, a children's carnival, food booths, and a closing night dance. *907-586-2201*

Sitka: Summer Music Festival. Chamber-music artists from all over the world perform over three weeks to standing-room-only crowds. Instructional workshops and evening concerts characterize this musical gala. *907-747-6774 or 907-277-4852*

August

Ketchikan: Blueberry Arts Festival. Arts and crafts, blueberry pies, blueberry crêpes, blueberry cheesecakes. Slug race, pie eating contest, and spelling bee. *907-225-2211*

Haines: Southeast Alaska State Fair. Popular regional event featuring crafts, home-made foods, a horse show, and a parade. *907-766-2234 or 800-458-3579*

October

Sitka: Alaska Day Festival. A three- to five-day festival celebrating the 1867 purchase of Alaska from the Russians. Festival highlights include a costume ball, Russian dancing, parade, and ceremonial reenactment of the purchase. *907-747-5940*

November

Sitka: Holiday Fest. Holiday celebrations are continued through January and include Russian Christmas and Starring festivities. *907-747-5940*

Totem poles near Kasaan Prince of Wales Island

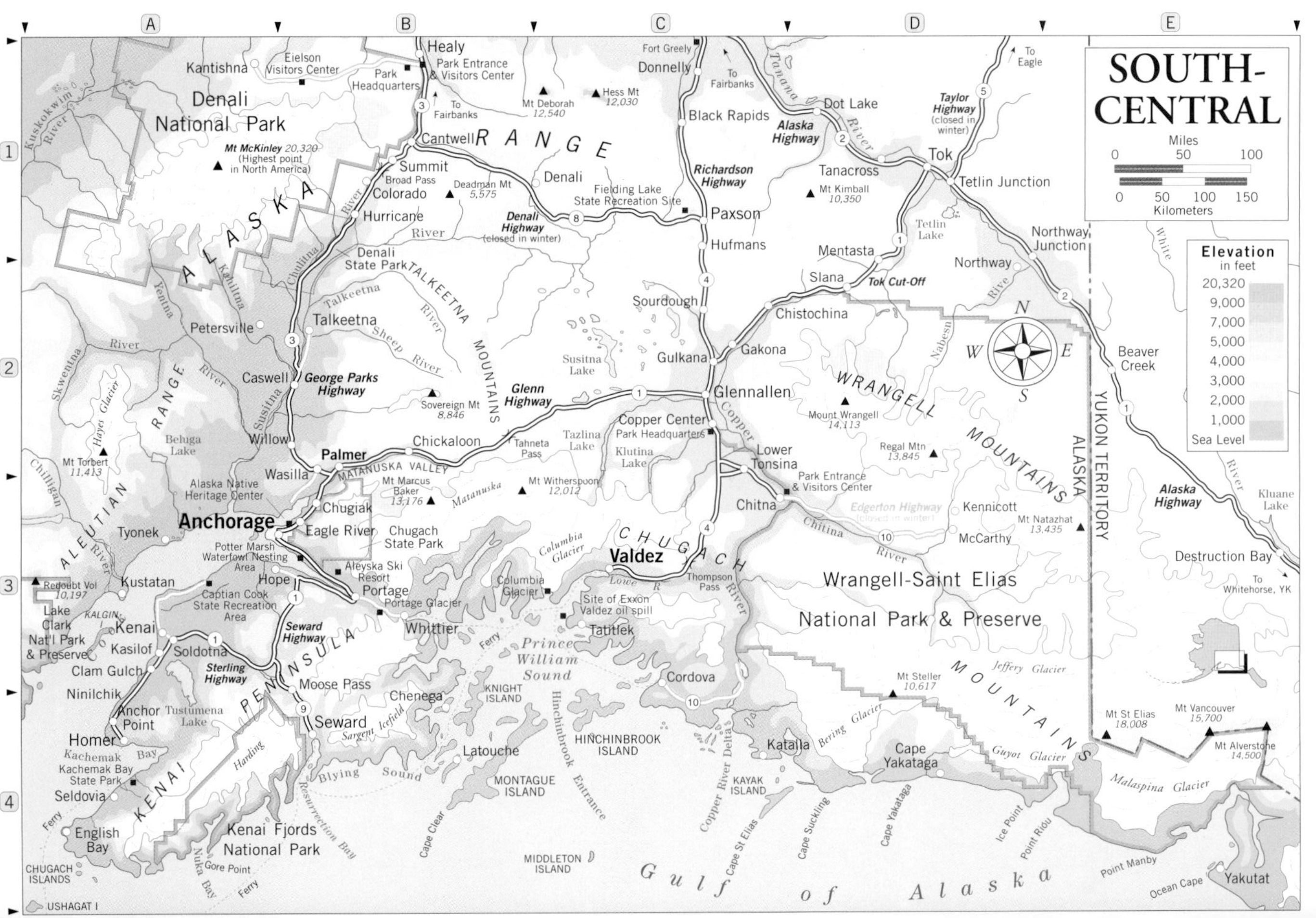
SOUTH-CENTRAL
Miles
0 50 100
0 50 100 150
Kilometers
Elevation in feet
20,320
9,000
7,000
5,000
4,000
3,000
2,000
1,000
Sea Level
A
B
C
D
E
1
2
3
4
YUKON TERRITORY
ALASKA
Kantishna
Eielson Visitors Center
Denali National Park
Park Headquarters
Healy
Park Entrance & Visitors Center
To Fairbanks
Mt McKinley 20,320 (Highest point in North America)
ALASKA RANGE
Mt Deborah 12,540
Hess Mt 12,030
Denali
Cantwell
Summit
Broad Pass
Colorado
Hurricane
Deadman Mt 5,575
Denali Highway (closed in winter)
Fielding Lake State Recreation Site
Fort Greely
Donnelly
To Fairbanks
Black Rapids
Richardson Highway
Paxson
Hufmans
Sourdough
Gulkana
Gakona
Glennallen
Copper Center
Park Headquarters
Klutina Lake
Tazlina Lake
Susitna Lake
Glenn Highway
Tahneta Pass
Mt Witherspoon 12,012
Chickaloon
TALKEETNA MOUNTAINS
Sovereign Mt 8,846
Denali State Park
Talkeetna
George Parks Highway
Petersville
Caswell
Willow
Wasilla
Palmer
MATANUSKA VALLEY
Mt Marcus Baker 13,176
Chugach State Park
Chugiak
Eagle River
Anchorage
Alaska Native Heritage Center
Potter Marsh Waterfowl Nesting Area
Alyeska Ski Resort
Portage
Portage Glacier
Whittier
Hope
Seward Highway
Sterling Highway
Captian Cook State Recreation Area
Soldotna
Tustumena Lake
Kenai
Kasilof
Clam Gulch
Ninilchik
Anchor Point
Homer
Kachemak Bay
Kachemak Bay State Park
Seldovia
English Bay
CHUGACH ISLANDS
USHAGAT I
Kenai Fjords National Park
Gore Point
Nuka Bay
Harding
Sargent Icefield
Seward
Moose Pass
Resurrection Bay
KENAI PENINSULA
Lake Clark Nat'l Park & Preserve
KALGIN I
Redoubt Vol 10,197
Kustatan
Tyonek
ALEUTIAN RANGE
Mt Torbert 11,413
Hayes Glacier
Beluga Lake
Chilligan
Skwentna
Yentna
Kahiltna
Susitna
Chulitna
Kuskokwim River
Tanana River
Dot Lake
Tanacross
Alaska Highway
Mt Kimball 10,350
Tok
Tetlin Junction
Taylor Highway (closed in winter)
To Eagle
Tetlin Lake
Tok Cut-Off
Mentasta
Slana
Chistochina
Northway
Northway Junction
Beaver Creek
Destruction Bay
To Whitehorse, YK
Kluane Lake
White River
Nabesna
WRANGELL MOUNTAINS
Mount Wrangell 14,113
Regal Mtn 13,845
Mt Natazhat 13,435
Kennicott
McCarthy
Edgerton Highway (closed in winter)
Park Entrance & Visitors Center
Lower Tonsina
Chitna
Chitina River
Copper River
Wrangell-Saint Elias National Park & Preserve
CHUGACH MOUNTAINS
Thompson Pass
Valdez
Lowe R
Site of Exxon Valdez oil spill
Tatitlek
Columbia Glacier
Prince William Sound
Cordova
Copper River Delta
Katalla
KAYAK ISLAND
Cape St Elias
Cape Suckling
Bering Glacier
Cape Yakataga
Mt Steller 10,617
ST ELIAS MOUNTAINS
Guyot Glacier
Jeffery Glacier
Malaspina Glacier
Mt St Elias 18,008
Mt Vancouver 15,700
Mt Alverstone 14,500
Yakutat
Ocean Cape
Point Manby
Ice Point
Point Riou
HINCHINBROOK ISLAND
Hinchinbrook Entrance
MONTAGUE ISLAND
MIDDLETON ISLAND
KNIGHT ISLAND
Latouche
Chenega
Blying Sound
Cape Clear
Gulf of Alaska
Ferry

SOUTH-CENTRAL

■ HIGHLIGHTS

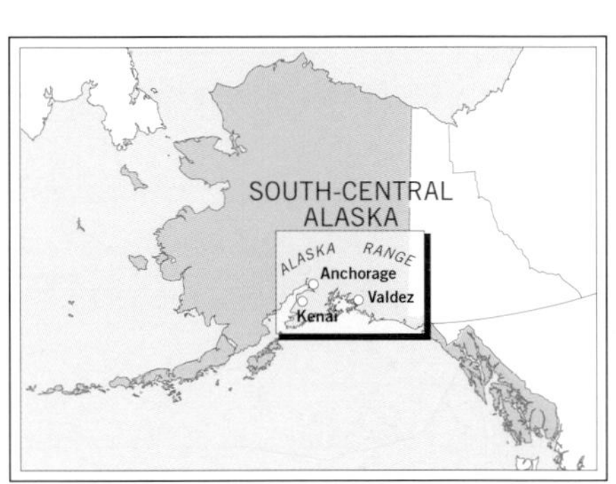

◆ MAPS

◆ PRACTICAL INFORMATION

■ LANDSCAPE AND TRAVEL

South-Central Alaska encompasses two worlds—the crenelated coastline of the northern Pacific and the complicated mountain country south of the Alaskan Range. Here is everything from seaweed-covered beaches to permanently frozen glacial ice fields. In this region you will find some of the tallest peaks in North America, and by my count about one hundred of the most beautiful valleys. Some of the fjords on the Kenai Peninsula look like pictures from Norway. Nearby old-growth rain forests appear to have been transplanted from the Amazon. There are soaring trees in those coastal forests with enough wood in one tree to build a good-sized country church, and there are ancient wind-flagged krumholtz trees at timberline that could fit in your hat. Retiring moose call this place home, as do wolves and grizzlies. In the rivers you will find the biggest salmon in the world.

The core city of **Anchorage** offers the amenities of a sizable metropolis, and paved roads lead to the **Kenai Peninsula,** which juts out south of Anchorage between Cook Inlet and Prince William Sound. Many people consider this the most beautiful area in Alaska, and it has several delightful towns, in particular Homer and Seward. A tour boat or marine ferry will take you out to explore the coastline of **Prince William Sound** and to see its glaciers, fjords, and wildlife. To reach it drive south to Portage and take the train to Whittier. Or travel north, then east of Anchorage via the Glenn Highway. At Glennallen the road meets the Richardson Highway which turns south to Valdez.

Many visitors drive or take the train from Anchorage to **Denali National Park** (*described on page 212 in the following chapter*).

■ ANCHORAGE AND VICINITY

◆ HISTORY

Anchor-age. The name says it. Anchorage was in the beginning a convenient place for ships to rest awhile from the stormy north Pacific, a shallow quiet stretch of salt water at the head of a long inlet, surrounded by moose forest and fox meadow. A place to throw out the heavy rusted anchor, and lower the wooden longboats, and venture forth in search of fresh water, fresh meat, fresh berries—anything so long as it did not taste of sea. The Russians visited, and the British, and later the

Downtown Anchorage in 1915 (above) when the city was just a year old. Today the city is the financial hub of the state (right) and has more than 257,000 residents. (Photo above from Anchorage Museum of History and Art)

ARCO

Americans. Everyone seemed to like it, but not even aboriginal Alaskans had built a permanent settlement. In 1914, the future arrived in the form of a pioneering federal railroad north into the gold-and-silver mining country around Fairbanks. Anchorage was the logistical center between Fairbanks and the southern terminus at Seward, and the rest, as they say, is history.

In the 1930s, concerted efforts were made to turn the Matanuska Valley north of Anchorage into an agricultural paradise—cattle, barley, potatoes. Most of these well-intentioned attempts did not meet with success, but the various government-sponsored experiments at least drew hordes of hardy homesteaders into the area. Other events conspired to bring Anchorage more and more toward center stage in Alaska—especially support activities surrounding the Aleutian battles of World War II and the growing popularity of Mount McKinley National Park, now Denali National Park.

By the 1970s, Anchorage had become an important international air crossroads, the financial and commercial center for the state, and the corporate headquarters for the oil pipeline running from Prudhoe Bay south to Valdez. Revenues from the pipeline brought an enormous amount of money into the state, and especially into Anchorage. Increasingly, Juneau—the state capital—began to fade behind the rising star of its big sister to the north. In 1974, state residents voted to move the capital to Willow, a small town north of Anchorage, but then, in the often contradictory spirit of democracy, refused to fund the project. The result is that Juneau remains the ever-remote seat of government.

◆ ANCHORAGE TODAY

Downtown Anchorage has a haphazard, frontier feel to it. Stern hotels overlook parking lots and empty lots; a few oil company office buildings and a federal building rise above disheveled cottages and new apartment buildings. The excellent art and history museum (more attractive inside than outside) and an architecturally interesting performing arts facility exude a public spirit also evident in parks ablaze with flowers in the summer. Good restaurants and hip bars are lively in the evening. Nearby are both upscale and dingy arts and crafts shops, fur outlets, pawn shops, a memorial to homicide victims, and dive bars (outside of which drunks reel around and curse each other). On a gray summer Saturday, downtown can appear damp and half-empty, except at the Saturday Market in the parking lot by the Hilton. But if the clouds part and the setting reveals itself, the effect is

ART AND CULTURE IN ANCHORAGE

In Anchorage, cultural juxtapositions abound. Inupiat teenage girls adopt gangsta styles fresh out of South Central L.A. Samoan, African-American, and Korean churches are tucked in unlikely buildings in less likely mini-malls. A horse-drawn carriage lumbers down asphalt lanes built as early as the Carter administration. A bank that once gave away a .44 Magnum with every $10,000 certificate of deposit turns into a donut shop. Two years ago your bed-and-breakfast was an after-hours bar that served the massage parlor that's now a 7-11. Lacking major historical sites to visit, tour-bus drivers take passengers through suburban neighborhoods, pointing out well-kept lawns.

"**Fine art**" muddles through somehow, although a flood of "moose and mountains" imagery tends to dominate the market. **Books** seriously examining the recent massive transformation of Alaska exist but require a little seeking out.

In Anchorage, artists nonchalantly cross disciplines and genres. A friend who was the concertmaster for the Anchorage Opera also played fiddle with a rock band called Sportin' Woodies. Another friend writes travel books, news articles, puts out a political magazine called *POL*, and sits on the Anchorage Municipal Assembly. A young poet and Denali train waitress is an accomplished jazz dancer. In one week I judged a high school poetry contest, opened my painting studio as part of a city-wide tour, and played an Earth Day festival as a rhythm guitarist in a band named after a trailer court.

There is a unique vibrancy and piquancy to the arts here. You only have to look as far as Tom Bodette of NPR fame and John Adams, Alaska's notable musical composer; and on to author John Haines, who has left the state he evoked so well in his writing, claiming Alaska's institutions did not support him.

Anchorage symphony, opera, and concert associations present increasingly vigorous programs. Small theater companies like Out North flex their muscles, fed by a nationally respected University of Alaska (Anchorage) theater program. Private galleries like the Decker-Morris and the International Gallery for Contemporary Art push to expand visual horizons. Cafes like **Kaladi Bros., Side Street, Cyrano's, Q [Qupqugiaq] Cafe,** and **The Firehouse** provide forums for poetry slams and live readings.

An original modern **rock music scene** that was non-existent eight years ago got a boost from UAA radio station KRUA 88.1 FM (worth checking out for the broad music variety and hilarious PSA's), and now bands like Freedom 49 and Ill-Gotten have given Anchorage teenagers that elusive something-to-do. A nascent **jazz** scene, numerous summer **folk and bluegrass festivals** and even a **Klezmer** band offer a decent variety of music that is steadily growing. The *Anchorage Daily News* "8"section and the *Anchorage Press* give extensive listings of just about every little event in town.

—*Jamie Bollenbach*

exhilarating. To the west lie the gray waters of Cook Inlet, rimmed with sand and clay cliffs topped by birch and spruce. In every other direction rise the jagged, snowcapped Chugach Mountains.

As with so many other cities, the local commercial life of Anchorage has been sucked into the neighborhoods where most people live, and like their counterparts in the Lower 48, shoppers head to nearby malls, rather than driving into the old downtown. This residential part of Anchorage can be difficult for the visitor to penetrate, and there isn't much incentive to do so, as artery boulevards are lined with the same chain food outlets, blank-walled discount stores, and landscaping-free malls that pockmark the rest of the United States. Yet, if you know someone to help you negotiate the terrain, they'll point out with great enthusiasm such places as City Market, a specialty food store and cafe where you can sit outside and mingle with the hip crowd; the solarium of Bell's nursery cafe; the big new chain bookstores; and a great Thai restaurant in an old Dairy Queen.

Fourth Avenue—1943 *by Anchorage artist Byron Birdsall. (Courtesy Artique Ltd. and Byron Birdsall)*

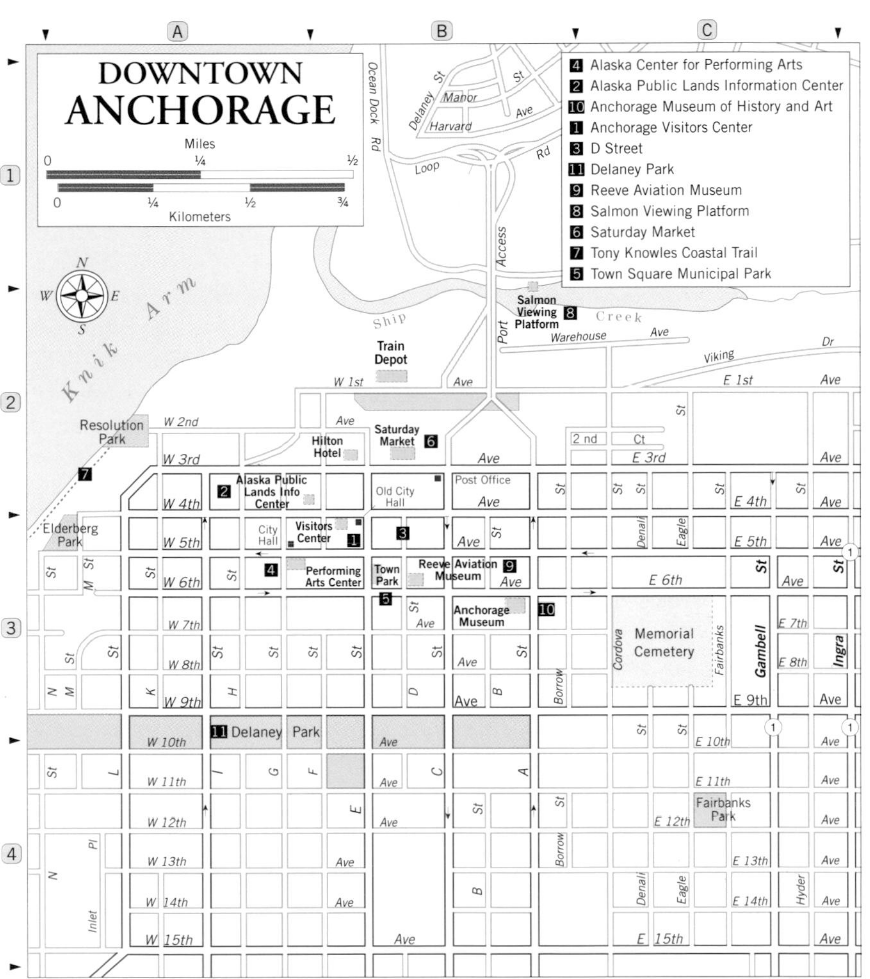

More than half of all Alaskan residents live in Anchorage and its surrounding suburbs. The majority of the city's 250,000 inhabitants trace their ancestry to Europe, yet there is a sizable population of Native Alaskans here—Eskimo, Athabaskan, Aleut, and Tlingit, as well as African-Americans, Russians, Hispanics, and folks from the Pacific Rim countries (Korea, Japan, Taiwan). The result of this mixture is a cosmopolitan, multicultural community in a city that retains the sort of informality associated with the frontier.

◆ EXPLORING ANCHORAGE

map page 151

1 Anchorage Visitors Center

Located on the corner of Fourth Avenue and "F" Street, the visitor center is open daily during the summer tourist season. This place is exploding with pamphlets, brochures, maps, coupons, and all manner of information. On the same block is the Old City Hall, where signs will tell you where to meet for the city walking tour offered every afternoon during the summer.

2 Alaska Public Lands Information Center

Located in the Old Federal Building also at Fourth and "F," the center features informational videos, wildlife exhibits, historical displays, and also includes a good selection of books, posters, and videotapes for sale. The highly trained desk staff can provide information on lands from the wildlife refuges in the Aleutians to the critical habitat area near Yakutat.

You will notice that these two visitors centers are at the center of downtown's shop and restaurant district, and that flowerpots overflowing with beautiful bright flowers hang from the Fourth Avenue lamp posts (in summer).

3 D Street between Fourth and Fifth

Here you'll find several arts and crafts stores selling original works, many by Native Alaskan artists. There are also many mass-produced imitations. (A recent scandal involved a new twist in the game of artistic misrepresentation, when a Vietnamese artisan bought the right to use the name of a Nome Eskimo and sold his work as "Native American.") Cyrano's Books is on this block, a center of Anchorage intellectual life for a decade. The store has a small cafe and a theater, and its owner a deep knowledge of Alaskan literature. For sale here is a tape of the poetry of Robert Service—a chronicler of gold rush and sourdough life, who wrote humorous, nostalgic, rhymed poetry—wonderful to have for long drives into the wilderness. (The opening lines of *The Shooting of Dan McGrew,* page 247, have inspired many Malamute Saloons.) Around the corner on Fifth is Cook Inlet Book Company, which offers a wide choice of books about Alaska.

4 Alaska Center for the Performing Arts

Located on Fifth Avenue and G Street, the center was built in the mid-1980s and furnished by Alaskan craftsmen. Check the schedule to see what new plays, musicals, dances, or symphonic performances are currently being featured; *907-263-2787.*

5 Town Square Municipal Park

This park, just east of the performing arts center, is—in the summertime—abloom with flowers so improbably colored, you'd swear they'd been dipped in paint. Rather, this color is testimony to the effect of 20 hours of daylight and plenty of rain.

6 Saturday Market

Held on summer Saturdays in the parking lot across from the Hilton, on E Street at the corner of Third. Nearly 300 vendors set up their blue and white tents herein selling: three-foot carved bears, Asian food (lumpia, yakatori, and pork buns from one vendor, but all good), Russian piroshki, popcorn, wolf-fur boots, knives, implements made from antlers, nesting dolls from Russia, decorated birch bark baskets from Siberia (Dersu Imports), hats and scarves made from qiviut (underfur of the musk ox).

7 Tony Knowles Coastal Trail

This lovely trail is reached by walking west down Third Avenue to the southern end of Resolution Park. Governor Knowles owned the Downtown Deli, then served as mayor of Anchorage for much of the 1980s. The trail named in his honor is one of the true pleasures of Anchorage. Following it, you'll see lovely residential neighborhoods, views across Cook Inlet, wildflowers, trees, and, honking in the tidal flats, dozens of Canada geese. Many Anchorage lodgings provide their guests with bicycles, and if yours does, take advantage of the offer and bike the trail. The trail extends south for many miles along the western shores of the inlet, passing Earthquake Park, so named when the 1964 earthquake caused the soil to slump and rendered the area unsuitable for residential development.

8 Salmon Viewing Platform

During the summer months, salmon migrate up Ship Creek and can be observed easily from this point, reached by continuing north on C Street across the railroad tracks to the bridge over Ship Creek. The banks are crowded with fishermen, shoulder to shoulder as they fish for salmon—quite a sight to behold in the midst of a major American city. Salmon in the 50-pound class have been caught in this creek.

9 Reeve Aviation Picture Museum

Located at 343 W. Sixth Avenue between D and C, this photo archive has more than a thousand photos of Alaska's most famous bush pilots. (Also well worth a visit for aviation buffs is the **Alaska Aviation Heritage Museum** with its classic aircraft collection, near the airport at 4721 Aircraft Drive.)

10 Anchorage Museum of History and Art

Located on A Street between Sixth and Seventh, this major facility offers an outstanding collection of historic and contemporary Alaskan art, and a special section for children. The wide interior atrium is a truly inviting space, airy and light. Alaskan artisans display and sell their wares here, and the ambiance is such that it's easy and pleasant to stand about and talk to them about their work. A cafe serves informal food at tables around a fountain (which is supposed to look like it's built of ice, but looks more like glass bathroom tiles). Downstairs galleries exhibit the works of Sydney Laurence, Thomas Hill, and Fred Machetanz, well-known Alaskan painters, whose romantic and realistic visions of an earlier era convey a sense of the mythic and spiritual effect the Alaskan landscape can have on those who live here. Upstairs, the crafts of Native Alaskan and early Russian communities are artfully displayed in domestic settings that give these tiny artifacts life and meaning. Especially beautiful are a narrow nude female figure caved in walrus ivory that served as a needlecase and an ancient stone bowl that served as a seal-oil lamp.

Among the many treasures in the collection of the Anchorage Museum of History and Art are this Haida argillite box (above) made by John Cross, circa 1900; the seal-oil lamp (below), circa A.D. 1000, which was found on the Kenai Peninsula.

11 Greenbelt/Delaney Park

South of the art museum in a long narrow strip from A to P streets between 9th and 10th, lie lovely bicycle and walking trails that wind through woods and meadows and eventually meet up with the Coastal Trail.

Alaska Native Heritage Center

map page 144, A/B-3

Located 12 miles north of Anchorage on 26-acres of land, this marvelous new site will encompass five "historic village" exhibits representing Native Alaskan traditions. Call for directions and information as this is a new facility, *907-263-5170.*

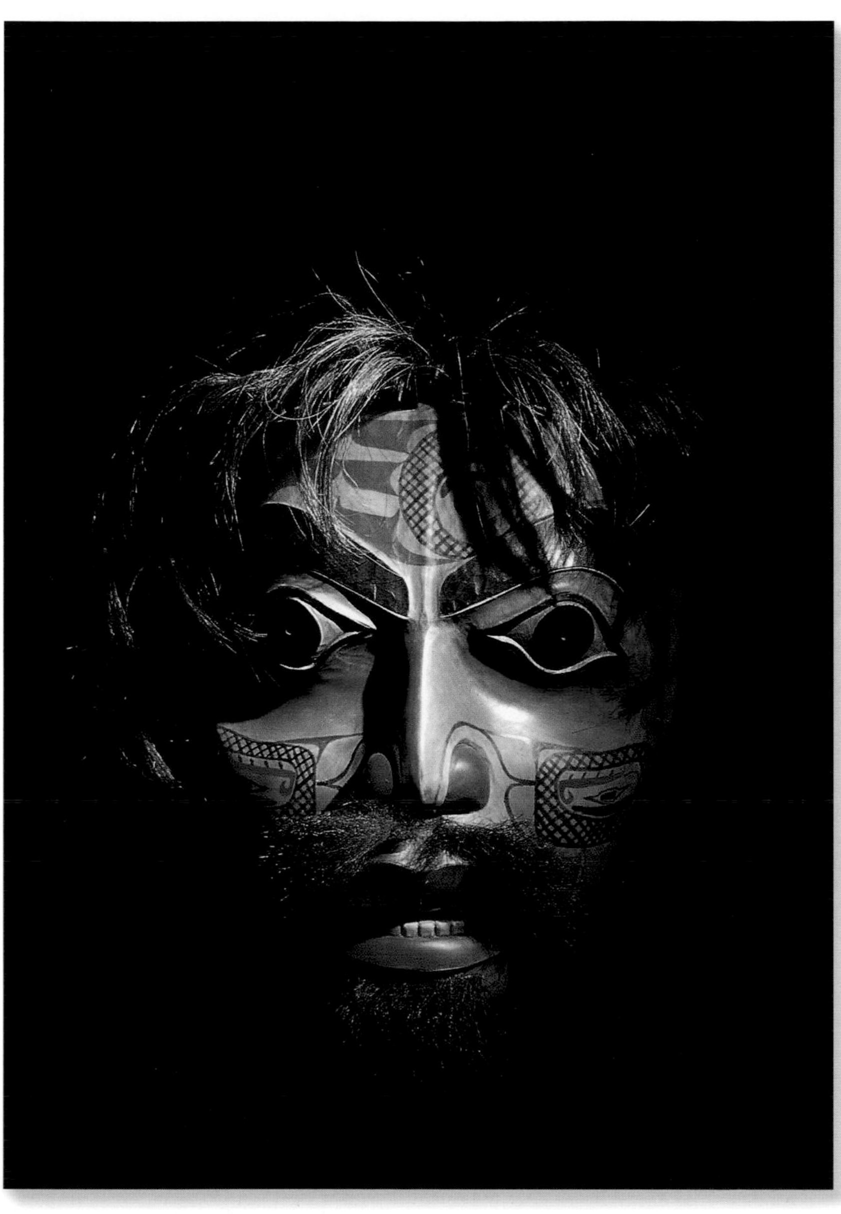

A contemporary Tlingit mask carved by artist Nathan Jackson.
(Anchorage Museum of Histrory and Art)

Alaska Politics

In Alaska, you'll see some version of the following: an abused, encrusted 4 x 4 Subaru with two bumper stickers, "Think Globally, Act Locally" and "An Armed Society is a Polite Society."

Nothing fits neatly in Alaska politics. Idealistic, reactionary, frontier-practical, isolated, and apathetic or actively paranoid, Alaskans insist on their own interpretation of everything. The people sort of lead, candidates sort of follow, and parties limp behind. Without a major sports team, politics has to suffice for entertainment. Most voters are Independents, and cross-party coalitions frequently determine the leadership of the state legislature.

Alaskans also have voted for every Republican presidential candidate since 1968, but three of the last four governors were Democrats, and the last Republican, a lighthearted moderate named Jay Hammond, was narrowly elected in 1978. Hammond looks and sounds like a governor of Alaska from central casting, and was partly responsible for the state's famous Permanent Fund, now a $20 billion reserve of public money from oil revenues.

Jay S. Hammond, governor from 1974 to 1982, is considered by many to be the quintessential Alaskan politician.

As a territory in the 1950s, Alaska was left-leaning enough that New York congressman John Pillion claimed that the future state's two senators and one representative would be "selected by communist agents." Current representative Don Young (R), who originally lost the election in 1972 to Rep. Nick Begich (who was deceased at the time), is famous for impersonating rabbits dying in leg traps, speaking obscenities in front of school children, and declaring happily that perseverance will beat out intelligence in the end.

Third parties such as Libertarians, Greens, or even Bull-Moose Republicans often bubble up. The "Alaska Independence Party" actually elected former Nixon Secretary of the Interior Walter Hickel as governor in 1990, but his adopted party's platform of "Alaska sovereignty" never resulted in substantive policy. This former Republican was far less cooperative with the oil corporations than current Democrat and former oil worker Tony Knowles. A centrist Democrat, Knowles has been liberal on social issues and has proved remarkably popular.

The 1971 **Alaska Native Claims Settlement Act** set up public corporations whose stockholders are composed of the 80,000 Alaskans of at least one-quarter Native heritage. These corporations provide stock dividends, jobs, resources, health care, and other quasi-governmental services to their stockholders, and function as major players in Alaska politics. The act, which gave control of 44 million acres of Alaska land to Natives fostered major divisions within these highly diverse ethnic groups. A Native corporate culture associated with the cities, business careers, and modern American lifestyles has developed, while a more traditional group has remained in small bush communities. The corporations gain revenue by resource development of their lands, thus Alaskan aboriginal peoples find themselves on both sides of such issues as clear-cutting trees for export to Japan or oil development in the Arctic National Wildlife Refuge.

Another effect of ANLCSA was the revitalization of Native Alaskan culture. Corporations have made it more economically viable for Native people to remain in their villages, and as a result, there has been a modest but pronounced renaissance of Native language, arts, and culture.

Oil development transformed Alaska politics, professionalizing the players and flooding the state treasury. The stakes of public decisions are now in the billions of dollars, and lobbyists and organized interests have become prominent. Oil development also imported a large number of people from oil industry states with a conservative Baptist political culture, who challenge Alaska's traditional social liberalism.

Oil interests, social conservatives, and development groups, such as the mining or lumber industries, have had a common interest in defeating more socially liberal and environmentally protective legislators. The resulting coalition has made the Alaska Legislature increasingly conservative. The pro-development/social conservative alliance continues its efforts to open up environmentally sensitive areas for developement, but the live-and-let-live traditions of a frontier culture remain as a force to be reckoned with.

—Jamie Bollenbach

◆ Nearby Hiking Trails

There is great mountain hiking right in Anchorage. The Chugach Mountains rise dramatically from the eastern suburbs, only a few miles from the core area of the city. If you drive east on O'Malley, Huffman, or DeArmoun roads—or virtually any other major road—you will reach trailheads. Once up these trails, you might catch a glimpse of Dall sheep, grizzly bears, black bears, moose, coyotes, wolves, foxes, eagles, hawks, ravens, and ptarmigan, to name just a few. (To avoid surprising large animals and putting them on the defensive, make noise as you walk by, talking loudly, whistling, singing, or otherwise making yourself noticeable.) The **Flattop Mountain trail** at the end of Huffman Road is one of the best, a four-mile round trip with a good view from the top. Another fantastic hike is the trail up **Rendezvous Peak**, offering even better panoramic views than Flattop Mountain. The trailhead is at the end of the Arctic Valley Road.

Given all the trails that lead directly into Anchorage, it's not surprising that wildlife lives on the city's fringes and often wanders through suburban neighborhoods. Three hundred moose are thought to live in the areas year-round, and

Within a short distance of Anchorage are recreational opportunities ranging from the extreme to the sublime. (left) Ice climbing above Turnagain Arm; (above) blueberry picking in Chugach State Park.

another 700 come into the city when the snow gets deep. In the winter of 1994, with snow banks reaching to the rooftops, some moose clambered up on top of houses in order to nibble at the lower branches of trees. And, Alaska Fish & Game Department biologists were amazed several years ago to find a pack of wolves living within the city limits of Anchorage.

◆ Nearby Sites of Interest: North

Eagle River Valley Nature Center

map page 144, A/B-3

The drive here from Anchorage is along a road lined with spruce and cottonwood that curves below spectacular mountains. At the end of the suburban town of Eagle River is the log cabin nature center, with displays about the area's natural history. In the summer, the center offers guided nature walks, including hikes into Chugach State Park along the historic Old Iditarod–Crow Pass Trail. Near the nature center are views of spectacular mountain scenery and the hanging glacier on Polar Bear Peak. Eagles, bears, and moose all live in the vicinity. *Drive north of Anchorage on the Glenn Highway, take the Hiland Road. exit at mile 13.5 and a right on Eagle River Road.*

Palmer and the Matanuska Valley

map page 144, B-3

Matanuska Valley (also referred to as Mat-Su Valley) is Alaska's primary farming region, known for the mammoth vegetables that grow here during the summer months, when photosynthesis is a 24-hour event. The valley was homesteaded in the Depression by struggling farm families relocated here by the U.S. government. Palmer, the valley's main town, is noted for its historical buildings. The **Palmer Visitors Center,** also known as the Matanuska Valley Visitor Center, provides extensive information on local hiking, boating, rafting, camping, and fishing. *Located in a log cabin on South Valley Way at East Fireweed Avenue.*

Musk Ox Farm

Just east of Palmer is the **Musk Ox Farm,** where the native musk ox is raised domestically. In Alaska, musk ox were hunted to extinction in 1865 but reintroduced to the area 70 years later. Their underfur, qiviut, is hand knit by Native Alaskans to make warm garments.

Eklutna Village Historical Park

The line of sofas overlooking the Glenn Highway at mile 26.3 tells you you're passing Eklutna. If it is a sunny day, residents of this Indian village sit back and watch the four lanes of traffic speed past on their way to or from "Los Anchorage." The town's park with its small museum and St. James Russian Orthodox Church provides an interesting view of local Native culture and history. The highlight of the guided tour is the "spirit houses"—funerary markers that combine elements of indigenous and Russian Orthodox tradition.

Hatcher Pass *map page 144, B-3*
North of Anchorage the road to Hatcher Pass leads 22 miles into the high mountains, through a historic gold mining area, and up to beautiful Summit Lake. This area is popular with the local population for hiking, wildlife observation, and, in winter, skiing and other winter sports. *North of Palmer on the Glenn Highway.*

◆ Seward Highway: Southeast

From Anchorage you drive toward the Kenai Peninsula on the most spectacular road in the country—the **Seward Highway.** Along the way you will be treated to views out of a picture book—towering snow-covered peaks rising from cold sea waters where pods of black-and-white orcas can sometimes be spotted hunting for salmon. A more common sight are beluga whales, riding the famous bore tides—high, rapid waves associated with incoming tides that are amazing to watch. Dall sheep are often visible along the highway, and throughout the summer, fantastic waterfalls and cataracts plunge from the mountain heights to the thick green valley forests. Don't walk out on exposed tidal flats to the side of the highway along Turnagain Arm. It's easy to get stuck in the mud, and eventually the tide comes in.

Potter Marsh Waterfowl Nesting Area *map page 144, B-3*
From this wooden boardwalk that winds through a wide green marsh along the edge of the Seward Highway, strollers occasionally see Canada geese (who nest here in the summer), trumpeter swans, arctic terns (who fly to Antarctica and back each year, 10,000 miles each way), ducks, and seabirds. Early July evenings are best. Sometimes park rangers set up telescopes focused on eagles or hawks—whose eagle-eyes are probably focused back upon the viewers. The constant sound of gunfire from a nearby rifle range and the roar of nearby freeway traffic adds a vaguely unsettling note to this bucolic scene. *About 10 miles south of downtown on the Seward Highway.*

Chugach State Park *map page 144, B-3*
Beginning at Mile 12, and for the next 24 miles, you drive through the 495,000-acre Chugach State Park between the mountains and Turnagain Arm on the Cook Inlet. (Supposedly Captain Cook came in here and turned around again when he saw the inlet didn't connect to Prince William Sound.) There are numerous hiking trails that lead from the highway up into the Chugach, offering varied terrain and breathtaking views. On the water side of the highway you'll see a pullout at Beluga Point, popular with windsurfers.

Alyeska Ski Resort *map page 144, B-3*
At Mile 37 on the Seward Highway, the spur-road to Alyeska Ski Resort leads into a scenic valley where you can get out and

stretch your legs or take some photographs of the wildflowers or mountains. The Westin Alyeska Prince Hotel has exceptionally beautiful public rooms and lovely terraces leading out to views of the mountains. A tram ride will take you up to a restaurant perched on the mountainside. During the winter Alyeska offers the finest downhill skiing in the state.

Portage Glacier *map page 144, B-3*
Along the Seward Highway, at the far end of Turnagain Arm, you'll meet the turnoff to Portage Glacier. Don't miss it! As you drive through the lovely green valley, if you see what looks like an enormous piece of blue plastic looming ahead: it's an iceberg. The **Begich-Boggs Visitor Center,** manned by Chugach Forest Service rangers, provides information about the natural wonders in the vicinity. Blue and green icebergs float in Portage Lake and, behind them, striking glacial mountains rise from the deep cold waters. Portage Valley also has several observation decks where you can see red and dog salmon during their spawning season—the best place is just past the bridge at Mile 4.1, on the turnoff to the campground.

■ KENAI PENINSULA *map page 144, A&B-3&4*

The Kenai Peninsula is a microcosm of Alaska. In it you will find representative samples of nearly every biogeographic province of the state, from permanent glaciers (Harding Ice Field) to crab-filled tide pools (Homer), from high mountain tundra where herds of caribou run (Russian River headwaters) to thick rain forest haunted by brown bears (Kachemak Bay State Wilderness Park), from salmon-filled coastal streams (Kenai River drainage) to mountain lakes supporting prodigious lake trout (Kenai Lake).

To be honest—and I'm certainly not alone in this—the Kenai Peninsula is my favorite part of Alaska, and it was on the Kenai River that I landed the enormous Dolly Varden that now hangs above my desk, forever reminding me of a wonderful day. The king salmon I caught on the Kenai—nearly 60 pounds—would have been too expensive to mount, and so it is represented by a framed photograph. But you get the picture—an outdoorsman's paradise.

From mid-June through mid-August the Kenai Peninsula becomes crowded, especially along the salmon streams, where RVs line the margins of the road and fishermen stand shoulder to shoulder in the water. Because the area is only a three- or four-hour drive from Anchorage, the roads, towns, and campgrounds fill

(previous pages) Avalanche and Flattop Mountains rise above the eastern flanks of Anchorage in Chugach State Park, the city's most popular recreation area.

up. If possible make reservations in advance. If you're making plans day by day, go anyway: you'll probably find accommodations in one of the many private campgrounds or B & B's.

◆ From Portage to Seward

From Portage the road turns west and then south onto the Kenai Peninsula. There are numerous turnoffs and side roads and public campgrounds where you can leave the busy road and enjoy the sites.

Hope *map page 144, A/B-3*

At Mile 70 there is a turnoff to the old mining village of **Hope** (another 18 miles distant), and there are several good public campgrounds down this road.

Upper and Lower Summit Lakes

Ten miles farther on you'll drive past Summit Lakes, a good spot for Dolly Varden fishing. This is also a nice place for a restorative picnic if the road is particularly busy.

Kenai Mountains

Ten miles past the lakes you'll find yourself deep in the Kenai Mountains and approaching the turnoff to the Sterling Highway, which leads west to Cooper Landing, Soldotna, Kenai, and Homer.

Moose Pass *map page 144, B-3/4*

If you continue straight, you'll be on your way to Seward, which is the gateway to Kenai Fjords National Park. The road reaches **Moose Pass** at about Mile 98 (motel, store, restaurant).

Kenai Lake

Five miles farther south you'll see the glacially fed, bright green-blue **Kenai Lake** off to the west—great lake trout fishing here. The rest of the drive consists of a steady descent through a heavily forested valley to the busy fishing town of Seward, at the head of Resurrection Bay.

Exit Glacier

Four miles before you arrive in Seward you'll reach the turnoff to Exit Glacier on the west side of the Seward Highway. This is the easiest and safest glacier to touch in all Alaska, and well worth the trip.

◆ Seward *map page 144, B-4*

Once known primarily as the southern terminus of the Alaska railroad and as the departure point for thousands of prospectors and miners, Seward (pop. 2,500) is today associated with the commercial fishing industry and the tourist business attached to Kenai Fjords National Park (formed in 1980). Seward was severely damaged in 1964 during the Good Friday earthquake, after which a tidal wave over 100 feet tall thundered in from the sea and pretty well leveled the seafront. Since then, Seward has been rebuilt and is now a charming town of wood-frame houses and fine summer gardens. Facing a deep blue bay and surrounded by snowcapped peaks, with impassable cliffs and ridges that soar up from the back of town, Seward is famous for its nasty weather, in both summer and winter.

You'll find the **Kenai Fjords National Park Visitor Center** along the boardwalk in the small boat harbor. The Chugach Forest Service office is located at the corner of Jefferson Street and Fourth Avenue. There are numerous private charters operating out of Seward that can take you on ocean-going tours of Kenai Fjords National Park, or on fishing trips, or both. Anything that gets you out on the water and into this fantastic park is highly recommended. Also, sea kayaks can be rented in Seward and transported to remote areas of the park for secluded wilderness adventures. Information on all of this can be obtained at the park visitor center.

Also on the waterfront is the new **Seward SeaLife Center,** an architecturally impressive aquarium that focuses on the marine life of south-central Alaska.

Playing with Steller's sea lions at the recently opened Alaska Sealife Center in Seward. (above). Seward, a year-round deep-water port, is the jumping off point for boat excursions to nearby Kenai Fjords National Park (right).

NUNATAK

◆ Kenai Fjords National Park *map page 144, A&B-4*

Stretching over 100 miles from Seward very nearly to Point Graham, this park is distinguished by its many rocky narrow inlets, or fjords. In these deep cold fjords live sea otters, sea lions, harbor seals, Dall's porpoise, harbor porpoises, sea lions, orcas (killer whales), and gray, humpback, and minke whales. Worldwide, the Steller sea lion population has declined 75 percent in the last two decades; and the majority of those remaining live off the coast of Alaska. Once while I was sea kayaking in Resurrection Bay a huge bull sea lion surfaced near my kayak and almost swamped the craft. He was much larger than the kayak, and rangers later told me that mature sea lions can exceed 13 feet in length and weigh in the neighborhood of 2,400 pounds.

The horned and tufted puffin colonies are also a sight to behold, as these gaudily colored birds fly in and out of their rocky cliffside nests.

■ Western Kenai Peninsula

The **Sterling Highway** begins at Mile 90 of the Seward Highway and leads west into the Kenai Peninsula. The scenic 173-mile-long road provides access to the Kenai River and various coastal communities and sites, including Captain Cook State Recreation Area, Kenai and Soldotna, Clam Gulch, Ninilchik, Deep Creek, Homer, and Kachemak Bay.

The road is two to four lanes and early on traverses lush green valleys ablaze with purple fireweed, hills on either side forested with conifers, rising to green scrub, then brown rock rims. Along the edge of the road are white- or gray-barked alders and aspen. Road signs read Give Moose a Chance, followed by the year's tally of road kill (about 250 by July). Although cars and moose are a danger to each other, chances are you'll drive along the highway and see no wildlife at all. The Sterling Highway continues on through spindly dwarfed forest before turning south along Cook Inlet. It ends at the end of the Homer spit. At certain times of the year—from Memorial Day to Labor Day, essentially—the road carries far more traffic than it was designed for years ago, so always drive cautiously.

◆ Sterling Highway to Soldotna *map page 144, A-3*

Kenai Lake

West of the Tern Lake Junction you will soon meet up with Quartz Creek and the lovely shore of Kenai Lake, a high glacial lake that is the source of the Kenai River. The glacial till, or ground-up rock, from the glaciers causes the lake to have a distinct blue-green color—the same is true of the river. At Mile 100.5 (from Anchorage) you'll pass the Bean Creek Road, which provides access to the Kenai Princess Lodge and RV Park.

Cooper Landing

About one mile farther is the sleepy little community of **Cooper Landing,** which also serves as an important headquarters for several major fishing outfitters and guides serving the Kenai River. There are restaurants and a store here, as well as private and public campgrounds, an RV park, and other visitor services. It is a very friendly place—one of my "homes away from home" in Alaska. The public campgrounds in this area—in fact on the whole Peninsula—are very well designed, with many excellent sites available.

Five miles farther down the road is the Russian River Campground, which is very crowded in the summer during the fishing season (by contrast, in May and September the place is virtually empty).

Resurrection Pass Trail

At Mile 106 from Anchorage you will find the trailhead for the Resurrection Pass Trail—this is one of Alaska's finest road-accessible wilderness trails, but is infested with mosquitoes in the summer (the country is also thick with black and grizzly bears). I recommend venturing up this trail (and all others on the Kenai Peninsula) with a topographic map, a compass, bug juice, and a briefing from the forest rangers.

Skilak and Swan Lakes

At Mile 111 there is a side-road south to Skilak Lake, a popular fishing area. Four good campgrounds are found along this 15-mile-long sideroad, which can offer a pleasant respite from the highway on a particularly busy day. Another sideroad at Mile 136 leads north to the Swanson River and Swan Lake area, which is a popular canoeing, fishing, and big-game hunting area on the north end of the Kenai Peninsula.

Soldotna

You'll reach the good-sized town of Soldotna at Mile 147 (again, from Anchorage), and there you'll find the road lined on either side with parking lots, cinderblock discount outlets, and chain restaurants, all unrelieved by landscaping. (If there are city planners here, their message seems to be: don't come here for recreational purposes.)

At this point you have a choice—head north in the direction of Kenai and Captain Cook State Recreation Area (excellent beach camping area, but often full), or head south toward Homer. Most choose the latter, and head over the Kenai River bridge toward Kasilof and points south. Along the way, if the sky is clear, you'll see magnificent snow-draped volcanos that rise above Cook Inlet on the Alaskan Peninsula: Mount Redoubt (10,197 feet) and Mount Iliamna (10,016 feet).

◆ Sterling Highway to Homer *map page 144, A-3&4*

Tustumena Lake *map page 144, A-3*
South of the little village of Kasilof (another great fishing town on a lovely salmon and steelhead river), there is a turnoff (east side of the road) to Tustumena Lake that is worth taking (Mile 164). Tustumena is an ideal place for camping, fishing, and canoeing. A person with a good boat can penetrate nearly 40 miles into the wilderness just by following the lake shoreline—lots of opportunities here for observing moose, bears, and bald eagles.

Clam Gulch *map page 144, A-3*
Clam Gulch at Mile 169 is another favorite place in May with the saltwater fisherman—the king salmon pass by here on their way north to the Kasilof and Kenai rivers, and you'll see the ocean dotted with skiffs as freezing-cold fishermen stubbornly troll for them.

Ninilchik and Anchor Point
map page 144, A-4
Ninilchik, at Mile 189, is one of the major ports for fishing outfitters on the coast—if you're interested in halibut or salmon fishing at sea, stop here or at Anchor Point, 25 miles farther on.

If you'd like to drop by an oldtime roadside bar try the one at the Happy Valley turnoff. Built of stones and cut logs, it's close and dark inside, as if hunkered down against the elements. In the entryway, locals have posted signs describing what they'd like to sell or acquire, such as: "LOOKING FOR WOMAN WHO LIKES TO FISH, CAN CLEAN FISH AND SEW, WHO OWNS A FISHING BOAT." The bar and its eight barstools run the length of the room; the jukebox features the Beatles, Hank Williams, and Buddy Holly. The wall above the two small tables is hung with a wolf skin and there's a snow crab under glass behind the bar.

(previous pages) Bishop's Beach near Homer is typical of the beauty of the western shores of the Kenai Peninsula.

◆ HOMER *map page 144, A-4*

At about Mile 220 you will have your first view of one of the prettiest little towns in North America: Homer. First you'll catch glimpses through spruce trees of the deep, cold, blue waters of Kachemak Bay. Then as you crest the hill and head down, you'll see a green swath of land before the bay, a small town, and Homer Spit gracefully curving away from it. Across the bay huge peaks soar from sea level into high steep permanent snowfields, and a light blue river of ice, Grewingk Glacier, flows around a conical mountain. Ships of every size and description are busily going this way and that, wild dark forests lie everywhere, and there are lovely homes, a clean waterfront, the genuine feel of an artistic community.

In recent years Homer ("Halibut Fishing Capital of the World") has grown beyond all predictions (except mine). Once you've spent five minutes in Homer, you'll understand its allure. The inspiration of nature's beauty is everywhere. Painters, sculptors, poets, songwriters, dancers, novelists, playwrights—you will find them here in greater concentration than anywhere else in Alaska. Their presence makes for a nice ambiance, a mixture of vitality and creative spirit. The spirit of *nouveau* cooking has also arrived in Homer, and travelers who've been dining for weeks on steak and potatoes, halibut and potatoes, and salmon and potatoes, along with iceberg lettuce salads, will feel they've arrived in a safe harbor. Good restaurants thrive in Homer, as do pretty B&Bs and hillside inns.

Alaska Maritime Refuge

As you approach Homer on the Sterling Highway, you will see the Alaska Maritime Refuge Center on the right. Rangers here provide valuable information, including maps of tidal pool areas, brochures on marine life, and specific suggestions for wilderness hikes, sea kayak rentals, halibut or salmon charters, aerial glacier tours. They also have a listing of B&Bs.

Homer Information Center

On the Sterling Highway, near the intersection with Pioneer Avenue, is the Homer Chamber of Commerce Information Center. They offer maps of Homer and information on hikes, charters, accommodations, and tours. *907-235-7740.*

Bishop's Beach

Just past the visitor's center, Main Street leads down toward Bishop's Beach, a beautiful, wild strand facing Cook Inlet and the volcanos on the Alaskan Peninsula to the west.

Municipal Center

Half a mile past Main Street the road splits, with the left fork (Pioneer Avenue) heading up into the busy municipal center. Excellent art galleries can be found here as well as the **Pratt Museum** at the end of Bartlett Street, a fine natural history museum.

Homer Spit

Homer Spit Road aims straight down the center of a narrow, four-mile-long, windy, treeless, gravel spit that is bleak and humming with activity. On the west side is its greatest asset (except for the view): a large boat harbor where fishing, commercial, and pleasure boats moor. Also on the spit are logs piled up for shipment to Asia, a chip mill, and huge barges. Warehouses, the offices of private fishing charters and tour boats, seafood restaurants, and tour-boat companies compete for space with shops selling tourist gimmicks, ice cream stores, public fishing areas, restaurants, and campgrounds (the windiest campgrounds on earth). Lining both sides of the road are parked RV'S and cars. At the end of the Homer Spit you can park by Land's End Resort, walk along the stony beach, and gaze over at the wilderness on the other side of Kachemak Bay. Daily ferries cross the bay to the villages of Seldovia or Halibut Cove.

(above) A fresh catch of halibut is weighed in at the dock in Seldovia.

(left) Ninilchik Russian Orthodox Church located just north of Homer reflects the Kenai Peninsula's Russian heritage.

■ Prince William Sound *map page 144, B&C-3&4*

Beautiful Prince William Sound washes the eastern flank of the Kenai Peninsula. Valdez lies at its northern end, the towns of Whittier and Seward to its west and southwest. It is protected from roiling waters of the Gulf of Alaska by Montague and Hinchinbrook islands.

In Prince William Sound, you can see the magnificent Columbia Glacier, as well as a wide array of marine and terrestrial wildlife, including orcas, harbor seals, humpback whales, and sea otters. Salmon and halibut fishing can be very good in parts of the Sound.

Prince William Sound

Just as we entered the famous Prince William Sound, that I had so long hoped to see, the sky cleared, disclosing to the westward one of the richest, most glorious mountains I ever beheld—peak over peak, a thousand of them, icy and shining, rising higher, beyond and yet beyond one another, burning bright in the afternoon light, with great breadths of sun-spangled, ice-dotted waters in front. Grandeur and beauty in a thousand forms awaited us at every turn in this bright and spacious wonderland.

—John Muir, *The Harriman Expedition,* 1899

◆ Whittier *map page 144, B-3*

Located on the Kenai Peninsula just east of Portage, Whittier (pop. 300) provides recreational access to Prince William Sound. A recently completed road/tunnel connects Portage to Whittier, but many travelers still take the train between the two towns. Trains depart from a little rail station right off the road, with a large parking lot where you can leave your vehicle. Automobiles can be put on the train and transported in Whittier to ferries departing for Valdez, which is located about a hundred miles to the north and east on the other side of Prince William Sound.

The rail line between Portage and Whittier was hurriedly built during World War II to facilitate the movement of troops, fuel, and supplies to the interior of the state in the event of a Japanese invasion. Whittier offered a port that was ice-free during the winter months, remote and difficult to attack from air or sea, and also accessible—once the long tunnels were bored through the Kenai Mountains—to the Seward-Fairbanks rail line.

The neatly planned streets of Whittier still retain some of the ordered ambiance of a military outpost. Virtually every resident lives in a single, multistory concrete building. The town was essentially abandoned by the military in the 1960s, especially after the 1964 Good Friday earthquake and tidal wave destroyed the harbor and many of the buildings. Today, in Whittier you will find a hotel, a couple of bed and breakfasts, a campground, a few cafes, and some stores. You can rent sea kayaks to explore the local waters, charter boats for wilderness kayaking, fishing, hiking, or camping expeditions.

One bit of advice when planning a trip to Whittier—pack all of the rain gear you own.

◆ VALDEZ *map page 144, C-3*

Most people reach Valdez via the Richardson Highway which, on its final approach through the rugged Chugach Mountains and Lowe River Valley, is one of the more beautiful drives in the state. You will find that Valdez is set at the base of dramatic, soaring snow-covered peaks. It receives an enormous amount of snow each winter, yet the waters remain ice-free, making Valdez an important port and

Valdez is the snowiest town in Alaska. Annual accumulations of 30 feet are not uncommon.

the southern terminus of the 800-mile-long Alaska Pipeline, from which crude oil is then transported south.

Valdez forever lost its obscurity on a cold overcast day in March, 1989, when the oil supertanker *Exxon Valdez* grounded on Bligh Reef, releasing 11 million gallons of north slope crude oil into Prince William Sound. If you visit Valdez today you will see little direct evidence of the spill, although most species are fewer in number than in 1989. The good news is that 400,000 acres of habitat have been protected with settlement money from Exxon. Valdez's other modern disaster—the 1964 Good Friday earthquake and subsequent tidal wave—wrought enough destruction on the town and its environs to require relocating the townsite.

Valdez is a fairly large town for Alaska, with a population now approaching 4,000, and it exudes an air of prosperity. There is an extensive dock area here, as well as pipeline support facilities, governmental offices, and even a community college. As you drive into town, the Richardson Highway becomes Egan Drive, and at the intersection of Egan Drive and Chenenga Street there is a **visitors center.** Inside you will find lots of good advice about the many things to do during your stay in Valdez, including boating to one of the three local state marine parks, rafting down the Lowe River, hiking around the Valdez Glacier, and fishing for halibut and salmon (summer months offer some of the best fishing on the coast).

A trip to the famous **Columbia Glacier** (25 miles to the west), whose sheer ice face rises 300 feet from the water, is made by nearly everyone. The Valdez area is popular with salmon fishermen during the silver salmon run in July and is also busy during the fall hunting season (the surrounding Chugach National Forest offers outstanding deer, moose, and bear hunting). You will find all amenities in Valdez, from public campgrounds to well-appointed hotels, fast-food outlets to nice seafood restaurants.

◆ CORDOVA AND VICINITY *map page 144, C-3*

Cordova, a town of 2,500, six hours by ferry from Valdez, occupies a strategic location for nature lovers. Just east of town is the famous **Copper River Delta State Critical Habitat Area,** to the west is spectacular Prince William Sound, and to the north are the wild Chugach Mountains. Over 20 million migrating shorebirds and waterfowl visit the Copper River's broad delta each spring and fall. The surrounding tidal marshes and wetlands comprise one of the most important migratory bird resting areas in the Western Hemisphere. Other animals that can be seen in the delta, which is reached by the Copper River Highway east of Cordova, include moose, black and brown bears, sea otters, sea lions, harbor seals, and bald eagles. From spring to fall, the waters are filled with runs of red, silver, and king salmon.

From Cordova you can explore west into Prince William Sound. There are endless possibilities for sea kayaking, sport fishing, camping, hiking, and big game hunting forays. The same is true of the backcountry in the Chugach Mountains, which can be reached by aircraft charter from Cordova.

The town was originally built in conjunction with the Kennicott Mines, now part of Wrangell-St. Elias National Park to the north. It was in Cordova that the copper ore was shipped for processing after having been brought south on railroad from Kennecott. One of the most spectacular lines in the world, it closed in 1938. Today, Cordova is an important fishing and cannery center—the population explodes every summer when cannery workers, many of whom are college students, arrive. (Work in Alaska's canneries is often dangerous, tedious, and underpaid, as Hillary Clinton discovered when she came to work in a cannery during college.)

In town you will find a **Chugach National Forest Service office**, a campground, hotels, motels, bed and breakfasts, restaurants, a handful of bars, and the customary array of stores. The folks at the forest service office can tell you about recreational cabins that can be rented, floatplane tours, fishing charters, hunting trips, good berry picking areas, hiking trails, and, in the unlikely event that you arrive in January, the Mount Eyak Winter Sports Area east of town.

East of town, the famous Copper River Highway leads 50 miles across the waterfowl rich Copper River Delta. The road dead-ends at the famous and costly Million Dollar Bridge. The Copper River often sends icebergs careening down from upstream glaciers, and from an elevated boardwalk by the bridge you can view ice calving from The Miles and Childs glaciers, sometimes washing waves onto the banks in front of you.

■ Wrangell-St. Elias National Park *map page 144, D&E-2&3*

Wrangell–St. Elias National Park, conjoined with the adjacent Kluane National Park in the Yukon, forms the largest parkland on the planet. What was until recently the exclusive domain of prospectors, hard-rock miners, trappers, and big-game hunters was formally designated a World Heritage Site in 1979. Together these two sprawling parks protect over 19,000,000 acres—an area about four times the size of the state of New Jersey. In Wrangell-St. Elias National Park three great mountain ranges converge—Wrangell, St. Elias, and Chugach. One glacier in Wrangell-St. Elias National Park—the Malaspina—is larger than the state of Rhode Island. The country around it resembles the frozen cordilleras of the Himalayas. Nearby Mount St. Elias, at 18,008 feet, is the fourth largest peak north of the Andes. It towers over surrounding mountains—nine of which are among the sixteen highest peaks in the United States.

Although much of the Wrangell Mountains owe their origin to volcanism, only Mount Wrangell itself remains active, with distinct vents of steam issuing forth from the menacing summit. The last eruption was recorded in 1930. Because of the volcanism, there are valuable minerals in the surface rock, including copper, gold, and silver. In the early part of the century the Kennicott Mining Company

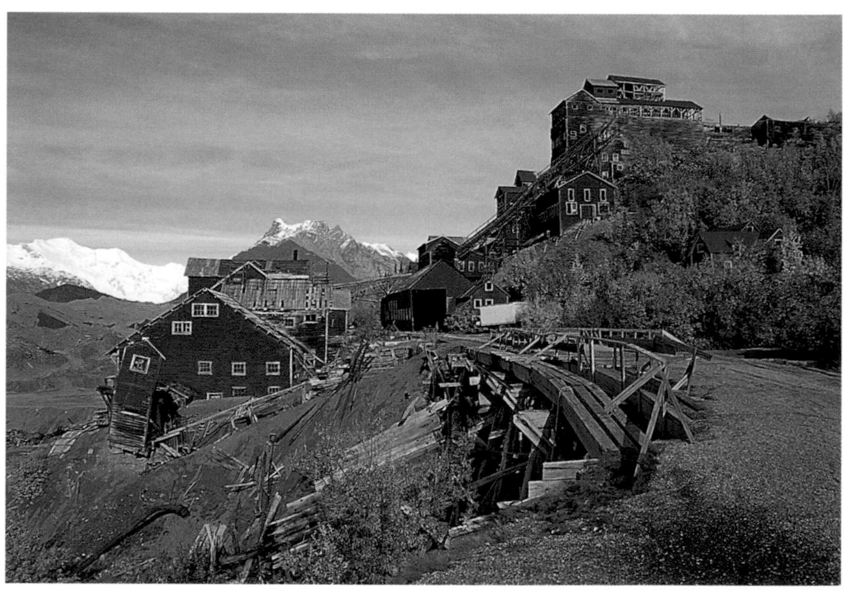

The abandoned Kennicott Copper Mine (above) sits on the edge of the massive Kennicott Glacier field, visible in the background covered in rubble. A rare aerial view of the Malaspina Glacier taken from 30,000 feet with 18,000-foot Mt. St. Elias visible in the background (right). The glacier is the largest in North America, encompassing a region the size of Rhode Island.

operated a highly productive copper mine near McCarthy, and the ruins of the mines are now on the National Register of Historic Places—it is one of the chief attractions of Wrangell-St. Elias, highly photogenic and unique, well worth the journey in itself.

The park is reached from Anchorage on the Glenn Highway. After passing Glennallen at Mile 189 (from Anchorage) the Glenn Highway shortly "T"s into the Richardson Highway (which runs north and south from Valdez to Delta Junction). Turn south here—the Park Headquarters is a short drive down the road just north of Copper Center. Most people enter the park on the Edgerton Highway, which is a well-marked turnoff south of Copper Center that leads over 90 miles east along the Copper River and deep into Wrangell-St. Elias National Park. At **Chitina,** where there is a district ranger station, you will turn onto an unpaved road that parallels the turbid, glacially fed **Chitina River.** Gas up before proceeding onward to McCarthy. Take your time; the road, narrow in places but well-engineered, isn't built for highway speeds. The road stops just short of McCarthy, ending in a gravel parking lot. A foot bridge leads across the river, and there is a shuttle service to carry visitors the five miles to the ruins of the Kennicott mine. The heavily wooded valley is wild and scenic, set between the rugged Chugach Mountains on the south and the soaring Wrangells to the north. Flightseeing tours are very popular, opportunities for hiking, camping, and photography abound.

■ NORTH OF ANCHORAGE

◆ TALKEETNA *map page 144, B-2*

Talkeetna is a small town located at the end of a spur road that turns northeast 99 miles above Anchorage on the George Parks Highway. At the junction, there's an excellent log cabin visitors center with a helpful staff aid to recommend tours and places to stay.

Talkeetna serves the vast region south of the Alaska Range in a number of ways. Every spring Talkeetna is the headquarters for those climbing Denali (Mount McKinley), the highest peak in North America, during the busy mountaineering season. Here the courageous (or insane) climbers bring their supplies and board small fixed-winged airplanes for the ride up to the Great Gorge, where they establish their base camps prior to the long and dangerous ascent *(for more on climbing Denali, see page 254).*

The National Park Service maintains a ranger station at Talkeetna from April through September, and off and on during the winter months.

Talkeetna has a good airport with a 4,000-foot paved runway, and you can fly here directly from Anchorage on a charter, then board a local flightseeing and air taxi plane and fly out to land on a glacier or see the great mountain. The airport becomes particularly busy during the big-game hunting season, which in most years runs from late August (Dall sheep) through early October (grizzly, caribou, moose). The Talkeetna Mountains are some of the most famous mountains in the world for big-game hunting—many record-class trophies have been taken from this area, in which the wildlife is carefully managed as a renewable resource.

During the summer fishing season, there is excellent salmon fishing on nearby Montana Creek, the Susitna River, and upstream on the Talkeetna River. Many fishermen prefer to be transported by floatplane or by boat to more remote wilderness fishing sites, far from the crowds near the road.

You'll find everything you need in Talkeetna—motels, B&Bs, restaurants, stores, and friendly people. Some of my nicest students at the university over the years came from Talkeetna. It is a small, hard-working community where people tend to have the old values. Two of Talkeetna's most well-known citizens were Don Sheldon and Ray Genet: the first, one of Alaska's great bush pilots, the second, an inveterate mountaineer, who at one time held the record for the most climbs on Mount McKinley, and who died at 27,000 feet on Mount Everest. To learn more about Sheldon, Genet, and about the history of the area visit the **Talkeetna Museum**, housed in an old red schoolhouse one block off Main Street and opposite the Fairview Inn. Talkeetna also hosts an annual bluegrass festival in midsummer (*see page 209*).

◆ DENALI STATE PARK *map page 144, B-1/2*

Of the nearly 100 state parks scattered across Alaska, Denali State Park (not to be confused with Denali National Park) is one of the most accessible and popular. Located on the George Parks Highway about 130 miles north of Anchorage, it offers visitors a viable alternative to the often packed national park up the road. Visitors at Denali State Park will see wildlife identical to that present in the national park: Dall sheep, moose, caribou, grizzly bear, black bear, fox, lynx, river otter, wolf, eagle, ptarmigan, and raven (of course you're not going to see all of this on one day, or in one place). There is a well-maintained campground at Mile 147

near Byers Lake. Trails lead from that campground east to Kesugi Ridge and Curry Ridge, both excellent areas for wildlife observation.

Before leaving Anchorage (or Fairbanks) you should purchase topographic maps if you intend to hike in the backcountry of the park. Denali State Park is a big place—at 324,240 acres it is about half the size of Rhode Island—and it is easy to get lost in unfamiliar country. You should also familiarize yourself with proper precautions in bear country, as there will not be as many rangers around to provide instructions as in the national park. The best thing about Denali State Park is that you have some unusual and spectacular views of Denali (Mount McKinley), including Ruth Glacier and the Great Gorge. The view from Curry Ridge is particularly sublime. It was from this area, accessed originally from the railroad, that famed Alaskan artist Sydney Laurence painted some of his memorable oil paintings of Denali earlier in the century.

Denali National Park, where Mount McKinley is located, is described in the following chapter, beginning on page 212.

A gaggle of geese (left) take flight off Fish Lake near Denali State Park. Red fox (above) are another of the park's many residents.

■ Travel Information

◆ Getting there

South-Central Alaska is easily accessible by water, land, and air. As Anchorage is the state's largest city, it is served by major national and some international airlines, including Alaska Airlines, Delta, and United *(see page 351 for toll-free airline numbers).*

Driving distance by car from Seattle to Anchorage via the Alaska Highway is 2,435 miles, and quite an adventurous journey. Take a *reliable* car and be prepared for emergencies. A good guide to this highway route is *The Milepost, Alaska.*

Alaska state ferries originating in Bellingham, Washington, will take you and your car as far as Haines, from which it is a 775-mile drive to Anchorage. Some ocean liners travel from the U.S. to Anchorage, but most cruise ships do not. The Alaska Marine Highway System ferries serving the Inside Passage of the Southeast do not connect to the ferries serving Prince William Sound and South-Central Alaska.

◆ Getting Around

By Plane

From Anchorage it is possible to travel to rural towns and scenic areas by commuter carriers offering intrastate scheduled air service, or chartered air service provided by local pilots. Inquire at Alaska Airlines for connectors from Anchorage, or check with your travel agent. To travel to this region's many off-road destinations, a scheduled air-taxi run from Anchorage to outlying villages will range from less than $100 per person on up. Bush plane charters go by the hour, and can be much more expensive. Air-taxi and charter services are located at Merrill Field and at Lake Hood near Anchorage International Airport. **The Federal Aviation Administration,** Anchorage, *907-271-2000,* has a list of certified air-taxi operations throughout Alaska, including the Alaska Airlines commuter **PenAir,** *800-448-4226,* which flies to Unalakleet, Dillingham, King Salmon, Dutch Harbor, Akutan, Cold Bay, and the Pribilof Islands; and **Reeve Aleutian Airways,** *907-243-4700,* which services Bethel, King Salmon, Unalaska /Dutch Harbor, and St. Paul (Pribilof Islands tours in summer).

By Car

In peak season (June through August), rental car reservations should be made as much as two months in advance. All the major car rental companies (Avis, Budget, Hertz, National, et al.) operate from Anchorage and offer rates of about $50 per day with unlimited mileage.

By Bus

The **Homer Stage Line** travels the Sterling Highway between Anchorage and Homer (218 miles). *907-235-7847 or 907-272-8644.*

By Ferry

The statewide ferry system offers scheduled service to many of the coastal towns in the South-Central area. Service in the summer season (May through September) is frequent, but ferries do not make daily stops at all ports; check your schedules carefully when planning your itinerary. Reservations for the state-run ferries are necessary on all routes, and may require up to six months advance notice for summer travel. For reservations call the main office in Juneau, *907-465-3941 or 800-642-0066.* There are many privately owned tour companies that service Prince William Sound and run boats between Whittier and Valdez, each offering varied tours, schedules, and accommodations. Some tour companies are listed by town on the following pages. Many are available and advertisements for tour companies abound throughout Alaska.

By Train

Alaska is not connected by rail to the Lower 48, but year-round rail service operates between Anchorage, Denali National Park, and Fairbanks, Anchorage and Seward, and Portage and Whittier. Rural services in and around Anchorage take passengers into remote areas and past breathtaking views. A one-way trip covering the 350 miles from Anchorage to Fairbanks costs about $135 and runs daily in the summer; reservations should be made 40 days prior to travel. Contact the **Alaska Railroad Corportation,** *907-265-2494*; or for more luxurious train travel from Anchorage to Fairbanks, try the **Midnight Sun Express,** *800-835-8907.*

CLIMATE

South-Central contains an enormous diversity of microclimates, covering as it does coastal islands under the mild maritime influence of the Japanese current (Montague Island holds the state record of the most rainfall in any one year, 332"!), abruptly rising coastal mountains where the rains become prodigious snows (Thompson Pass outside of Valdez holds the state's all-time snowfall record of some 975" in one year), and then inland valleys in the precipitation shadow of the mountains but open to bitterly cold arctic winds during the winter (as represented by Glennallen, a crossroads in a valley beyond the Chugach Mountains north of Valdez).

SUNLIGHT

SUMMER MAXIMUM	SUNRISE	SUNSET	# OF HOURS
Anchorage	4:21 AM	11:42 PM	19:21

WINTER MINIMUM	SUNRISE	SUNSET	# OF HOURS
Anchorage	10:14 AM	3:42 PM	5:28

While visiting Anchorage one may expect mild and sunny summers punctuated by periods of rain. The cold and snowy winter is from October through April and spring consists of a couple of weeks in May.

TEMPS (F°)	AVG. JAN.		AVG. APRIL		AVG. JULY		AVG. OCT.		RECORD	RECORD
	HIGH	LOW	HIGH	LOW	HIGH	LOW	HIGH	LOW	HIGH	LOW
Anchorage	20	9	42	28	65	50	40	29	86	-38
Glennallen	-3	-28	43	17	70	42	35	12	90	-56
Homer	28	15	42	28	60	45	45	30	80	-21
Valdez	25	11	43	26	60	45	43	31	83	-24

PRECIPITATION (INCHES)	AVG. JAN.	AVG. APRIL	AVG. JULY	AVG. OCT.	ANNUAL RAIN	ANNUAL SNOW
Anchorage	0.8"	0.6"	1.9"	1.9"	16"	70"
Glennallen	0.3"	0.1"	1.5"	0.6"	9"	41"
Homer	1.7"	1.1"	1.7"	3.4"	23"	60"
Valdez	5.8"	3.0"	4.7"	8.0"	62"	245"

The Iditarod

The longest dogsled race in the world, the Iditarod begins in Anchorage the second Saturday in March and ends in Nome about ten days and 1,049 miles (1,678 kilometers) later. The trail follows an old dog team mail route first blazed in 1910, and crosses two mountain ranges, then follows the Yukon River for 150 miles, passing bush villages and crossing frozen Norton Sound. The race's origins lie in the advent of a diphtheria epidemic which broke out in Nome in 1925. Dog sledders relayed over 674 miles in six days in order to deliver an anti-toxin serum to inoculate children. Two great sled dogs—the speed-racer Togo and Balto, who guided the final sled through a blizzard—were the real heroes. Balto's statue is in Central Park in New York City.

Today's race has a first prize of $52,500 but the cost of launching a team can be twice as much. Participants pass through 26 checkpoints in the wilderness along the way and between Ophir and Kaltag (in the interior southwestern part of the state). There are actually two different routes the course follows on alternate years. One heads north, passing through Ruby and Nulato, and the other south through Iditarod and Anvik. Big winners over the past twenty years have included Rick Swenson and Susan Butcher. The winning time of the race, which officially began in 1974, shrunk from 20 days to little over nine.

FOOD, LODGING, & TOURS

REGIONAL INFORMATION

Hotel and Motel Chains: You may get a better nightly rate by using these numbers to request the local hotel phone number, then calling directly.

Best Western. 800-528-1234
Days Inn. 800-325-2525
Hilton Hotels. 800-HILTONS
Holiday Inn. 800-HOLIDAY
Quality Inns. 800-228-5151
Ramada Inn. 800-228-2828

For detailed lodging information send for brochures from the following organizations:

Alaska Public Lands Information Center. nps.gov/aplic; 605 4th Ave.; Anchorage, AK 99501; 907-271-2737
One-stop source of information on all public lands, state or federal. Highly recommended

Alaska Private Lodging. P.O. Box 200047-MP, Anchorage, AK 99520; 907-258-1717
Statewide B&B reservation service

Alaska Sourdough Bed and Breakfast Association. 889 Cardigan Circle, Anchorage; 907-563-6244

Restaurant Prices
Per person, without drinks, tax, or tip:
$ = under $12; $$ = $12–$20; $$$ = over $20

Room Rates
Per night, per room, double occupancy:
$ = under $70; $$ = $70–$100; $$$ = over $100

= lodging
= restaurant
= campground
= wilderness lodge

ANCHORAGE

map page 144, A/B-3

population 257,780
visitors information 907-276-4118

Arctic Roadrunner. 2477 Arctic Blvd; 907-279-7311 and 5300 Old Seward Hwy.; 907-561-1245. $
A no frills, order-at-the-counter spot for beef and salmon burgers, french fries, and fixings.

Club Paris. 417 W. 5th Ave.; 907-277-6332 $$$
Considered by locals the quintessential old-time Anchorage restaurant; serves steaks and

seafood in the old-fashioned American way. Huge trophy fish mounted on dark wood walls beside fine old-time realist paintings by Byron Birdsall. The curved wooden bar, glasses, and bottles of liquor gleam in an intimate darkness, and there is an air here of retreat and masculine comfort from a harsh environment.

✕ **Crow's Nest Restaurant.** At the corner of "K" Street and Fifth Ave. in the Captain Cook Hotel; 907-276-6000 $$$
Considered by many to be the city's finest restaurant. The dining room is unexpectedly formal—white tablecloths, silver place settings—and has beautiful panoramic views. Menu changes seasonally; features local seafood. Housed in the popular Captain Cook Hotel.

✕ **Downtown Deli and Cafe.** 525 W. Fourth Ave.; 907-276-7116 $–$$
A downtown cafe convenient for tourists, as it's located across the street from the visitors center. Atmosphere is simple and open. Sandwiches, seafood, fresh vegetables, bagels, and blintzes. Wholesome and simple.

✕ **Glacier Brew House.** 737 W. 5th Ave.; 907-274-BREW $$–$$$
Sprawling, open-beamed rustic atmosphere in a downtown location, specializing in wood-fired oven pizza, rotisserie chicken, steaks, and seafood. Fine microbrew selection, including the house brand.

✕ **Gwennie's Old Alaska Restaurant.** 4333 Spenard Rd.; 907-243-2090 $
Sourdough pancakes and reindeer sausage; breakfast served all day long.

✕ **Hogg Bros. Cafe.** 1049 W. Northern Lights; 907-276-9649 $
Gigantic breakfasts; burgers. Very crowded on weekends.

✕ **Humpy's Great Alaskan Alehouse.** 610 W. Sixth Ave.; 907-276-2337 $
A favorite Anchorage hangout. Hearty food and beer in a loud, lively atmosphere.

✕ **Jen's Restaurant.** 701 W 36th Ave.; 907-561-5367 $$$
Don't let its strip-mall location turn you away. The innovative dishes, the conviviality of host Jens Hansen, and excellent wine list make this the place for those in the know. After 10:00 p.m. or so, dance to swing or bebop music.

✕ **La Cabaña.** 312 E. Fourth Ave.; 907-272-0135 $
The oldest Mexican restaurant in Alaska. Good Americanized Mexican food and the best margaritas in town.

✕ **L'Aroma.** 3700 Old Seward Hwy.; 907-562-9797 $
A first-rate Italian bakery and deli in the New Sagaya complex. Try one of the amazing little pizzas from a wood-burning oven.

✕ **Qupqugiaq "Q" Cafe and Eatery.** 640 W. 36th Ave.; 907-563-563 $
The conventional exterior disguises one of the marvels of Anchorage interior design. Sip a latte or eat a satisfying panini or soup.

✕ **Rice Bowl.** 810 E. Sixth Ave.; 907-276-7423 $$$
Scrumptious Chinese cuisine downtown. Also known for its steaks.

ANCHORAGE
continued

✕ **The Marx Bros. Cafe.** 627 W. Third Ave.; 907-278-2133 $$$
Intimate dining, lovely views, as well as exquisite food. Sets the culinary pace for Anchorage, with its original menus and local seafood and berries in unique combinations. The wine list is excellent. Our favorite Anchorage restaurant.

✕ **Moose's Tooth Pub and Pizzeria.** 3300 Old Seward Hwy.; 907-258-2537 $
Gourmet pizzas, hearty salads, and locally brewed beer. Arrive early to avoid a wait.

✕ **Sacks Cafe.** 328 G St.; 907-276-3546 $
Fresh, wholesome food.

✕ **Simon & Seaforts.** 420 L St.; 907-274-3502 $$
One of Anchorage's fine restaurants, where people come to celebrate a special event. Large and breezy with panoramic view of Cook Inlet, comfortable booths, and an air of elegance and sophistication. Fresh Alaskan seafood. "Frontier" paintings in the bar are actually newly minted and feature Anchorage locals. Reservations recommended.

✕ **Sourdough Mining Company.** 5200 Juneau; 907-563-2272 $
Big, open, unfinished "miners'" decor; this is the place for ribs, hushpuppies, and fried seafoods.

✕ **Tempura Kitchen.** 3826 Spenard Rd.; 907-277-2741
Good Japanese food; known for gyoza.

✕ **Thai Kitchen.** 3405 E. Tudor Rd.; 907-561-0082 $
There are several fine Thai restaurants in Anchorage, but poll after poll makes this one the clear winner. But go for the food or for take-out, not the atmosphere—it's located at the rear of a convenience store.

✕ **Villa Nova.** Corner of Arctic and International; 907-561-1660
Dark, cozy Italian restaurant with real atmosphere and good pasta.

Alaskan Frontier Gardens B&B. Corner of Alatna St. and Hillside Dr.; 907-345-6556 $$
A lovely three-room B&B ten miles outside of town in a gorgeous wilderness setting. The Ivory Suite has a sauna and Jacuzzi.

ALASKAN FRONTIER GARDENS

Anchorage Hilton. 500 W. Third Ave.; 907-272-7411 $$$
This dark 22-story highrise dominates downtown Anchorage. Rooms have nice views of the city and Cook Inlet. It has a heated indoor pool and stuffed brown bears and polar bears in the lobby. Rooms in peak season can cost $300 per night.

Anchorage Hotel. 330 E St.; 800-544-0988 $$$

Established in 1916 and recently renovated; complimentary continental breakfast.

Anchorage Mariott Downtown. 820 W. 7th Ave.; 907-279-8000 $$$

Newly built full service hotel with 390 rooms.

Anchorage Sheraton. 401 E. Sixth Ave.; 907-276-8700 $$$

Towering above the Anchorage skyline, this Native corporation-owned hotel may be Alaska bland on the outside, but inside the lobby, with its marble murals and jade tiles, it's like a museum of Native Alaskan art.

Anchorage Youth Hostel. 700 H St.; 907-276-3635 $

Open year-round; dormitory rooms with bunk beds, some private rooms, kitchen and laundry facilities, and common rooms. Fills up in the summer; reservations advised.

Arctic Pines. 3310 Lois Dr.; 907-278-6841 $$

Five minutes from the airport. A B&B with city conveniences in a wilderness setting.

Herrington House. 702 Barrow St.; 800-764-7666 $$$

Renovated cottage with two large private rooms; separate entrances; fireplaces. Complimentary breakfast. Flowery, elegant decor. Near the museum and the federal building in a neighborhood of old cottages and highrises. Complimentary bicycles are provided, and it's easy to bike from here to the wonderful bikepath along Cook Inlet.

Hotel Captain Cook. 939 W. Fifth Ave. at K St.; 907-276-6000 $$$

A landmark hotel owned by well-known character and ex-governor Walter J. Hickle. The spacious main floor, appointed in dark wood and oil paintings, houses restaurants and shops. Guest rooms are in the three gold towers, nicely decorated in muted tones, and supplied with all the amenities. The rooftop restaurant, Crow's Nest (see restaurants), is the finest in Anchorage and the Whales Tail is a popular bar often featuring live music.

HOTEL CAPTAIN COOK

Merrill Field Motel. 420 Sitka St.; 907-276-4547 $

A less expensive alternative to the high-rise hotels downtown. And you can watch airplanes taking off and landing at nearby Merrill Field. A couple of good restaurants within easy walking distance.

ANCHORAGE *continued*

Rainy Pass Lodge. Reservations: 200 W. 34th Ave., Suite 430, Anchorage, AK 99503; 800-773-7735 $$$

Deluxe accommodations, horseback riding, fishing, and secluded cabins, situated in the pristine wilderness 125 miles north of Anchorage. Guests fly in past Mt. McKinley and stay along the historic Iditarod Trail.

REGAL ALASKAN HOTEL

RAINY PASS LODGE

Regal Alaskan Hotel. 4800 Spenard Rd.; 907-243-2300 or 800-544-0553 $$$

A beautiful, popular luxury hotel situated against the backdrop of snow-covered mountains. A roaring fire in the lobby fireplace and a trail along Lake Spenard add to its pleasures. Sauna and exercise room. Excellent restaurant. Provides airport transportation and has the world's largest floatplane base.

Riversong Lodge. Reservations: 2463 Cottonwood St., Anchorage, 907-274-2710 $$$

On Yentna River at Lake Creek (45 minutes by floatplane from Anchorage) and in a prime fishing area, the lodge has 10 cabins and a homey main building constructed of hand-hewn spruce logs and pine paneling. Its excellent food was celebrated in the August 1996 *Bon Appetit.* Truly one of Alaska's fine and unique restaurants.

RIVERSONG LODGE

Snowshoe Inn. 826 K St.; 907-258-7669 $
Shared and private baths, continental breakfast.

Tours

Alaska Available. Bed & Breakfast Reservation Service; 1325 O St.; 907-277-9900
Custom-designed tours may include hotel accommodations, B&Bs or wilderness lodges, glacier cruises, fly-in and charter fishing, ferry and railroad reservations, and car rentals.

Alaska Native Heritage Center. 10080 Heritage Center Dr.; 907-330-8000
A major new 26-acre facility showcasing Alaska Native cultures. Performances, cultural displays and exhibits, artists in residence, and impressive recreations of traditional village settings from across the state.

Alaska Railroad. 800-544-0552 or 907-265-2494
Daily summer service between Anchorage and Fairbanks via Denali Park; between Portage and Whittier or Prince William Sound; and between Anchorage and the Kenai Peninsula. Reduced service in winter.

Anchorage Historic Guided Walking Tour. 907-274-3600
Summer only. Begins inside the Old City Hall at 524 West 4th Ave., downtown next to the visitors center. M–F 1:00 P.M. Fee.

Chugach Express. Girdwood; 907-783-2266
Dogsled on a trail south of Anchorage.

Downtown Bicycle Rental. Corner of 5th & C; 907-279-5293
Anchorage has a great bike-trail network; you can also bring a bicycle on the state ferry system free of charge.

Equinox Wilderness Expeditions. 618 W. 14th Ave.; 907-274-9087
Coastal kayaking tours into Kenai Fjords National Park and Prince William Sound and river journeys on the Copper River.

Era Aviation. 6160 South Airpark Dr. (south side of Anchorage Int'l Airport); 800-866-8394
Provides round-trip flights on the *Spirit of the North*, a DC-3, to Prince William Sound and Mount McKinley.

Kenai Fjords National Park Wildlife & Glacier Tours. 907-276-6249 or 800-468-8068
Day-long cruises from Seward on the Kenai Peninsula through exquisite Resurrection Bay. The small, comfortable ship has a well-informed crew who direct you to viewing wildlife. An unforgettable day, well worth the price of roughly $100 per person.

Great Northern Air Guides. 4151 Floatplane Dr.; 907-243-1968
Located at Lake Hood near the Anchorage Int'l Airport; floatplane or wheel-plane trips available.

Anchorage Bars and Nightlife

Pioneer
739 W. Fourth Ave.
907-276-7996

Club Paris
417 West Fifth Ave.
907-277-6332

Chilkoot Charlie's
2435 Spenard Rd.
907-272-1010

Humpy's
610 W. Sixth Ave.
907-276-2337

Darwins' Theory
426 G St.
907-277-5322

Cabin Tavern
264 Muldoon Rd.
907-338-9905

Cheechako
317 W. Fireweed Ln.
907-274-6132

Office Lounge
545 E. Nor. Lights Blvd.
907-276-9150

Fancy Moose
Regal Alaskan Hotel
907-243-2300

Simon and Seafort's
420 L St.
907-274-3502

F-Street Station
325 F. Street;
907-272-5196

Anchorage's nightlife reflects its contradictory cultures. Some of the oldest bars like the **Pioneer** and **Club Paris** are now attracting a hipper crowd at night due to their honest shots and old West Coast city feel. You will no doubt hear about **Chilkoot Charlie's,** an overpriced meet-meat market that's made an industry out of getting the rocker crowd sloshed and (consequently) less lonely. On the good side it is expanding its live music offerings. If you live here, both Chilkoot's and **Humpy's** (with its rich kids and upscale beer menu) are the places to go to run into people you tried to avoid in high school. Humpy's can be very pleasant in the afternoon, but the gold card patrol prowls shamelessly at night. At least at Chilkoot's you can get through the entire evening saying nothing but "OWWW!" and "Bud!"(as long as you're wearing a Scorpions T-shirt), and likely as not a cash-happy fisherman from Kodiak will buy you drinks until he's distracted by a compelling placement of Spandex.

Darwin's is a good little bar to meet people from around the world, although its beer selection is limited and the place gets a little close at times. The **Cabin Tavern** in Muldoon is an old log roadhouse with a military scene, and another log bar, **The Cheechako,** is a pretty good softball hangout. For sheer strangeness visit the **Office Lounge,** shaped like a crown and covered inside with paisley velvet. It has an amiable alky crowd and weird rotating bar.

The Fancy Moose in the Regal Alaskan hotel is the nicest place to wait for the plane, but the drinks are a little uneven.

With excellent food as an attraction, bars for lawyers like **Simon and Seafort's, Fletcher's,** or **F-Street Station** are worth a slower, more expensive visit. Simon's especially is an enjoyable experience, with first-rate service and a great view of Cook Inlet.

Also worth a look are several microbreweries. The **Glacier Brew House** is in a genuinely old building for Anchorage, dating back to the 1930s—prehistoric!—and has good food and a warm though touristy atmosphere. Beer and fine inlet views for outside diners is the draw at the **Snow Goose Restaurant and Brewery. The Railway Brewery** situated beside the Alaska Railroad Depot is also a nice choice for a late summer afternoon repast on its sprawling deck.

Sadly lacking are first-rate dance clubs, but Chilkoot's, the **Gaslight**, and others are able to support a good time. Older visitors might enjoy the 1950s-oriented **Hot Rods** and its attached pool hall with a truly amazing collection of antique pool tables.

—Jamie Bollenbach

Fletcher's
Hotel Captain Cook
907-276-6000

Glacier Brewhouse
737 W. Fifth Ave.
907-274-2739

Snow Goose
Third Ave. at G St.
907-277-7727

Railway Brewery
421 W. First Ave.
907-277-1996

Gaslight
721 W. Fourth Ave.
907-277-0722

Hot Rods
4848 Old Seward Hwy.
907-562-5701

Anchorage
continued

Major Marine Glacier Tours. 800-764-7300 or 907-274-7300
A six-hour cruise from Anchorage through Prince William Sound to Blackstone Glacier. Wildlife viewing and up-close views of the many glaciers. Dinner optional.

Sport Fishing Alaska. 1401 Shore Dr.; 907-344-8674
Personalized fishing trips planned statewide. Run by former supervisor of Alaska State Fish & Game Department.

Nova. novaalaska.com; P.O. Box 1129, Chickalon, AK 99674 907-595-1363
Variety of rafting trips, flat to whitewater.

Cooper Landing
map page 144, A/B-3

population 390

Chugach National Forest. Cabins: 907-271-2599 Campgrounds: 907-224-4111
Choose between 41 recreational cabins, rustic but comfortable, for $25 a night, or several campgrounds along Sterling Hwy. between Cooper Landing and Kenai. Tends to be full during fishing season.

Gwin's Lodge. Mile 52, Sterling Hwy. ; 907-595-1266 $$
Modern cabins. Good place to headquarter a fishing operation—stone's throw from the Kenai and close to the Russian River, as well. Restaurant, bar, and tackle shop.

Hamilton's Place. Mile 48.5, Sterling Hwy.; 907-595-1260 $$
Restaurant/bar look with view of the beautiful river; general store, tackle shop, cabins, and camping area. Great place to hang out and talk to the fishing guides, most of whom will tell you their life story for a couple of beers.

Kenai Princess Lodge. Mile 47.8, Sterling Hwy.; 800-426-0500 $$$
A sprawling, luxurious complex on a bluff overlooking the wild beauty of the Kenai River. Restaurant, exercise room, shuffleboard.

◆ Tours

Alaska River Adventure. 907-595-2000
Half- and full-day fishing or scenic tours of the Upper Kenai Peninsula, and wilderness trips throughout Alaska.

Alaska Wildland Adventures. 800-478-4100
Scenic floats on the Kenai River. Four trips daily.

Kenai Lake Adventures. 907-595-1363
Customized packages for chartered flight-seeing tours, air service, daily fly-out fishing excursions, and deluxe lodge accommodations.

Cordova *map page 144, C-3*

population 2,580
visitors information 907-424-7260

Killer Whale Cafe. First Ave., inside the Orca Bookstore; 907-424-7733
This comfy breakfast and lunch spot, perched

above a fun browsing bookstore, serves up great sandwiches and baked goods. Sit upstairs for a nice view of the harbor.

Cordova Rose Lodge. 1315 Whitshed Rd.; 907-424-ROSE $
This maritime-themed inn on a landlocked 1924 barge has five guest rooms (some with private baths). Full breakfast included.

HOMER *map page 144, A-4*

population 4,350, greater population 11,000
visitors information 907-235-7740

Alaska's Italian Bistro. *(seasonal)* Central Charters Boardwalk on Homer Spit; 907-235-6153; and **Pepe's Downtown Bistro.** *(year-round)* 475 E. Pioneer Ave.; 907-235-4943. $-$$
Italian food, tapas bar, and Mediterranean specialities at two locations: on the Homer Spit with a view of Kachemak Bay and downtown on Pioneer Ave. between the Fireweed Gallery and Ptarmigan Arts.

Café Cups. 162 W. Pioneer Ave.; 907-235-8330 $
Homer is known for good food, and this is one of its best restaurants. Come here for relief from the slabs of salmon and steak you've been eating for days, and enjoy innovative, interesting dishes. Desserts are elegant, microbrewery beer is on tap, and local artists' work decorates the walls.

Chart Room at Land's End. At the end of Homer Spit; 907-235-0406 $$
Overlooking Kachemak Bay, this casual restaurant serves seafood and burgers.

The Homestead. Mile 8.2, East End Rd. (8.2 miles past the corner of Lake St. and Pioneer Ave.); 907-235-8723 $$$
In a log building with pleasant ambiance, a view of bay and spruce trees. Widely regarded as the finest dining in the Homer area: seafood, steaks, etc.

Saltry. Halibut Cove; 907-296-2223 $$-$$$
To reach Halibut Cove, take the Danny J ferry from the Homer harbor. Saltry's menu features Alaskan seafood prepared in exotic dishes, and accompanied by a great selection of imported beers. Wide open feeling, big windows, and glossy blond wood.

Smith Family Restaurant. 412 E. Pioneer Ave.; 907-235-8600 $-$$
Good plain American food.

Smoky Bay Natural Foods. 248 W. Pioneer Ave.; 907-235-7252 $
Organic food available in groceries and for lunch: quiches, chicken, and a variety of vegetarian dishes. Local hangout.

Two Sisters Bakery and Restaurant. 106 W. Bunnell Ave. (turn right on Main St. as you come down the highway into town); 907-235-2280 $
An endearing, funky breakfast-and-lunch cafe. The coffee is rich and the pastries fragrant and homemade. A longtime local favorite. Closes at 6:00 p.m.. *(See picture on next page.)*

HOMER *continued*

TWO SISTERS BAKERY AND RESTAURANT

Beeson's Bed & Breakfast. 1393 Bay Ave.; 907-235-3757 $$

Six of the inn's eight guestrooms have views of the mountains and the bay. All rooms have private baths, including the cottage which can sleep up to seven people. Hot tub.

BEESON'S BED & BREAKFAST

Crane's Crest B&B. 59820 Sanford Dr.; 907-235-2969 $$

Panaromic view of Kachemak Bay. Sandhill cranes feed in the yard and entertain guests.

Driftwood Inn. 135 W. Bunnell Ave.; 907-235-8019 or 800-478-8019 $$–$$$

Three blocks from Bishop's Beach, this 20-room inn has kitchen and laundry facilities, a playground, and picnic table and barbeque on the deck. Upstairs rooms are themed "Grandma's Place" and decorated with old-fashioned furnishings; downstairs, rooms in the "Ships' Quarters" are patterned after the Alaska State Ferry.

Kachemak Bay Wilderness Lodge. Reservations: P.O. 956, Homer, AK 99603; 907-235-8910 $$$

Private cabins near wilderness hiking trails, kayaking, and canoeing. Staff naturalists lead guided hikes and boat trips across Kachemak Bay. Five- to 12-day vacation packages available.

Lands End Resort. 4786 Homer Spit Rd.; 907-235-0400 or 800-478-0400 $$

At the end of wide, windy, industrial Homer Spit, this motel/inn of 61 rooms faces a magnificent bay rimmed with snowcapped mountains. Bayside rooms have fabulous views; other rooms face a parking lot. Restaurant both inside and on a wide wooden deck overlooking the bay; serves hamburgers, steaks, prime rib, and seafood.

Old Town Bed & Breakfast. 106 W. Bunnell Ave. (Main St.); 907-235-7558 $$

Housed in the Old Inlet Trading Post, this wonderful B&B has three clean, airy rooms. Down the road is Bishop's Beach, a wild strand facing Cook Inlet, with a view of the Southwest Peninsula.

OLD TOWN BED & BREAKFAST

Seaside Farm. Mile 5, East End Rd.; 907-235-7850 $
Backpackers' hostel, housekeeping cottages, and tent campsites.

Shorebird Guesthouse. 4774 Kachemak Dr.; 907-235-2107 $$$
Private separate cottage with beach access, wildlife viewing of birds and seals.

Skyline B&B. 60855 Skyline Dr., off East Hill Rd.; 907-235-3832 $–$$
Five bedrooms with private baths; full breakfast. Wonderful panoramic views from the house and sitting room.

◆ Tours

Alaska Maritime National Wildlife Refuge Visitors Center. On the highway leading into town; 907-235-6961
Free birding walks and beachcombing walks. Drop by and ask for current times and meeting places.

Alaska Wilderness 4-Wheeler Tours. 907-235-8567 or 907-235-8996
Scenic hill country tours, wildlife viewing, beach tours, and clam digging.

Bald Mountain Air Service. 800-478-7969 or 907-235-7969
Floatplane trips to Katmai National Park across Cook Inlet, for bear viewing (about $450 per person for one-day trip); also one-hour glacier/wildlife flightseeing tour.

Center for Alaskan Coastal Studies. In the National Bank Building, on Lake St.; 907-235-6667
Daytrips with a naturalist to tide pools and through forests by Peterson Bay and China Poot Lake. Other, shorter wilderness tours lead visitors along a boardwalk through lutz spruce forest.

Coastal Outfitters. 907-235-8492
Close-in bear watching along the katmai coast. Overnight stays on comfortable yacht.

Fishing Charters.
There are about 40 fishing charters, most of which can be found on Homer Spit. Some are **Capt. Mike's Charters** 907-235-8348; **Daniel's Personalized Guide Service;** *907-*235-3843; and **Thompson Halibut Charters;** 907-235-7222.

Kachemak Bay Ferry. 907-235-7847
Summer only. Daily ferry service to Halibut Cove from Homer Spit.

HOMER *continued*

Kachemak Bay Wilderness Lodge. 907-235-8910
Five-day natural history trips with professional guides. Programs focus on rain forest ecology, marine biology, and ornithology.

Kenai Fjords Outfitters. 907-235-6066
Provides floatplanes, flightseeing trips, and fishing getaways in remote streams. Flights to Katmai or Kodiak to see brown bears.

Rainbow Tours. 907-235-7272
Naturalists lead boat tours to Gull Island sea bird rookery, the village of Seldovia, or a natural history tour in Peterson Bay.

Timberline Outfitters. 907-235-2688
Seven- to 12-day custom horseback adventures into remote parts of the Kenai National Wildlife Refuge.

Trails End Horse Adventures. 11.2 miles, East End Rd.; 907-235-6393
Guided horseback tours in the Homer hills or tothe head of Kachemak Bay.

True North Kayak Adventures. 907-235-0708
Sea kayaking on Kachemak Bay with wildlife viewing. Guided day trips out of a base camp on Yukon Island. Longer multi-day expeditions available.

KENAI *map page 144, A-3*

population 6,610
visitors information 907-283-1991

Great Alaska Fish Camp. Reservations: (summer) 33881 Sterling Hwy., Sterling, AK 99672; 800-544-2261; (winter) Box 2670 Poulsbo, WA 98370; 800-544-2261 $$$
The lodge overlooks the confluence of the Kenai and Moose rivers and offers a variety of fishing options: driftboats, ocean cruisers, bush planes, etc.

◆ TOURS

Fishing Tours.
Numerous guides offer fishing tours for king salmon; try **Alaskan Adventure Charters**, 907-262-7773, or call visitors information *(see above).*

Great Alaska Fish Camp and Safaris ferries its clients to mountain lakes on a seaplane for trout fishing on the Kenai Peninsula.

SOUTH-CENTRAL

PALMER AREA

map page 144, B-2/3

population 4,100
visitors information 907-745-2880

Forks Roadhouse. Mile 19, Petersville Rd. Peters Creek; 907-733-1851 $$
Rustic lodge with three cabins and 10 rooms (shared bath). Restaurant and bar. Open year round with the main business during winter.

FORKS ROADHOUSE

Hatcher Pass Lodge. Independence Mine State Historic Park, Mile 17, Willow-Fishhook Rd.; 907-745-5897 $$
Four hours from Denali and two hours north of Anchorage. The lodge has private cabins, mountain views, outdoor sauna, and offers lunch and dinner. Nearby is historic gold mining village.

Mat-Su Resort. 1850 Bogard Rd., Wasilla; 907-376-3228 $$
Overlooking Wasilla Lake with float plane and boat dock. Lodge, and cabins with kitchenettes. Gourmet restaurant.

Motherlode Lodge. Mile 14 Palmer Fishhook Rd.; 907-746-1464 $$
B&B in historic bilding. Eight private rooms with private baths. Fine dining by reservation.

Valley Hotel. 606 S. Alaska St.; 907-745-3330 $
Thirty-three rooms, 24-hour coffee shop, a liquor store, and lively lounge.

SELDOVIA *map page 144, A-4*

population 310
visitors information 907-234-7612
Seldovia is accessible only by boat from Homer.

The Buzz. Main St.; 907-234-7479 $
Home-style bakery. Breakfast and lunch.

The Mad Fish. Main St.; 907-234-7676 $$-$$$
A tiny place overlooking the water. Exceptional regional cuisine worth flying in for.

Boardwalk Hotel. 907-234-7816 $$
Fairly modern, basic hotel with 13 guest rooms, all with bath. Overlooks harbor.

Dancing Eagles B&B. 907-278-0288 $$
A little funky, but a lovely spot.

Seaport Cottages. 907-234-7483 $
One-bedroom cottages with kitchens.

Swan House South B&B. 907-346-3033 or 800-921-1900 $$$
Right on the water; wonderful views. Private bath. Will arrange your transportation.

SEWARD *map page 144, A/B-4*

population 3,000
visitors information 907-224-8051

Apollo Restaurant. 229 Fourth Ave.; 907-224-3092 $
Eclectic menu includes pizza, pasta, and Greek food.

Chinook's Waterfront Restaurant. Small Boat Harbor (on the other side of Coast Guard Station); 907-224-2207 $
Fresh Alaskan seafood with a view of Seward and the harbor.

Harbor Dinner Club. 220 Fifth Ave.; 907-224-3012 $–$$
A family-run, Alaska-casual restaurant with bar. Full lunch and dinner menu.

Ray's Waterfront. 1316 Fourth Ave.; 907-224-5606 $$
Serves large portions of excellent seafood; view of the harbor and the mountains beyond. Colorful bar.

Resurrect Art Gallery and Coffee Center. 320 Third Ave.; 907-224-7161 $
Featuring the work of local artists, this church-turned-cafe offers coffee, espresso drinks, and pastries. Live music most Saturday nights.

Best Western Hotel Seward. 221 Fifth Ave.; 907-224-2378 $$$
Standard amenities amid colorful, gold-rush-themed decor. Near the waterfront and several restaurants.

Fox Island Wilderness Lodge. 800-478-8068
A lovely wilderness lodge in a beautiful, remote area, featuring peace and quiet.

FOX ISLAND WILDERNESS LODGE

Marina Motel. 1603 Seward Hwy.; 907-224-5518 $$–$$$
Eighteen rooms, some with harbor view. Walking distance to train station and waterfront. Clean and comfortable.

Sea Treasues Inn. At Sixth and Adams St.; 907-224-3401 $$
One of the few downtown b&bs; reservations recommended.

Seward Hostel. Reservations: No telephone, P.O. Box 425; Seward; AK 99664 $
Just off the end of Lost Lake Trail, 16 miles north of Seward, hikers find this a convenient place to stay; 14 beds, two baths, kitchen, and common room.

Summit Lake Lodge.
Mile 46 on way to Seward past Moose Pass; 907-244-2031 $$
Set in a beautiful area, this upscale roadhouse next to Tenderfoot Creek Campground has become quite popular.

Van Gilder Hotel. 308 Adams St.; 907-224-3079 $$–$$$
National Historic Site, built in 1916; furnished with antiques; some rooms have views of the inlet.

Waterfront Campground. Ballaine Rd. and Madison St.; 907-224-3331 $
A nice public campground, with picnic tables, on the water.

◆ Tours

Kenai Fjords Tours, Ltd. 800-478-8068.
Offers several options for wildlife and glacier tours in Kenai Fjords area. Highly recommended. Excellent nature talks by the crew, lofty views, and a chance to see otters, eagles, sea lions, and orcas.

Talkeetna

map page 144, B-2

Also see Denali National Park, Page 264

population 440
visitors information 907-733-2330

Talkeetna/Denali Visitors Center. At the junction of the Parks Highway and the Talkeetna spur road; 800-660-2688
On highway at turnoff for Talkeetna is this excellent visitors center run by the Chamber of Commerce. Helpful staff will give you advice on accommodations, phone ahead for you, make plans for you to river raft, flightsee, or take horseback trips.

Talkeetna Roadhouse. Main St.; 907-733-1351 $
Home-style country fare served in a rustic log-cabin setting. Popular with locals and climbers on their way to Mount McKinley.

TALKEETNA ROADHOUSE

Denali View B&B. Mile 3 Talkeetna Spur Rd. turnoff; call for directions; 907-733-2778 $$
Cedar-sided house in a wilderness setting overlooking valley with view of Denali. Three rooms.

TALKEETNA/DENALI
continued

Fairview Inn. Mile 1 Talkeetna Spur Rd.; 907-733-2423 $
Six guest rooms with shared baths in a 1923 inn. Rowdy bar downstairs.

FAIRVIEW INN

Moose Dropping Inn Bed & Breakfast. Mile 1 Talkeetna Spur Rd.; 907-733-3128 $$
Clean rooms, smoke-free environment and Moose Dropping gifts. Sourdough pancake breakfast; great fishing nearby.

Swiss-Alaska Inn. East Talkeetna by the boat launch; 907-733-2424 $$
A family-run rustic inn with homey rooms and a restaurant.

Talkeetna Motel, Restaurant, and Lounge. Downtown Talkeetna, 907-733-2323 $–$$
Roadside motel with restaurant, cocktail lounge; dancing.

Trapper John's Bed & Breakfast. Downtown Talkeetna, near river; 907-733-2353 $$
Log cabin sleeps four and has full kitchen facilities. Reputedly has the finest outhouse in town. Rates include breakfast.

VALDEZ *map page 144, C-3*

population 4,070
visitors information 907-835-2984

Mike's Place. 201 N. Harbor Dr.; 907-835-2365 $
Italian and Greek specialities such as pizza and gyros, and seafood.

Oscars. 143 N. Harbor Dr.; 907-835-4700 $-$$
Family establishment serving breakfast, lunch, and dinner.

Pipeline Club. 112 Egan Dr.; 907-835-4332 $$–$$$
Lounge and restaurant featuring fine steaks and Alaska seafood. Nightly entertainment.

One Call Does It All. *907-835-4988*
Books lodging and activities in Valdez area.

Guest House Inn Valdez. Corner of Egan Dr. and Meals Ave.; 907-835-4445 $$$
Rooms with fridge and microwave, continental breakfast.

Westmark Valdez. Fidalgo Dr.; 907-835-4391 $$-$$$
The largest and most popular hotel in town fills up early in the summer so reserve early. Located next to a small boat harbor. Adjoining bar and restaurant overlooks the water and serves steaks and seafood.

◆ Tours

Keystone Raft and Kayak Adventures. Mile 16.5, Richardson Way; 907-835-2606
Five daily raft trips down Keystone Canyon; 10-day kayaking and rafting excursions.

Stan Stevens Cruises. 907-835-4731
Tour-boat cruises and wilderness camps in Prince William Sound.

Whittier *map page 144, B-3*

population 300
visitors information 907-472-2327

Sportsman Inn. 88 Front St.; 907-472-2352 $
A 20-room motel with laundry facilities, and sauna. ✕ Bar and 24-hour restaurant.

◆ Tours

For a complete list of boat tours into **Prince William Sound** contact the Harbor Office, *907-472-2330.* A few tour opertors include:

Alaska Sightseeing Cruise West. 206-441-8687

Major Marine Tours. 907-274-7300;

Renown Charters. 907-224-8023

26 Glacier Cruise. 907-276-8023

SoundEco Adventures; 907-472-2312; Gerry Sanger, former biologist, has been giving tours and transporting kayakers in Prince William Sound since 1987.

Wrangell-St. Elias *map page 144, C&D-2&3*

visitors information 907-554-4402

P.O. Box MXY via Glen Allen, AK 99588

The Caribou Hotel. Mile 186.5 on Glenn Hwy.; 907-822-3302 $$–$$$
A newly renovated hotel with 55 rooms, all with private bath. The **Caribou Cafe** out front serves standard fare.

McCarthy Lodge. McCarthy; 907-554-4402
A cozy lodge built in 1916; 16 rooms with shared baths. Lodge arranges rafting, hiking, and sightseeing excursions.

MCCARTHY LODGE

◆ Tours

Girdwood Chugach Express. In Girdwood; 907-783-2266
Sled trips in winter, kennel tours and dog cart rides in summer.

Festivals and Events

January

Anchorage: Sled-Dog Racing. The season begins in mid-January and hold sprints every Saturday and Sunday until February. *907-562-2235*

Seward: Polar Bear Jump-Off. Only in Alaska—costumed participants jump into the frigid waters of Resurrection Bay. *907-224-5230*

February

Anchorage: Fur-Rondezvous. Probably the most popular festival in Anchorage. World Championship sled dog races, parade, city-wide exhibits and events. *907-277-8615*

Soldotna: Peninsula Winter Games. Festivities include the Alaska State Championship Sled Dog Races and Dog Weight Pull Contest, as well as ice sculpture contests, ice bowling, and snow volleyball. *907-262-9322*

Valdez: International Ice Climbing Festival. Held in mid-February. *907-835-5182*

March

Anchorage: International Ice Carving Competition. Artists sculpt large blocks of ice in Town Square. *907-276-5015*

Wasilla: Iditarod Trail Sled Dog Race. The most famous event in Alaska. Festivities include the actual race, a reindeer potluck and awards banquet.

Valdez: Alaska Extreme Skiing and Snowboard Trials. Competitions held at the Alyeska Ski Resort. *907-754-7669*

April

Valdez: World Extreme Skiing Champions. The world's best daredevil skiers come to Valdez to compete. *907-835-2108*

May

Cordova: Copper River Delta Shorebird Festival. Celebrate the arrival of millions of migrating shorebirds.

Homer: Kachemak Bay Shorebird Festival. Celebrating the arrival of 100,000 migrating shorebirds. *907-235-7740*

Prince William Sound Regatta. Procession of boats from Whittier to Valdez.

July

Seward: Mount Marathon Race. A race up the 3,000-foot mountain; the best vantage point is right below the trail's starting point. *907-224-8051*

Talkeetna: Moose Dropping Festival. Parade, entertainment, food, and moose dropping throwing contests. *907-733-2330*

August

Palmer: Alaska State Fair. Eleven-day event near Anchorage features agricultural exhibits from farms throughout Alaska, and is particularly noted for its oversized vegetables. Also features rides, concerts, and food. *907-745-4827*

Seward: Silver Salmon Derby. The second Saturday of August marks the beginning of the annual nine-day fishing derby; local merchants sponsor prizes up to $10,000 for the largest salmon caught. *907-224-8051*

Talkeetna: Bluegrass Festival. Weekend long music festival. *907-733-2599*

October

Anchorage: Quyana Alaska Native Dance Festival. In celebration of Alaska's Native culture. *907-274-3611*

The World Extreme Skiing Championships are held at Thompson Pass each year in April.

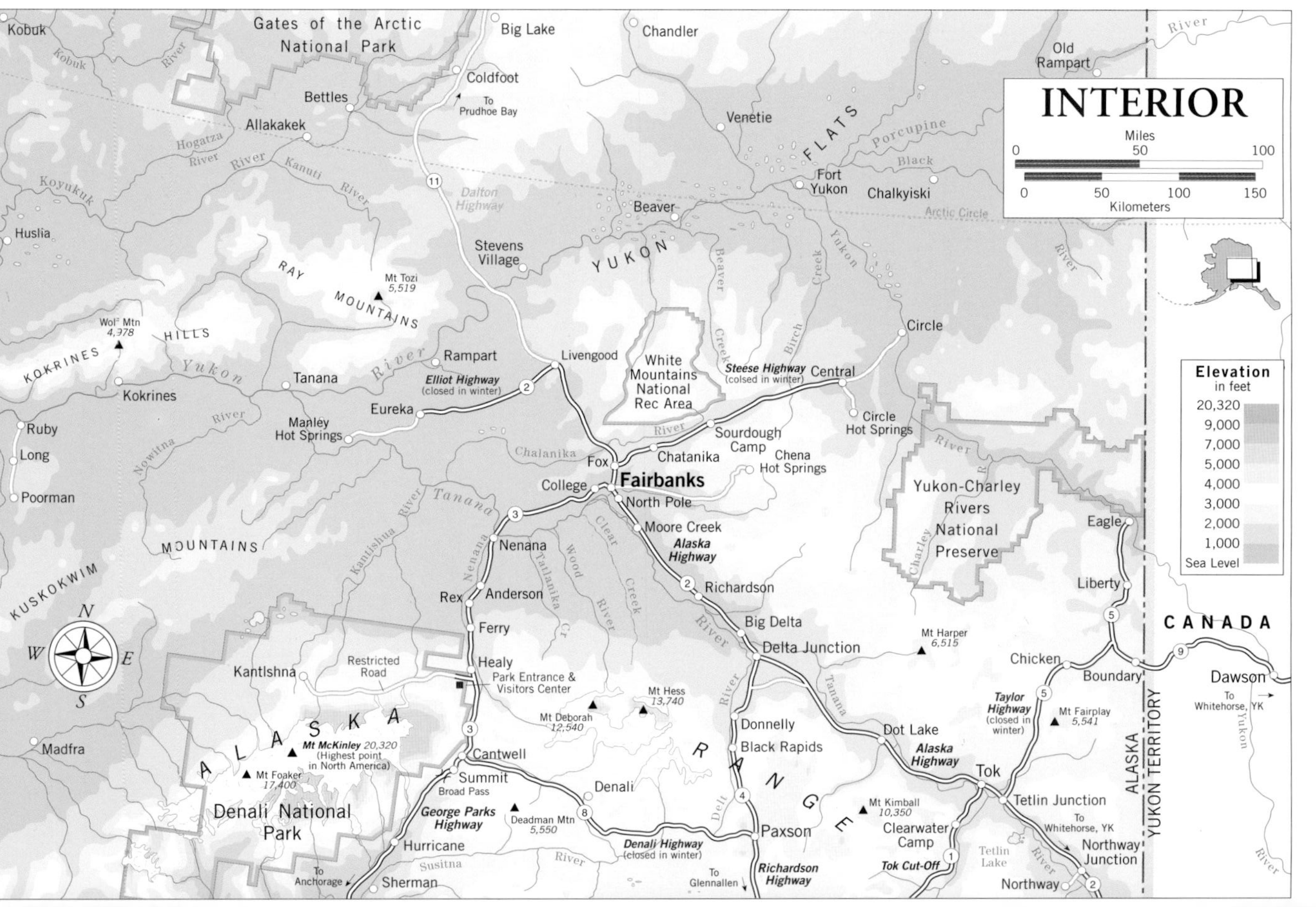
INTERIOR
Miles
0
50
100
Kilometers
0
50
100
150
Elevation
in feet
20,320
9,000
7,000
5,000
4,000
3,000
2,000
1,000
Sea Level
CANADA
ALASKA
YUKON TERRITORY
Dawson
To Whitehorse, YK
Eagle
Liberty
Boundary
Chicken
Mt Fairplay 5,541
Taylor Highway (closed in winter)
Tetlin Junction
To Whitehorse, YK
Northway Junction
Northway
Tetlin Lake
Tok
Alaska Highway
Tok Cut-Off
Clearwater Camp
Mt Kimball 10,350
Dot Lake
Mt Harper 6,515
Yukon-Charley Rivers National Preserve
Circle
Circle Hot Springs
Central
Steese Highway (colsed in winter)
Chena Hot Springs
Sourdough Camp
Chatanika
Fairbanks
North Pole
Moore Creek
Alaska Highway
Richardson
Big Delta
Delta Junction
Donnelly
Black Rapids
Paxson
Richardson Highway
To Glennallen
Denali Highway (closed in winter)
Mt Hess 13,740
Mt Deborah 12,540
Denali
Deadman Mtn 5,550
Cantwell
Summit
Broad Pass
George Parks Highway
Hurricane
Sherman
To Anchorage
Denali National Park
Mt McKinley 20,320 (Highest point in North America)
Mt Foaker 17,400
Kantlshna
Restricted Road
ALASKA RANGE
Park Entrance & Visitors Center
Healy
Ferry
Anderson
Nenana
Rex
College
Fox
Livengood
White Mountains National Rec Area
Elliot Highway (closed in winter)
Rampart
Eureka
Manley Hot Springs
Tanana
Stevens Village
Beaver
Venetie
Fort Yukon
Chalkyiski
Chandler
Big Lake
Coldfoot
To Prudhoe Bay
Dalton Highway
Old Rampart
Arctic Circle
YUKON FLATS
Gates of the Arctic National Park
Bettles
Allakakek
Mt Tozi 5,519
RAY MOUNTAINS
KUSKOKWIM MOUNTAINS
KOKRINES HILLS
Kokrines
Wolf Mtn 4,378
Ruby
Long
Poorman
Huslia
Kobuk
Madfra
N
S
E
W

I N T E R I O R

■ HIGHLIGHTS

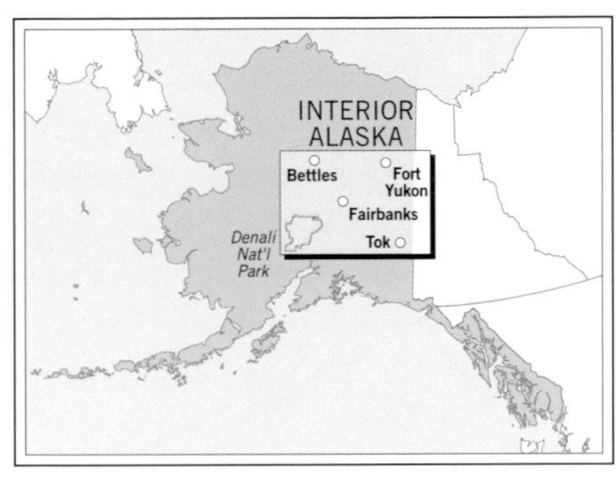

◆ MAPS

◆ PRACTICAL INFORMATION

■ LANDSCAPE AND TRAVEL

For many, the sprawling territory north of the Pacific Coast and south of the land of the Eskimos is the real Alaska. It certainly is the "heart" of Alaska. And it is vast—larger than Texas and Oklahoma combined. To the south is the imposing Alaska Range. Mount McKinley—tallest mountain on the continent at 20,320 feet—can regularly be seen from Fairbanks 120 miles away. Several other peaks nearby are also in that range: Foraker, Deborah, and Hess. Surrounding Denali (or Mount McKinley) is Denali National Park, where herds of caribou, colossal Alaskan moose, lumbering grizzlies, and wolves can be seen, and heard. To the north of Fairbanks is the Brooks Range, which though only half the height of the Alaska Range rises like an immense protective barrier between the Arctic Ocean and the rest of the state. In between the two mountain ranges are thousands of lakes, great rushing rivers, and vast expanses of taiga (spruce-birch woodlands). Although nearly a thousand miles from the ocean, the center of this area has an altitude of less than 500 feet. In the late spring, flocks of migratory waterfowl gather in assemblages so vast, those viewing them feel as if they'd stepped between the lines of the Book of Genesis and were witnessing the dawn of creation.

Along the river cutbanks of the Interior, the ivory tusks and skulls of mammoths are found each summer, as well as the skeletons of steppe bison and other fauna of the Pleistocene. During the last ice age, the Interior of Alaska was one of the few places of the far north not covered by glaciers. As a result, it became a refuge for the great mammals of the period, and part of an ice-free corridor leading toward the south.

Fairbanks is the central city of this region. From Fairbanks, it's possible to rent a car and drive south to Denali National Park, or to set out east for Chena Hot Springs, and the town of North Pole. In your own very well-equipped car you might set out along the Dalton Highway for the Arctic Ocean. Or you can arrange for bush planes to take you to arctic villages and remote wilderness areas.

Temperatures range widely in the Interior. In the winter, temperatures of 50 below zero are not uncommon. In July, when the sun beats down for 22 hours a day, the temperature often rises to 90 degrees.

■ Denali National Park *maps pages 210, 214, and 215*

◆ History

In 1794, Captain George Vancouver, exploring the north Pacific inlet named for his former commander James Cook, took note of "distant stupendous mountains covered with snow." This glaciated white massif was what the ancient Athabaskans called Denali, the high one. In 1794 the world was both a similar and a different place. By that date the Spanish universities of Latin America, for example, had been in existence for two centuries. Calculus was taught, as was human anatomy and physiology, the plays of Shakespeare, the novels of Cervantes. Telescopes mapped the heavens. Despite these advances, the interior of Alaska—even its highest mountains—remained a question mark to most of the civilized world.

Another century passed. Short arctic summers came, and long winters. And still Denali and its environs were the sole domain of caribou and moose, lynx and snowshoe hare, moccasined feet and wooden dogsleds. Then, in 1896, a prospector named William Dickey, wandering near the headwaters of the Chulitna River, took out his transit and made some crude measurements. To his amazement, the peak in his viewfinder proved to be more than 20,000 feet high. That made

Denali the highest mountain north of the Andes. As word of Dickey's measurement spread, excitement grew about the region. In a geological district of such stupendous vertical relief and uplift, might there be precious metals scattered near the surface and then exposed in stream and river beds? The answer to that question was yes, and in 1906 the Kantishna gold stampede brought more than 2,000 miners to the vicinity of Moose Creek and Wonder Lake.

When Charles Sheldon arrived by riverboat at Kantishna mining camp in 1906, he was already a self-made millionaire, having retired four years earlier at the age of 35 after making a fortune in a Mexican mining venture. A graduate of Yale University, an activist in the Boone and Crockett Club, and a personal friend of President Theodore Roosevelt, Sheldon would devote the rest of his life to traveling, big-game hunting, writing, and conservation causes. As soon as he saw Denali and the spectacular countryside and wildlife surrounding the peak, Sheldon, now known as "The Father of Denali National Park," realized that the area should forever be withdrawn from private development and designated a national park. For the next ten years Sheldon worked tirelessly toward that end, and in February 1917, as war ravaged Western Europe, President Woodrow Wilson signed the bill that established Mount McKinley National Park in the distant, little-known territory of Alaska.

By this time Mount McKinley had been climbed by two different parties of pioneering mountaineers. In the first attempt, which occurred in 1910, the four-member Sourdough Expedition made it to North Peak (19,470 feet), which they mistakenly believed was the summit. Interestingly enough, the Sourdoughs made their ascent with little more than doughnuts and thermoses of hot chocolate in their packs, quite different from the elaborate supplies taken today! Three years later, Episcopalian minister Hudson Stuck, Harry Karstens, Walter Harper, and Robert Tatum completed the first successful ascent of the South Peak (20,320 feet). While on the summit, they observed the 14-foot flagpole on the North Peak left by the previous expedition.

In the late 1930s, an intense controversy developed in the fledgling McKinley National Park. Park officials believed that if the wolves were exterminated (as had already been accomplished in Yellowstone National Park), the numbers of ungulates—Dall sheep, moose, caribou—would naturally increase. Because tourists came to observe wildlife, wouldn't it make sense to provide them with more wildlife to see? Before implementing the plan, the park service brought in zoologist Adolph Murie, who had previously studied coyote predation in Yellowstone,

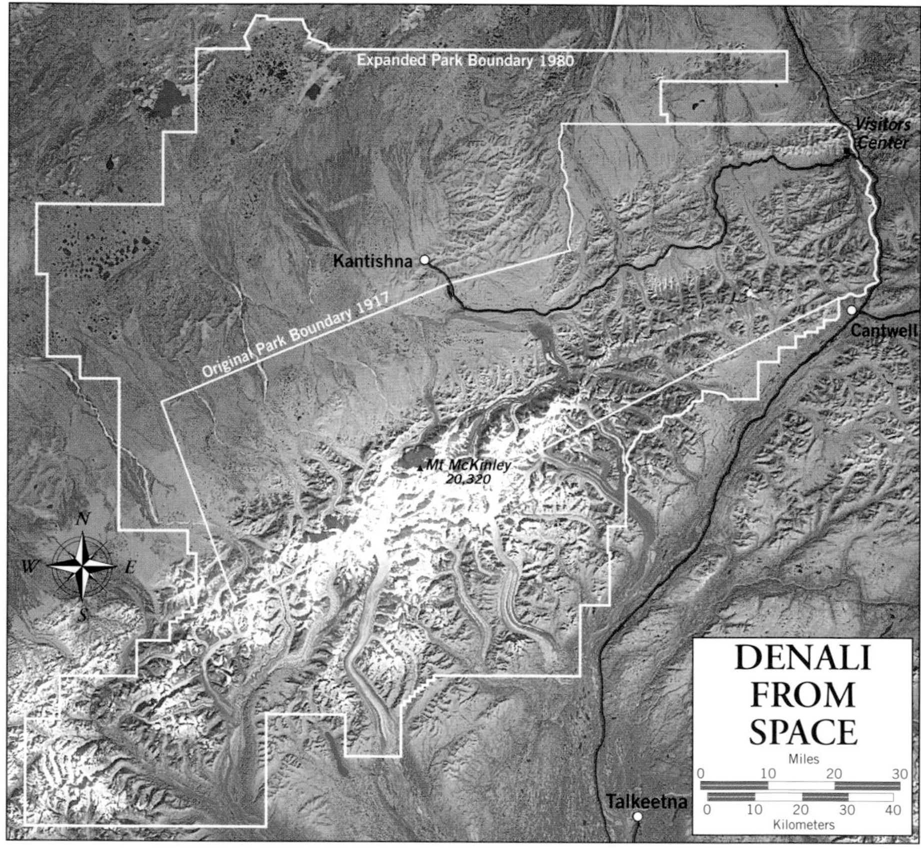

to determine the relationship between wolf predation and ungulate populations, especially Dall sheep. Murie determined that the wolves had a "salutary effect" on populations, culling out the weak, infirm, and old individuals to the benefit of the whole population. Despite Murie's findings, the National Park Service conducted a limited wolf control program until 1992, when a rebounding sheep population made it unnecessary. Nowadays, Denali's wolf population ranges from 50 to 150 animals; its Dall sheep population is at 2,500 and its caribou population at 2,000.

The other major development in Denali's recent history was the 1980 Alaska National Interest Lands Conservation Act, which enlarged the boundaries of the park by nearly four million acres (for a total of six million acres). The act also

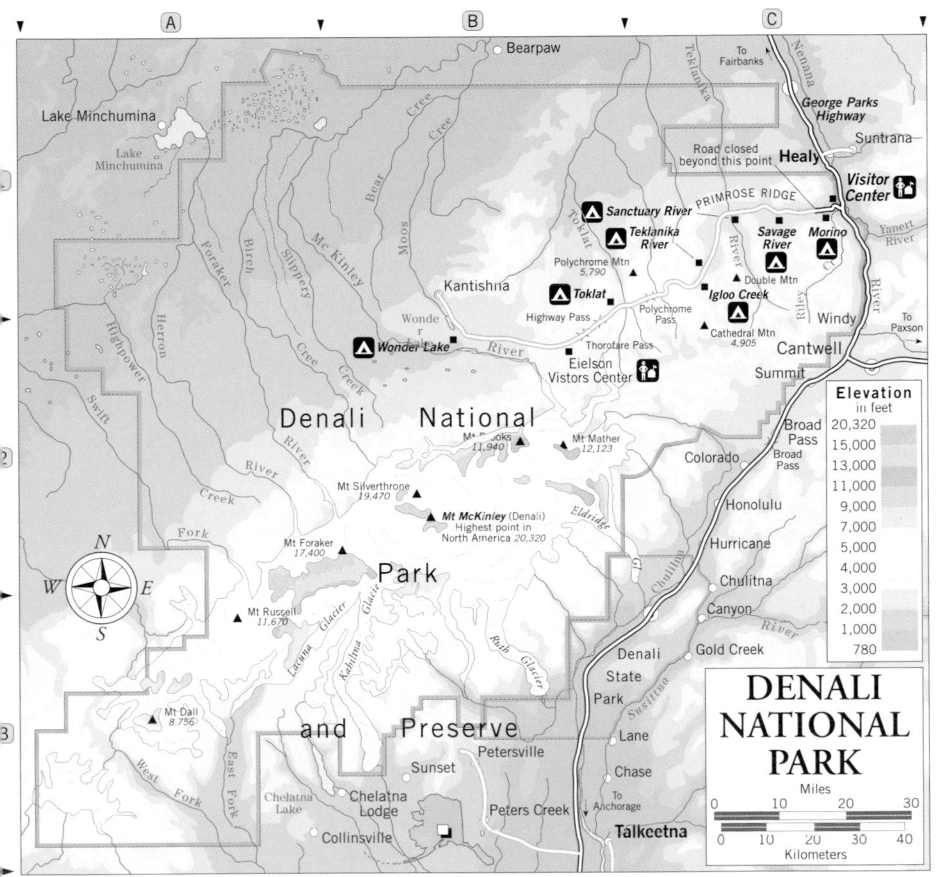

changed the name of McKinley National Park to Denali National Park and Preserve (Mount McKinley is still officially known as McKinley, though it is commonly referred to as Denali). Although hunting is prohibited in the central parklands, the surrounding new parkland and preserve allow sport hunting as well as subsistence hunting by Native Americans.

◆ Approaching Denali

Most visitors to Denali come from far away. And in that resides much of the delight. You advance slowly, over hundreds of miles, like one of Chaucer's pilgrims, with every third thought of that "stupendous" inspirational place over the horizon.

At last, from a rail car north of Anchorage or an automobile south of Fairbanks, depending on your approach and the weather, you see this immense white mass. This enormous feature dominating the western sky is no cumulus cloud, no cloud of smoke from a burning forest, no hallucination. It is a mountain, a solid ancient block of rock and snow and ice that rises almost four miles above the level of the sea. Like a fortified castle of the Wagnerian gods, Denali stands alone, cold and aloof, remote and isolated, not married by ridge or range to other mountains. Crowned with snow and ice, it looms above a vast green sea of spruce and birch and meadow and slow subarctic river.

Seeing the peak itself depends on the weather. Sometimes you can see it every day for two weeks. At other times, during the same season, it will rain every day for two weeks. (One-third of visitors actually see the mountain.) Generally, if people plan to spend at least five days in the park, they have a good chance of seeing Denali, especially if they rise early before the clouds begin to form.

◆ Visiting Denali National Park

Park Entrance *map page 215, C-1*

The entrance to Denali National Park lies along the George Parks Highway (AK 3), 250 miles north of Anchorage, and 120 miles south of Fairbanks. (If you're coming from Anchorage, also see the description of the town of Talkeetna, page 182.) At the entrance (and there's only one), you will be greeted by a sign informing all visitors that they must stop at the **Visitor Center** just up the road on the right. At this immense wood building you will obtain bus passes, backcountry camping permits, and road-accessed camping permits. There is also an auditorium, an information area, and a marvelous gift shop well-stocked with books, maps, postcards, posters, wildlife videotapes, and "Area Closed—Bear Danger" signs you can purchase and hang in your office back home. Here you can also pick up a copy of the park newspaper which will tell you how to respond if you encounter a grizzly. *907-683-1266.*

Transportation

Entry into Denali is restricted to shuttle buses, tour buses, official park vehicles, and the cars of those who own property at the end of the 90-mile park road. If you arrive at peak season (mid-June through mid-August), you can expect a delay of one or two days before you can obtain one of these bus tickets—unless you make reservations in advance by calling the Public Lands Information Center in Anchorage or Fairbanks. The same goes for camping sites. *907-456-0527.*

Most people see Denali via the shuttle buses that leave from the visitor's center every half hour beginning at 5:00 a.m. during the summer. Denali bus drivers are characters: freelance entertainers and naturalists, who will stop whenever someone cries "Wolf!" and answer questions all day long. Buses leave the visitors center with enough extra space so that they can pick up hikers along the route, which means that you can get off any time you'd like, hike about, then come back to the road and hail down a bus going in either direction.

Tour buses, a bit more expensive, offer shorter trips. Private vehicles are allowed to drive the first 15 miles of the park highway to the Savage River closure point.

Campgrounds

Near the park entrance, **Riley Creek Campground** has 102 spaces, with facilities for campers, trailers, and tents, as well as flush toilets and tap water available. This is the only campground open year round. **Morino Campground,** also near the entrance allows only tent camping for backpackers (up to 60 spaces). **Savage River Campground,** at Mile 19.2 on the park road just before the Savage River Check Station, is a popular overnight facility with 34 spaces and the same set up as Riley Creek. There are some nice views from Savage. **Teklanika Campground,** at Mile 29 on the park road, is the only other campground accessible to vehicles. There are excellent hiking possibilities in the countryside around Savage and Teklanika, and wildlife abounds near both.

Sanctuary (seven sites) at Mile 22, **Igloo** (seven sites) at Mile 34, and **Wonder Lake** (20 sites) at Mile 85—are accessed only by park bus, which means you must obtain a bus ticket at the same time you secure a camping permit, and you must carry all your gear with you on the bus.

In the event camping sites are closed for a couple of days, don't worry—private campgrounds are located at Lynx Creek about a mile north of the park turnoff on the George Parks Highway, and also at Healy, about 10 miles north of the park turnoff on the Parks Highway. There are also facilities just to the south on the Parks Highway at Grizzly Creek.

◆ The Road to Wonder Lake

Park Entrance to Mile 10.5

map page 215, C-1

Moose are often seen browsing among the trees in the forested areas close to the center. Birding can be good in the early summer (June through early July). About seven miles up the road, which climbs steadily up from the Nenana River valley, you leave the spruce forest and enter the tundra, where there are few if any upright trees. At about Mile 9.5 (if the clouds lift) you will have a good view of Mount McKinley to the southwest. There are numerous pull-outs where you can photograph the peak, and shuttle bus drivers will pull over if the view is good. One of the best views is about Mile 10.5, where McKinley is flanked by Double Mountain and Sable Mountain.

(following pages) The classic view of Mount McKinley taken from the road to Wonder Lake.

THAT DENALI SHUTTLE BUS: *IT CAN BE THE WORST ...*

Here's what a bad day is like:

A freezing rain pelts 35 people huddled in line at 7:00 A.M. before the Denali shuttle bus. Several people's shoes are soaked. The bus driver's glasses are steamed up, and by the time the bus is underway the bus windows are steamed up inside. The bus driver turns up the pace of his window wipers, and adjusts his receptionist-microphone. "Today, my job will be driving the bus," he says in a mechanical voice. "Your job will be looking for wildlife." Passengers in window seats turn sideways and try to open the steamed-up windows. "When you open a window on a day like this, the rain will blow onto the seat behind you. The rolls of paper towels on the overhead racks can be used to wipe the steam off the windows. This is what we call a *three-roll day.*" He laughs a mirthless laugh, then resumes his sing-song. "We often see moose in this area. Moose live in the forest here."

An hour passes and no one sees an animal. "If it weren't for the clouds," says the driver, "you'd see Mount McKinley from the road." Another hour passes. "Dall sheep are probably up there on the slopes, behind those clouds."

More time passes. "It's important to stay seated on Polychrome Pass because there's a thousand-foot drop off. It will be especially important on a day like this when there is no visibility and buses are coming in both directions. When it rains hard the road sometimes washes out."

A blonde woman pulls eyehades and earplugs from her purse. Everyone under the age of 20 is asleep. Everyone else is fretting.

Several hours later, the bus has turned around and is heading back. If anyone has seen an animal, they haven't mentioned it. The driver feels he should respond to the increasing air of dissatisfaction. "Many people come to Denali hoping to see the grizzly bears, and they are not visible every day. We have many other animals here. Ground squirrels are abundant. "

"I didn't come here to see ground squirrels," says one man loudly.

"You want to see grizzlies?" says his companion. "Wrap yourself in bacon and get out at Mile 38." The two men glower at one another.

Eight hours after they began that morning, 35 passengers, none of whom have seen ground squirrels, arrive back at the Visitors Center, exhausted. They'll remember this day and bring it up whenever someone mentions Alaska.

... OR THE BEST OF EXPERIENCES ...

Here's what a great day is like:

It's 7:00 A.M and 35 people dressed in REI jackets and walking shoes climb aboard a green school bus that will travel through Denali National Park. The driver says his name is John, not Driver, so anyone who wants to ask him a question should ask for John.

He's hardly pulled the bus out of the parking lot when a teenage girl cries, "Moose!" Every day passengers shout at John: "Moose!" and every day he pulls over the bus, his eyes riveted with apparent excitement on the forest. Binoculars are focused, light meters consulted. People are generous to strangers. "Here, take my seat. Can you see him there at 11 o'clock?"

During the next hour, the shuttle passes three bull caribou with 40 pound antlers, standing silhouetted against the sky on the top of a ridge. Then the clouds open wide, sunlight comes streaming across the vast landscape. "That's Denali!" cries the driver. "Mount McKinley! Only 30 percent of those who come here see it!"

The bus continues to the Toklat River, and soon the driver is choking with excitement. "Look down . . . that's fantastic . . . a grizzly is chasing wolves . . . away from a kill!" Thirty-three human beings strain out the bus windows, snapping pictures. The other two passengers tell the driver they'd like to get out here to hike. Get *out?* Here? Surely the driver will refuse to let them, but he opens the door and says, *"Have fun."*

The bus continues. At a rest stop everyone sees a sow grizzly cross a wide gravel bar, jump into a rushing glacial river, swim across, get out, and shake herself. Her two cubs are scared to jump in. They race back and forth on the bank, then take the plunge. Caught in the current, they flail around. The mother is not trying to save them. She seems to be saying: you want to be a bear? You swim rivers. The cubs make it.

Three and a half hours after it left the visitors center, the bus turns around at Eileson. Heading home, more caribou appear, and a fox runs along the road. Dall sheep appear on a far hillside, and Mount McKinley shows itself three times. The light on the snowy peaks is a brilliant, burnished silver. All the way home, there's laughter. A German family is speaking in broken English about the wonders of America, pleasing everyone. The couple who got off to hike appear on the road and get on again, uneaten. A magical feeling drifts over the crowd. It's been one of the best days of their lives. One of the days they'll bring up again and again whenever someone mentions Alaska.

Savage River Area *map page 215, C-1*
Past the Savage River Check Station there is excellent hiking on undeveloped trails. The canyon behind the station is narrow and beautiful with wildflowers and caribou tracks along the river bank. You can hike along the broad braided portion of the Savage River, across the road, as well in the highlands to the north. Several important words of caution: first, the glacial water, especially during the run-off, is freezing cold and deadly swift (keep children at your side at all times); second, grizzlies can be encountered anywhere and are unpredictable animals; third, if you are climbing on Primrose Ridge just to the west, be aware that storms can develop quickly and create dangerous "white-out" conditions.

Wildlife photographers track huge Dall sheep rams in the Savage River canyon and surrounding uplands both early and late in the season (they migrate south to the big peaks in the summer). From the bus you'll see them as specks of white high against brown-ochre cliffs, and you might see a wildlife photographer as a blue speck. He's got a special permit to drive in his car; he's been lying on his stomach in his blue parka and crawling forward in the rain for hours; and now he's focusing his telescopic lens on a ram, hoping it will shift position slightly, so he can take a picture unlike anything you've ever seen before. Don't pass up the chance to get off the shuttle bus and bushwhack up the mountain (whistling the whole time to warn grizzlies), crawl on

Grizzly bear cubs check out the tourists in Denali National Park. (Photo by Kerrick James)

your belly, and take out a pair of binoculars, to see a ram up close.

Primrose Ridge *map page 215, C-1*

For the first few miles past the Savage River bridge, the road parallels Primrose Ridge, a 4,500-foot tundra range that in a good year can have some pretty nice wildflower displays around the summer solstice in late June. The ridge can also be very beautiful in September, when the tundra foliage turns brilliant colors of red and orange, yellow and purple. Caribou and sheep are often seen on Primrose Ridge. Grizzlies will appear, more often than not, as light brown or sunbleached "honeybee-like" shapes lumbering among the berry patches, often with cubs.

Sanctuary River Area *map page 215, C-1*

At about Mile 23 there is an old-fashioned ranger cabin just south of the road. This is the tiny Sanctuary Campground (accessible only by bus), one of the best campgrounds in the park. When Adolph Murie made his study of park wolves in 1939, he stayed for a time in the Sanctuary ranger cabin.

The road soon crosses the beautiful Sanctuary River—a good place to look for moose, especially cow moose. To the southwest you will see Double Mountain, which is best photographed late in the day, as the sun streams in from the west and brings out all the fine detail and shadowing in the mountain. Past Sanctuary River the road climbs a ridge (good place to look for

A Denali Park shuttle bus encounters caribou along the park road.

caribou in the autumn), and then descends into the valley of the Teklanika River.

Teklanika River *map page 215, C-1*

Teklanika Campground is reached at about Mile 29. This is the second largest campground in Denali National Park, though one of the most difficult to obtain permits for, because of its popularity. A little farther on, the road crosses the Teklanika River. Moose are frequently seen in the bed of the river, as are wolves, which den in the closed area upstream (closed meaning no one can hike there—be certain to consult park orientation maps). The road proceeds through a dense spruce forest (dense for the subarctic—elsewhere the trees would be considered few in number and small in size).

Igloo Ranger Cabin and Cathedral Mountain *map page 215, C-1/2*

At Mile 34, just past the Igloo Ranger Cabin and Igloo Campground, the really good country for grizzly-watching begins. Just past the cabin and to the south, on the flanks of Cathedral Mountain, I once observed and photographed a pair of mating grizzlies—an extremely rare sighting even by Denali standards. At about Mile 36 there is a soapberry patch due south of the road in which grizzlies can be seen feeding every August. Once past the Igloo Campground, you are in prime grizzly country and should always proceed, even if walking on the road, with extreme caution—make a lot of noise and travel in groups.

Tattler Creek *map page 215, C-1*

Tattler Creek is often recommended for hiking by rangers (but be sure to ask again for advice if you decide to go there). After you bushwhack up the creek a ways, a shoulder of tundra opens up between two steep mountainsides, and this is a lovely place to wander about for a few hours, picking blueberries and daydreaming. Grizzly tracks will probably be visible in the mud, and on the precipitous cliffs of the mountain, the narrow, inaccessible footpaths of Dall sheep.

Sable Pass *map page 215, C-1*

Beyond Tattler Creek—at Mile 38.3—all travel off the road is prohibited for five miles. This is known as the Sable Pass Critical Habitat Wildlife Closure Area. If you walk here, don't even think of leaving the road. It is, for many periods of the year, literally crawling with grizzlies.

The East Fork of the Toklat River is a good place to take a photograph of the Alaska Range, which is upstream and is especially striking early in the morning or in the evening. The cabin visible a mile to the south is the "Murie Cabin," where Adolph Murie and his family lived for about two years while he was undertaking his historic wolf study. At that time the Dall sheep population had declined drastically. The Park Service assumed this was due to their major predator, wolves, which they proposed to eliminate. Murie established that the sheep population had declined due to six winters of exceptionally heavy snow.

Today, wolves den on the tundra to the south of the cabin—this is all an area closed to hiking. Past the East Fork, the road climbs, and climbs, toward Polychrome Pass (3,700 feet).

Along the narrow, dizzying road over Polychrome Pass shuttle buses make a rest stop.

Polychrome Pass and Toklat River

map page 215, B/C-1/2

The summit of Polychrome Pass (where buses make a rest stop) offers a commanding view of the Plains of Murie (named for Adolph Murie) and the Alaska Range. This is an excellent location to look for wildlife, particularly caribou, wolves, and grizzly bear. Because there are no trees and the view encompasses dozens of square miles, animals are easily spotted. Behind the road, on the grassy ridges of Polychrome Mountain, Dall sheep are also visible, often quite near and even on the road. Marmots and pikas are also commonly seen near the rest area. Wolves hunt on this mountain, especially in the evening hours.

The road descends Polychrome Mountain by some tortured switchbacks and steep inclines, and then crosses wide swaths of tundra country on its way to the Toklat River, which is reached at Mile 53.1. Just downstream is a wolf denning area closed to hiking and the remnants of the cabin where naturalist Charles Sheldon spent one long, lonely winter early in the 20th century. Another rest stop is made at Toklat, and some buses turn back to the Riley Creek VAC at this point. If your ticket is for the Eielson Visitor Center or for Wonder Lake, your bus will proceed.

Highway Pass and Stony Hill

map page 215, B-2

The road past Toklat climbs toward Highway Pass, another famous location for wildlife photographers, where anything from grizzly bears to ground squirrels can be seen at any time. Keep your eyes open. At Mile 60.5, the road crosses Stony Creek, and then climbs up Stony Hill, where some of the finest wildflower displays in the park can be seen around the summer solstice. This is also an excellent area to see grizzly bears. Some buses park at the top of Stony Hill, where there is a sublime view of Mount McKinley, or Denali, to the west.

Thorofare Pass and Eielson Visitor Center *map page 215, B-2*

Thorofare Pass, about four miles farther up the road, affords another excellent view of the great peak, as well as opportunities to view caribou and, believe it or not, a small colony of gulls that make this area home every summer. Also, be on the lookout for long-tailed jaegers—scissor-tailed birds that nest on the tundra and are sometimes seen fighting off hawks, eagles, and foxes. Finally, at Mile 66, is Eielson Visitor Center, named for a pioneering aviator who landed his plane on the gravel bar of the McKinley River at the bottom of the hill. Ninety-five percent of all visitors go no farther, because the bus trip to this point and back (*sans* hiking excursions) is a seven-hour trip. The views of Mount McKinley from Eielson can be spectacular—I have spent many an hour in the middle of the arctic summer "night" waiting for the sun to rise (around 2:50 A.M.) to obtain a photograph of Denali from this vantage.

Wonder Lake *map page 215, B-1/2*

The road winds for another 24 miles to Kantishna. This portion of the road consists of magnificent rolling tundra-lake country, with scattered groves of spruce. Keep those binoculars close at hand—you're apt to see moose and grizzly bears lumbering about on the moist terrain. At Mile 83.5 you will have your first view of Wonder Lake and Wonder Lake Campground (one of the most popular campgrounds in the entire national park system—good luck in obtaining a camping permit). If you've come this far, you'll be eager to get off the bus and walk around. The views here may be the finest on the planet. And on a rare and beautiful day you might see a bull moose feeding on water lilies beneath a long forested ridge with Denali towering in the background. This is the location where Ansel Adams took his two famous pictures of the peak in June 1947. (He set up his tripod on the ridge above the Wonder Lake Ranger Cabin.)

Kantishna *map page 215, B-1*

Beyond the old park boundary now stretches the vast Denali Preserve, a buffer of protected land created by the Alaska Lands Bill of 1980. The town of Kantishna is a private inholding. The growth in this area is nothing short of astonishing—wilderness lodges, restaurants, overnight cabins, private tour buses. The Alaska congressional delegation has for years lobbied for the park road to loop through Kantishna and double back east another 90 miles to the George Parks Highway, making an immense circle through the last great wilderness. There has even been talk of a rail line from Healy to Kantishna. It is a familiar story, as old as America. Some call it progress, and others call it something else. In any event, if you have traveled the road to Wonder Lake, and made the journey on a clear day, you may count yourself lucky. Private tour buses and air charters serve Kantishna, where there are private campgrounds, a historic roadhouse, and upscale lodges (many hundreds of dollars per night), that offer hot tubs, saunas, excellent food, guided day hikes by trained naturalists, fishing excursions to Moose Creek, and wildlife viewing tours both inside and outside Denali National Park.

◆ Activities Near Denali National Park

Hiking

If you must stay outside the park for a few days, there are still dozens of things to do. There are a number of good hiking trails in the vicinity of the park entrance, and at the visitors center you can obtain maps and up-to-date information about each of them. These include the popular **Horseshoe Lake Trail,** which is accessed by a trailhead one mile west of the park turn-off from the Parks Highway, and just before the railroad tracks. The trail leads north about three quarters of a mile to a beautiful lake in the valley of the Nenana River. Moose are often seen here, especially in the morning and evening. As with all park trails, be aware that grizzly bears can be encountered at any time.

Another good trail in this area is the five-mile (round trip) **Mount Healy Overlook Trail,** which begins just behind the park hotel near the post office. A third easily accessed trail near the park entrance is the **Triple Lakes Trail,** which leads south from the Parks Highway three miles to some picturesque lakes near the Riley Creek drainage. Good USGS topographic maps for all three trails are available at the visitors center, as well as more specific guidance from rangers. Park rangers also lead fascinating nature hikes into the backcountry every day. These "discovery hikes" can range from two to five or more miles, and normally include talks on such topics as wildflowers, geology, glaciers, and wildlife.

Dogsledding

A dogsledding demonstration is given every day near park headquarters at the kennels for Denali's sled dogs. In the wintertime rangers patrol the park by dogsled, going from cabin to cabin on a well established route. At that time the ground is covered with snow and the temperature's cold, optimum conditions for these dogs. In summer, the dogs are biding their time, waiting for the weather to improve and get colder, but twice a day they have an opportunity to pull a ranger around a *mud* track on a big, old-fashioned sled. The moment the dogs see the rangers getting a team ready, they go wild, leaping up on their kennel houses, racing around trying to be noticed, yelping and yipping, and generally displaying that they are 100 percent worthy of being chosen. Those which are, from the lead dog to the two on the wheel, go joyfully into their harnesses. Those not chosen look like children left behind on picnic day, woofing around in their pens, or sitting down on their haunches with downcast eyes.

As there's no parking by the kennels you must walk there or catch a bus for the short trip from the visitors center. Departures are about 9:30 A.M. and 1:30 P.M., but check again when you arrive.

Rafting

Rafting the **Nenana River** near the Denali National Park entrance is a popular thing to do. Several licensed concessionaires operate from highly visible sites just off the Parks Highway in the vicinity of the Lynx Creek shopping and hotel area. Be forewarned—this is a dangerous activity on Class III to Class IV rapids.

Flightseeing

Park visitors often take **flightseeing tours**, either by helicopter or fixed-wing aircraft. Again, these businesses operate near the park entrance (an airfield is located directly behind the Denali National Park rail stop), as well as from airstrips in nearby towns such as Talkeetna and Healy. Such scenic trips provide a unique view of the park, especially of its dramatic geology. Opportunities for aerial landscape photography on a clear day are boundless. If you've been in the area for days, and the weather hasn't cleared, this is one way to get up above the clouds and see the mountain.

Sled dogs transport winter travelers in Denali Park. (Photo by Nick Jans)

Fireweed and white spruce trees predominate in the Interior.

Bicycling

Bicycling is increasingly popular in the park, with bicycle rentals available both in the park area and in Talkeetna. One of the advantages of bicycling is that you do not have to wait for a bus ticket to travel on the closed portion of the park road. The disadvantages include exposure to the subarctic environment (there can be snow on any day of the year), a rough gravel road with buses flinging sharp pieces of gravel unpredictably, and a possibile encounter with grizzlies, which can run faster than you can pedal.

■ DENALI HIGHWAY *map page 210, B–D-4*

The largely unpaved Denali Highway runs parallel to the Alaska Range for 135 miles, from Paxson on the east to Cantwell on the west. Along the way there are developed trails, canoe routes, campgrounds, and several traditional roadhouses providing food, lodging, and sometimes gasoline. Because the road is not surfaced, travel proceeds at a slow and civilized pace, enabling visitors to pull off and take photographs of the scenery or wildlife, have a long relaxed picnic, observe the interesting geological features (cirque basins, glacial moraines, kettle lakes) or stretch their legs. This freedom of activity stands in marked contrast to Denali National Park just down the road, where travelers are confined to often uncomfortable park buses (the park buses serve as school buses from September through May and are designed more for children on short rides to school than for adults on 12-hour jaunts to and from Wonder Lake).

The Denali Highway also offers visitors an opportunity to see the Alaska Range without the many restrictions encountered in Denali National Park. There are no park entrance fees, park bus tickets, campground permits, restricted hiking zones, patrolling park rangers, or prohibitions on big-game hunting or fishing (other than applicable state regulations).

The Denali Highway opened in 1957, providing road access to then McKinley National Park from the Richardson Highway. After the George Parks Highway was completed in 1972, enabling folks to drive directly from Anchorage to McKinley National Park, fewer people drove the Denali Highway. Today it is one of the nicest "back roads" in the state.

For many, the ability to enjoy the Alaska wilderness as it suits them is quite refreshing. Visitors will see the same wildlife—caribou, moose, Dall sheep, grizzlies, black bears, wolves, fox, coyotes, lynx, golden eagles, ptarmigan, and so forth—as in Denali National Park, and, with the exception of Denali itself, the subarctic scenery is virtually identical to that within the park. Much of the area along the road is managed by the Bureau of Land Management, which has a multiple-use philosophy of land use, unlike that in the national parks, which is aimed at preserving land and wildlife with minimal interference from humankind. Thus along the Denali Highway you will see off-road vehicle trails, snowmobile use areas, well-marked canoe routes, fishing camps, and, in the spring and fall, big-game hunting camps (the road is closed in winter).

Paxson to Tangle Lakes

map page 210, C/D-4

Most visitors begin their trip down the Denali Highway at the tiny village of **Paxson** (pop. 45), which is located on the Richardson Highway 135 miles east of Cantwell. For the first 20 miles the road climbs steadily from the Summit Pass area past Sevenmile Lake (Mile 6.8) toward **Tangle Lakes,** which are encountered at Mile 20. There are several hundred archaeological sites in the Tangle Lakes area, and summer off-road vehicle use is restricted to signed trails. Visitors will also find two BLM campgrounds, complete with toilets and boat launch (lake trout fishing is great). Visitors often see caribou, moose, and grizzlies at Tangle Lakes. In the fall it is a very popular area with guides, outfitters, and hunters.

Canoe Trails

map page 210, C-4

The 35-mile **Delta River Canoe Trail** begins at the Tangle Lakes BLM campground just north of the Denali Highway, with a take-out near Mile 212 of the Richardson Highway. The Delta River drains north into the Tanana, which ultimately discharges into the Yukon River, which in turn winds its way to the Bering Sea. A shorter boating excursion can be found on the Upper Tangle Lakes Canoe Trail, which involves portages through the Tangle Lakes to Dickey Lake and ultimately the Middle Fork of the Gulkana River, with a take-out near the Richardson Highway (this route involves dangerous rapids). Both canoe trails are managed by the Bureau of Land Management.

MacLaren Summitt

The next major feature on the Denali Highway is **MacLaren Summit** (4,086 feet) at Mile 35.2, which provides travelers with a commanding view to the north of Mount Deborah, MacLaren Glacier, and Mount Hayes. These are the highest mountains before the Denali massif—on a clear day these mountains are visible from downtown Fairbanks (70 miles north of the Alaska Range). There is a good hiking trail from the parking lot, which leads over the tundra to the north nearly three miles. After MacLaren Summit, the Denali Highway descends to cross the MacLaren River (caribou are often seen in this region) and, once past a series of ridges, Clearwater Creek.

(following pages) Dramatic views of Mount Hayes and the Alaska Range are afforded along the Denali Highway, as seen here in the Monahan Flats area.

Susitna River *map page 210, C-4*
Draining south from two enormous glaciers—West Fork and Susitna—is the enormous **Susitna River,** crossed at Mile 79 on a 1,036-footbridge. From here to its termination at the Parks Highway the Denali Highway has good populations of moose, bear, and caribou. Beaver are often seen on the smaller side streams that are free of the glacial till brought down on the major river. Fishing for salmon, trout, and arctic grayling can also be good at various times of the year. Once you reach the Parks Highway (always nice to be on a paved road again) it is only 27.5 miles north to Denali National Park's entrance area. Fairbanks is about a two-hour drive to the north, and Anchorage is a good four- to five-hour drive to the south.

■ FAIRBANKS *map page 210, C-3*

My memories of Fairbanks are primarily of the winters, which begin with a night of nonstop snow in September, reach a nadir in January with daily highs of 45 below zero, and linger, in terms of freezing temperatures and persistent snow drifts, through May. I can remember frozen car batteries, car tires flattened and frozen solid to the ground, alternator belts and coolant hoses shattered by the cold, my hand literally frozen to the door knob of the house (and my wife unfreezing it with a pan of warm water), the pan of water thrown into the yard that froze (in a musical tinkling sound) before it reached the ground, "days" in December that consisted of three hours of twilight, ice fog so thick that aircraft (including U.S. mail and Fed-Ex planes) could not land for a week, furnaces that died when the phone lines were down, frozen pipes and backed-up water in the house, starving moose eating campus shrubbery on the first day of spring, wolves that devoured pet dogs at suburban homes, caribou driven out of the mountains by snow and found wandering around town, people with dry coughs that lasted all winter, light planes that simply disappeared on winter flights (never to be found), violent drunken fights reported nightly in the wild frontier bars along First Avenue, and some amazingly rancorous political battles. No doubt about it, winter life in Fairbanks—about 100 miles south of the Arctic Circle—is a Category One ordeal.

In the summer, though, Fairbanks (pop. 31,850) changes into a friendly and interesting town, with some unusual sites and activities found nowhere else in North America. For one thing, at midnight on the summer solstice you can observe people golfing or playing baseball. For another, you can, at the annual Tanana Valley State Fair in mid-August, see vegetables—pumpkins, squash, carrots, zucchini, lettuce, cucumbers—of truly prodigious size, all grown under the continual bath of

Caribou Fog

The temperature dropped steadily as we left the foothills and started into the high country. Below us in the canyons we could hear the river ice booming like salvos of artillery. Occasionally a spruce tree beside the trail would groan, as its heart sap froze and expanded, and explode like a stick of dynamite. As the sun rose briefly above the mountain tops, the thin air seemed to be filled with iridescent frost spangles, brilliant crimson and blue and green as they flashed in the sun's rays. Frank nudged me and pointed. A low bank of fog seemed to be drifting slowly over the frozen river.

"Caribou," Frank explained. "When it gets this cold, their breath and body heat form a cloud of steam big enough to hide them." As I watched, the cloud parted for a moment, and I saw a herd of fifty caribou climb the far bank and trot into the spruces.

—Klondy Nelson with Corey Ford, *Daughter of the Gold Rush,* 1958

sunlight. And try putting children to bed at 10:00 or 11:00 P.M., with the sun still high in the sky, and you may find your persuasive abilities sorely tested!

◆ University of Alaska *map page 236, A-1*

Chief among the attractions in Fairbanks is the campus of the **University of Alaska.** The school is located on a wooded hill on the west end of town, and is easily reached via University Avenue or Farmer's Loop Road. The campus was originally established by the territorial legislature in 1917 as an agricultural and mining college. Among its first graduates was Margaret Murie, who was instrumental, with Supreme Court Justice William O. Douglas, in the formation of the Arctic Wildlife Range in 1960. Murie later authored such classic works as *Two in the Far North* and *Wapiti Wilderness.*

Today the Fairbanks campus is home to more than 8,000 students, many from Asian countries on the Pacific Rim, and supports more than 50 undergraduate and graduate degree programs, including degrees in geophysics (investigating greenhouse gases, global warming, plate tectonics, northern lights), anthropology (a perfect site to study indigenous cultures), and oceanography (this department should be near salt water, but universities are not always known for their common sense). UAF also owns the distinction of being the only university in the world with

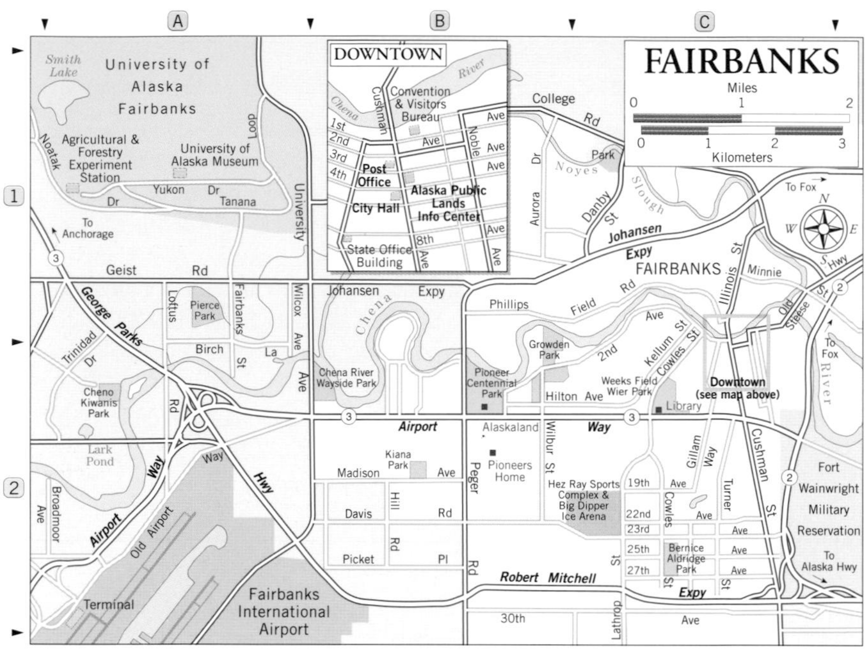

its own rocket-launching facility: Poker Flats, as it is called, is located north of town (not open to the public) and is used for studies of atmospheric physics.

Constitution Hall (just off Tanana Drive in the center of the campus) is where the original Alaskan constitution was signed. Also here is the superb campus bookstore which has the best collection of books on Alaska in Alaska. It's a short walk across campus (or ride on the free shuttle bus) to the **University Museum**. This state-of-the art facility is one of the "top ten" tourist sites in Alaska. Inside you will be treated to all sorts of marvels, such as Oscar, a ten-foot Kodiak bear that greets you at the door; Blue Babe, a perfectly preserved 35,000-year-old steppe bison; a pair of fossilized ivory mammoth tusks; various Eskimo artifacts; photographic and painting exhibits; and dioramas featuring wolves and other Alaskan fauna. The gift shop is worth a lingering visit, with books, cards, calendars, jewelry, musk ox fur, caribou antler artifacts, and some one-of-a-kind Alaskan posters.

Down the hill from the museum is the **University Experimental Farm,** where researchers grow high-latitude barley and wheat, as well as flowers and vegetables. A short drive to the south via Miller Hill and Yankovich Roads is the UAF **Large Animal Research Station,** which has large outdoor enclosures with musk ox and reindeer. Definitely plan to stop at both, and be sure to take a guided tour of "The Musk Ox Farm."

◆ Other Fairbanks Attractions

Alaskaland

Back toward town along Airport Way, visitors often stop at **Alaskaland,** a modest amusement park with a narrow-gauge train track and the riverboat *Nenana,* and the railroad car that carried President Harding from Fairbanks to Anchorage. Also here is the Pioneer Air Museum, gift shops, and the Alaska Salmon Bake—where fresh salmon and halibut is barbecued to suit your tastes.

Information Centers *map page 236, B-1*

Sites to visit downtown include the **Alaska Public Lands Information Center** at the corner of Cushman and 2nd Avenue (maps and books galore), the many gift shops and art galleries selling arts and crafts along Cushman, and the **Convention and Visitors Bureau Log Cabin** located along the Chena River just east of the Cushman Bridge. The friendly personnel have an encyclopedic knowledge of the recreational opportunities available in the Interior.

Pike's Landing is a popular Fairbanks restaurant situated on the banks of the Chena River.

Chena River

No trip to Fairbanks is complete without a half-day voyage down the Chena River on the wooden paddleboat *Discovery,* run by Captain Binkley from his landing off Dale Road on Airport Way. This exciting tour will lead you to an Athabascan village where Native Alaskans will demonstrate traditional fur preparation and the use of dogsleds. Captain Binkley will also take you to the confluence of the Chena and the Tanana, where you can watch the clear waters of the snow-fed Chena mix with the turbid, glacially fed waters of the mighty Tanana.

Flightseeing

You might also investigate taking a short flightseeing trip, which will give you a bird's-eye view of the Interior landscape. Many of these trips, which are very affordable, include a landing on a remote lake where you can fish for northern pike, salmon, or rainbow trout. You can also catch scheduled mail planes for one-day trips to Fort Yukon, Arctic Village, Anaktuvuk Pass, and Bettles. Most of the small charter companies are located on the south-end of the airport (toward the Alaska Range) where there is also a water runway for floatplanes.

Icefog on an average January day in Fairbanks.

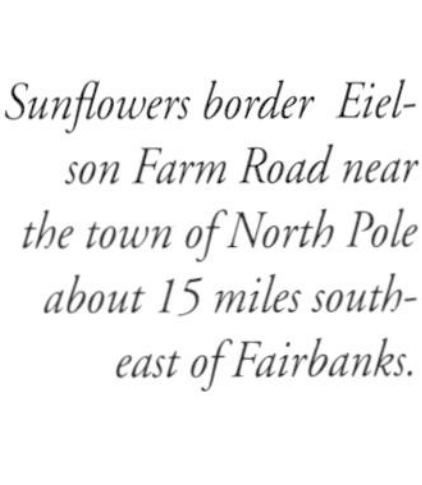

Sunflowers border Eielson Farm Road near the town of North Pole about 15 miles southeast of Fairbanks.

■ North and East of Fairbanks

Just north and east of town a number of places are worth investigating. At **Gold Dredge Number 8,** Mile 9 on the Old Steese Highway, visitors pan for gold with metal pans and sometimes find small nuggets. You can also pan for gold at **FE Gold,** Mile 27.5 on the Steese Highway.

◆ Chena Hot Springs *map page 210, C/D-3*

The road to Chena Hot Springs, reached via the Steese Highway, just a few miles north of town *(map page 210),* is one of the best places in Alaska to observe moose. There are sloughs, lakes, and beaver ponds on either side of the road where they feed among the lily pads. On the way, you'll see the town of Chena Hot Springs, which provides a partial sense of the casual lifestyle of the Alaskan bush. If you follow this 56-mile road all the way to its end, you can soak in warm geothermal springs at the Chena Hot Springs Resort. There are also cabins here, a bar, a restaurant, and camping at Chena State Park.

Excellent hiking trails begin at various trailheads along the road by the resort. Mid-July look for ripe raspberries growing on bushes alongside the gravel roads leading to the river. In early August, the wild blueberries will be ripe on the tundra domes in the 250,000-acre Chena State Park, as well as on Wickersham Dome (about Mile 26 on the Steese Highway) and Murphy Dome (ten miles south of

Fairbanks on Murphy Dome Road). Be sure to watch out for black and grizzly bears while berry-picking.

◆ North Pole *map page 210, C-3*

The town of North Pole, a 14-mile drive southeast of town on the Richardson Highway, serves the army and air force bases in the area. The **Santa Claus House**—filled with Christmas accouterments and, naturally, toys—is a favorite with children. Each December, thousands of letters from around the world arrive in North Pole.

◆ Circle *map page 210, D-2*

One of the most popular short drives from Fairbanks runs over the largely gravel Steese Highway through the scenic White Mountains to Circle. Along the way are ample opportunities for hiking, berry-picking in season, wildlife viewing, and fishing. The vistas at Twelvemile Summit and Eagle Summit are spectacular, especially

Panning for gold at Gold Dredge #8 (left). Another form of gold wrested from the landscape is birch syrup. Michael East at Kahiltua Birchworks boils the valuable sap down into a sugary refinement (above).

Sourdough's Weather Bureau

We had no thermometers in Circle City that would fit the case [reach low enough], until Jack McQuesten invented one of his own. This consisted of a set of vials fitted into a rack, one containing quicksilver, one of the best whiskey in the country, one kerosene, and one Perry Davis's Pain-Killer. These congealed in the order mentioned, and a man starting on a journey started with a smile at frozen quicksilver, still went at whiskey, hesitated at the kerosene, and dived back into his cabin when the Pain-Killer lay down.

—Recorded by William Bronson,
The Last Grand Adventure, describing late 1890s in Alaska

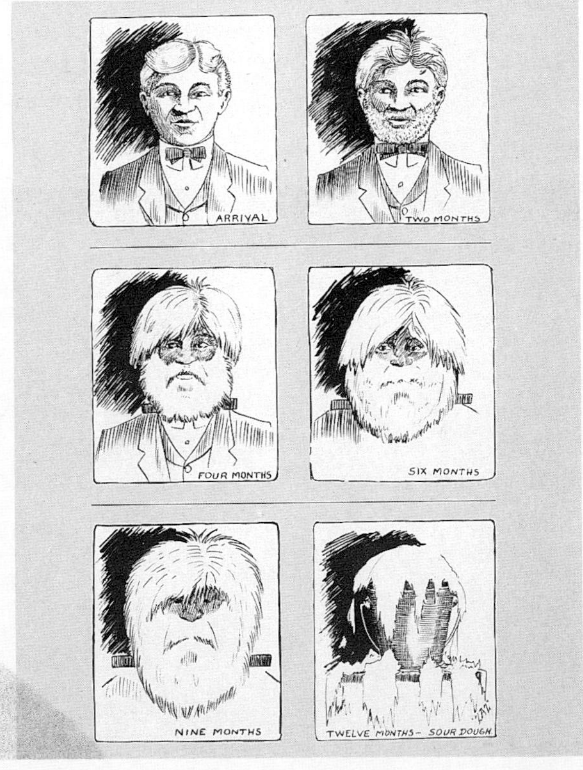

in late August and early September when the tundra begins to turn colors. You also get to see the Yukon River up close.

The town of Circle (located at Mile 162) offers an easily accessible "bush-like" environment for those who cannot make a plane or boat trip deeper into the Interior. There is a pioneer cemetery in Circle, as well as a trading post, a museum, old-time miner's cabins, and antique dog-freight rigs, a cafe, bar, and motel. The Circle Hot Springs Resort provides an Olympic-sized pool, hotel, and individual cabins. *(See page 263)*

■ Bush Villages

Few Interior bush villages can be reached by road. Most are visited via airplane or riverboat. In these villages time seems to move very slowly. The movement of the sun across the sky each day, the phases of the moon (especially to hunters and trappers), and the seasons are more important than calendars and clocks. In the remote villages, wild land is still seen as a physical home, while in the road-accessible villages, the "western" view of land as property predominates. In either case, the bush community is isolated for much of the year and develops a unique culture. People live close to the land, hunting, fishing, gardening, foraging for berries, and making their own winter clothes from the skins of wild animals.

◆ Fort Yukon *map page 210, D-1*

People either love or hate Fort Yukon, a village set near the confluence of the Yukon and Porcupine rivers. Those who love the place enjoy solitude, blueberry- and cranberry-picking, salmon- or pike-fishing, and wildlife-viewing. Those who hate it chafe at the isolation and the low, swampy terrain—busy with mosquitoes in the summer and deadly cold in the winter.

For hundreds of miles in every direction from Fort Yukon are myriad sloughs, ox-bows, lakes, ponds, bogs, rivers, forests, and meadows. Historically this was excellent trapping country, and the town was formed by a field agent for the Hudson's Bay Company in 1847.

Old timers were referred to as "sourdoughs," as opposed to "cheechakos," or newcomers, because of the pot of starter dough they maintained to make their bread. Another version of the term's origin is proposed in this magazine cartoon (left) from a 1907 edition of the Nome Nugget.

Fort Yukon is a short (less than one hour), inexpensive plane flight from Fairbanks, with daily service from several commuter airlines. There are two hotels in town, a general store, and several restaurants. The local inhabitants are Athabaskan Indians, and are related linguistically to the Navajo and Apache of Arizona and New Mexico. Today many Athabaskans pursue a modified subsistence lifestyle, which includes maintaining fishing wheels for salmon in the summer, picking berries and hunting moose in the autumn, fur-trapping in the winter, and hunting waterfowl in the spring. Although snowmobiles have largely replaced the dogsleds of old, many people still raise, train, and race their dogs in the snowy months.

◆ Manley Hot Springs *map page 210, B-2*

Manley Hot Springs lies north and west of Fairbanks at the end of the Elliot Highway and features a campground and the historic Manley Roadhouse. This is an excellent place to have a beer and meet the people of the bush, a colorful group

Alroy DeAngelis at his cabin in the "bush" near Peters Creek.

that includes professional fur trappers, mushers, gold and silver prospectors, hard-rock miners, and commercial and subsistence fisherman.

Surprisingly, this area produces an abundance of vegetables, due to the warm soil and long summer days.

The hot springs in Manley are superb and non-sulphurous, and visitors can enjoy the soothing waters in a large pool. Tours can be arranged to local gold mines and fishing camps.

◆ Ruby *map page 210, A-2*

Ruby is located on the Yukon River over 200 miles southwest of Fairbanks. Founded in 1907 during the gold rush, the town is one of the main checkpoints on the annual Iditarod Sled Dog Race. There is a roadhouse here, and you can charter aircraft to take you to remote lakes, mountaintops, and stretches of river. A stay here offers visitors a look at the bush lifestyle, which includes commercial and subsistence fishing for salmon, trapping, logging, and winter dogsledding.

Most bush villages are accessible only by plane. Here Michael East unloads supplies from a Super Cub at Quiet Lake.

From the Canadian Border to Fairbanks

The Alaska Highway has changed substantially since being constructed during World War II. Where it once was little more than a crude track in the wilderness, it is now a true paved highway over its entire length, easily traveled by a standard passenger car in good shape. Many visitors to Alaska make the long trek up through Canada via the Alaska Highway, which begins at Dawson Creek in eastern British Columbia near Alberta. The entire trip is an adventure in itself, and should be enjoyed as such. Slow down and take in the landscape. Stop to take day hikes, picnic, or make a few casts (with appropriate licenses). Buy a copy of *The Milepost* and study it.

A. A. Bennett of Fairbanks was one of the state's early bush-pilot heroes. Here he poses in front of his Swallow biplane in 1927. The photograph is from the collection of the Alaska Aviation Heritage Museum in Anchorage. This unusual museum displays 21 vintage aircraft and chronicles the exploits of the pilots who linked the rural communities of Alaska's interior to the larger cities.

Dangerous Dan McGrew

A bunch of boys were whooping it up in the Malamute saloon
The kid that handles the music-box was hitting a jag-time tune;
Back of the bar, in a solo game, sat Dangerous Dan McGrew,
And watching his luck was his light-o'-love, the lady that's known as Lou.
When out of the night, which was fifty below, and into the din and the glare
There stumbled a miner fresh from the creeks, dog-dirty, and loaded for bear.
He looked like a man with a foot in the grave and scarcely the strength of a louse,
Yet he tilted a poke of dust on the bar, and he called for drinks for the house.
There was none could place the stranger's face, though we searched ourselves for a clue;
But we drank his health, and the last to drink was Dangerous Dan McGrew.

—Robert Service, *The Shooting of Dan McGrew,* 1907

◆ Northway *map page 210, E-4*

On the south side of the Alaska Highway, just west of the border, is the 900,000-acre **Tetlin National Wildlife Refuge,** an important summer habitat area for hundreds of thousands of ducks, geese, cranes, and other waterfowl. The turn-off for the village of Northway is passed at about Mile 1264—the former leader of this village, Chief Northway, lived to be 114 and was annually featured on his birthday by Willard Scott of NBC'S "Today" show. Even in his 90s, Chief Northway worked every summer in the tribal fishing camp, where salmon are still caught in fishing wheels and prepared for winter use as human and as sled-dog food.

◆ TOK *map page 210, D-4*

The first major town encountered on the Alaska Highway as you drive from Canada northwest into Alaska is **Tok,** located at the junction of the Alaska Highway and the Tok cutoff to the Glenn Highway. You may notice some charred forests on the nearby hillside. A major forest fire in the summer of 1991 nearly destroyed the town, and was finally put out by the first fall snowstorms. There is an excellent Alaska Public Lands Information Center in Tok, which has an incredible quantity of excellent (free) information—maps, brochures, handouts—and a superb front desk staff.

◆ DELTA JUNCTION *map page 210, C/D-3*

While driving north on the Alaska Highway toward Delta Junction, keep your eyes open for bison on or near the roadway.

At Mile 1422 you will enter the sizable town of **Delta Junction,** located at the junction of two important roads—the Alaska Highway and the Richardson Highway (which leads south to Valdez). Delta Junction provides road travelers with their first view of the trans-Alaska pipeline, which stretches from the oil fields of Prudhoe Bay on the Arctic Ocean 800 miles south to the port of Valdez. The pipeline is best seen north of town, where it crosses the Tanana River on a bridge. This region has a number of year-round natural springs and better than average subarctic soil that supports potatoes, wheat, barley, oats, and hay.

On the final approach to Fairbanks you will encounter ever-increasing evidence of civilization—an air force base, the quaint town of North Pole, housing developments, and shopping malls. Finally, at Mile 1520, your journey is over. The Alaskan Highway is behind you, and the vast interior of Alaska is before you. You can turn north and drive all the way to the Arctic Ocean on the Dalton Highway (see the Arctic Alaska section) or turn south toward Denali National Park, Anchorage, the Kenai Peninsula, and the Pacific Ocean.

(previous pages) When winter temperatures fall to extreme levels the atmosphere seems almost to glow in an array of pink and blue colors.

■ TAYLOR HIGHWAY *map page 210, E-2&3*

The Taylor Highway begins at Tetlin Junction on the Alaskan Highway, about 79 miles west of the Canadian border. It leads 161 miles north to the village of Eagle on the Yukon River, with a cut-off east to Dawson City in the Yukon Territory. The Taylor also provides access to the Fortymile National Wild and Scenic River, popular with river rafters, and the Yukon-Charley National Preserve, a 2.2- million-acre area administered by the National Park Service, which maintains an office in Eagle. Like the Denali Highway between Paxson and Cantwell, the Taylor Highway between Tetlin Junction and Eagle enables travelers to get off into the real backcountry of Alaska.

The Taylor Highway (more like a logging road) heads north from Tetlin Junction through the **Tanana Valley State Forest,** a scenic area of spruce and birch forest and grassy meadowlands. Look for moose and black bear in this area, especially in the morning and evening hours. At about Mile 35 **Mount Fairplay** (5,541 feet) is visible just to the east—there is a nice turnout where you can stop and take photographs. In days gone by, caribou were plentiful in the Interior and

Paddle steamers once plied the Yukon River from Eagle to Dawson, transporting miners and materials. (Underwood Photo Archives, San Francisco)

summered on the tundra of Mount Fairplay and other alpine peaks. Their decline is probably due to overhunting.

The once bustling mining town of **Chicken** (pop. 17) is at Mile 64. If you are passing through in the morning, stop in for a hot cinnamon roll and a friendly tour of the ghost town with its 13 original log buildings including the 1905 schoolhouse.

At milepost 95.7 there is a turn-off to the right for the Canadian border, and the historic town of **Dawson City**. If you continue north, the road steadily climbs toward some beautiful alpine mountains, reaching an altitude of nearly 4,000 feet (comparable to around 12,000 feet at the latitude of Colorado, in terms of being above timberline). Caribou, moose, bear, and Dall sheep can be hunted to the west on **Walcutt Mountain**, an area where all motorized vehicles (ORVS, planes) are prohibited. Past the Walcutt Mountain area, the road more or less plunges down American Creek to Eagle, on the banks of the mighty Yukon River.

◆ EAGLE *map page 210, E-3*

Eagle (pop. 165) is an interesting place—a look at the Alaskan bush life in one of the few small communities accessible by road. There are all the accouterments of civilization here—gas stations, restaurants, a post office, various stores, a laundromat and shower, motels, cabins, and campgrounds. If the summer mosquitoes were not so bad, and the winters not so cold, dark and interminable, it would probably be a town of 20,000. But this is Alaska, and so the community consists of miners, trappers, dog mushers, and other bush types. There is much to do here, from fishing and hunting, to river rafting and hiking, to simple sightseeing around town. In recent years Westours (Gray Line of Alaska) has run the *Yukon Queen* riverboat between Dawson City and Eagle—a nice trip. Planes can be chartered here, as well as rafts. The folks at the Yukon-Charley Rivers National Preserve office will be happy to show you a video on the preserve, and to recommend activities. The noted nature writer Barry Lopez once visited the Yukon-Charley Rivers Preserve, and wrote a wonderful essay ("Yukon-Charley: The Shape of Wilderness") about his experience in the wild backcountry. Lopez wrote that he was surprised to find no rangers, no trails, no signs of development—only the pure and natural surface of the earth.

Enormous vegetables such as these cabbages are grown in the Interior valleys during the summer thanks to the warm temperatures and endless daylight.

Climbing McKinley

R. D. Caughron is one of America's premier mountaineers, having ascended peaks throughout the U.S., Canada, Europe, and Peru. He has been on five successful expeditions to the Himalayas, including Peak Korjaneska in Tajikistan, Gasherbrum II and Nanga Parbat in Pakistan, and Dhaulagiri in Nepal. In 1996 he participated in an international expedition to K2 from China. His story of Mount McKinley describes a climb he made in 1980 with two friends, Gerry Dienel and Dean Rau.

From Wonder Lake we're taking stock up to the base of the Muldrow Glacier, or at least as far as the horses and pack animals will go. In my mind, I'm going through the checklist of everything we brought, and our plan—which is to climb the mountain on the north side and go down it on the West Buttress side.

We come to the McKinley River. It's very wide, running fast, and you can't see into it at all. Gerry, my partner from Pennsylvania, heroically makes the first move with his pack unbuckled at the waist loop. Three seconds later, I'm stunned to see Gerry swept away downstream. He's paddling like crazy. Can he make it with his pack? Barely. He clings to the other side about 100 yards downstream. "Come on across!" he shouts. My legs tremble. Dean, our third partner, gives a shout. Here's our two packers. Say, do you mind if we catch a lift across the river? Thank goodness. Now it starts to rain, big time, and the river behind us is rising fast. Oh well, these conditions are what those sourdoughs who did the first ascent of McKinley's north peak from a bar in Fairbanks must have been comfortable with. Right. Gerry's okay, but now several miles farther toward McKinley, we're all equally wet. This is real.

We camp part way to the Muldrow Glacier. It's a beautiful campsite. Green all around. The sun even starts to show itself. Must be around 10 P.M., but who knows in the partial light? Bugs. Everywhere. Biting bugs. Up goes the tent and the bug net. You just have to love this stuff. Spirits are high. What was that for dinner now? Hamburger Helper with what?

Dawn

Dawn looks just like dark. We're up early. Sort of a gobble breakfast. Cold grains and coffee. We go by the packers still encamped, but they pass us by mid-morning. When we get to the moraine our stuff is all out on the ground. Thanks, Curly. See ya. We start to organize our loads. We'll have to make several carries up to where we can go down on the ice and use our sleds. First a cup of coffee. What's that? The stove doesn't work? I pump until the gas can't take any more pressure. Anyone got a match? It still doesn't work. What's that, a leak around the base of the burner? We jump back just in time to watch our stove explode about 30 feet into the air, spinning as it goes. Expletives. We tried both stoves in Anchorage and they worked just fine. Hell, we haven't even gotten to the glacier yet. Can it be fixed? One medical doctor, one Ph.D. in biochemistry, and one M.S. in mechanical engineering, and we give up after five minutes. The stove is absolutely repair proof. Whose idea was it to bring that latest and greatest piece of junk anyway?

We bury the stove. Nothing else to do. We now have one stove, and since our water depends on melting snow, that stove is a critical item in our kit. We cross our fingers. Time to go anyway.

To the Glacier

It's at least a mile and a half to the glacier. We make the trip three times apiece. At last we get all our gear to the overlook. The scenery is awesome. Bright sunny rays through the clouds, highlighting embedded rocks and gravel in the glacier's blue and black ice. Up above you can't see a thing. Cloud. Low hanging cloud at that. It's slippery but we get down to the glacier. It's so wide here, miles and you can see forever. What's this? It's a cache of ski gear left by some Japanese. Just junk, but historical junk. We're awed. I wonder if they made it.

Onward and upward. We come to the first crevasse. Who knows how deep it goes. Don't want to fall in. We rope up. Party of three for the Muldrow Glacier. Looks like we've reserved the entire route. No one, no where. An occasional bird flies overhead. Looks like a vulture. Great, but not really.

We're getting along well. Only one argument settled by an arm wrestling contest, which I lost. Didn't know an orthopedic surgeon could be so strong. Maybe I wasn't trying hard enough? Time to eat something. What was that again, with the Hamburger Helper? Tea. Great.

The weather remains cloudy, but as we head up, hauling our sleds behind us with about 100 pounds each of personal and group equipment, McKinley's sculpted ridges start to emerge through the mist. Wow, it's clearing. My goodness there's our route, all the way to Brown's Tower. Looks like a long way. Looks pretty level, through the ice field. We'll have to switch sides as we head up, but doesn't look like a problem as long as we don't fall into something.

The northwest face of Mount McKinley (the Wickersham Wall) is famous for the frequency of avalanches. (Photo by Kerrick James)

ASCENT

We've come to the up part. A steep slope requires some ice climbing, and a rope. Ever hauled a 50-pound orange plastic sled dangling from a line, up on ice and snow? Great fun. Well, we did it. We even recovered our ice screws we used to protect our ascent. The idea with the sleds is very simple. When the terrain is flatter, or gradual, the weight goes into the sled. When the terrain steepens, the load goes on your back.

What is this? Looks like a big snow cavern. Someone has been here before. We clear enough room to be comfortable. Guess we'll sleep here: What's that smell? Gas fumes. It's our stove. Well, at this altitude the gas doesn't burn completely. But we've no choice. We've only got one small stove, and that's all we've got to make water, which is what we really need desperately. Orange Tang and hot chocolate, that's what we all like best. Looks like we've got about five pounds of drink and 30 pounds of Hamburger Helper. Hum.

Good thing we brought that shovel. Better to have the restroom outside than in the cave. But it's steep around here. Don't slip now. Early morning, for the big push up to Brown's Tower. It's a humper. All the weight is on my back. We move slowly. It

Traversing a Mount McKinley ice field. (Photo by R.D. Caughron)

takes forever to gain elevation, but we're finally almost there. We round the corner. The scenery is gorgeous. Views as far as the eye can see. A sculpted ice ridge makes me think this is the Himalayas.

Dean, in charge of our orthopedic surgery department, is having a hell of a time with headache. It's the dreaded altitude sickness. Will Dean recover? Will we have to go down fast to save his life? I listen to his chest. No gurgling. Pass the Hamburger Helper. A day passes, and now Dean starts to feel better. Whew!

Storm and Cold

As we're heading up a large snow valley between the north summit and the true south summit, the wind picks up. It doesn't look good back down the valley toward Talkeetna. Right. Let's build a snowblock cave.

Very nice. Nothing for *Architectural Digest,* but good enough. And the wind does start to howl. The next day (actually it is pretty difficult to tell time here), we decide to keep going up. Big mistake. As we inch our way up this valley in snowshoes, whiteout to whiteout, we're literally pinned down by the wind. We dig in again. This time just enough time to dig a trench and pitch our tent. How many times did we have to get out and shovel snow from around our tent during the storm? Too many times to remember.

We survive. The storm clears, but now there's three feet of powder to navigate through, and the temperature has really dropped. Decision time. It's clear but cold. Really cold. Numbing cold. We inch forward making Windy Gap at 18,000 feet around 11 A.M. What should we do? We look over to see some lumps in the snow. I guess those are the bodies of the German couple that died here and haven't been evacuated yet. Tough to get a helicopter to 18,000 feet I guess. We shiver and move on.

The idea is to stash our stuff and mark the stash with wands so we can find it upon our return. We're going for the top today, tonight, whenever we get there. We move out. No wind. It feels really strange. So cold and clear. A jet, a big commercial passenger liner zooms overhead about 1,000 feet up. That must be a thrill.

The Summit

It's deep snow. Not hard crust. We plough our way around the 18,000-foot corner. We're laboring really hard, and all three of us have headaches now. It takes forever.

We reach the last rise. Looks like a 50-meter slope up to the summit ridge. We're 20 meters up the slope. One of our members announces he's finished and can't make it any farther. The other two of us just bend over and stare at the snow. We insist he go on, and we're pretty emphatic. Either you go up to the top, or we'll carry you up. No way are any one of us turning around now. Slowly, painstakingly slowly we reach the summit ridge. Only 75 meters horizontal to go. It's so cold a large ice crystal is hanging from my nose, and I look at Gerry to see rime all around his face. I've got on every piece of clothing I brought with me, including the baclava I found at Windy Gap, and I'm FREEZING. We're finally there. Hello. Goodbye.

A miniature Czech flag is flying on top of the summit of Mount McKinley. Picture time. Hugs all around. Two minutes go by. We've got the panorama recorded. We turn around and go down the direction we've come. Must be round 5 P.M. The snow is loose and light. It's still a chore to move. We inch forward. A long line appears in the distance. It's a guided party coming up from the West Buttress. Just about the time our paths intersect, we have to turn to head back to our cache. We're freezing. The arctic air mass coming in from over the Pole is about 40 below. The Himalayas are warmer. We've only got about half the oxygen to breathe that one has at sea level,

On the summit of Mount McKinley. (Photo by R. D. Caughron)

and our heat metabolism is about 50 percent of that at sea level too. This is going to be a struggle.

Descent

We do it. We reach our cache. There are those bodies again. Dreadful. Up goes our little tent. Our stove hums away for one cup of water, and after remembering to turn the stove off, we all fall into a deep sleep.

Our route plan is pretty simple. Head down the west side of the mountain to the 17,000-foot-level camp. Down some very steep slopes, windswept and crusty. The going is treacherous, awkward and we're exhausted. At last, we're on the level above the rocky west buttress. The slope appears very avalanche prone.

We're greeted as heroes by the climbers in the 14,000-foot camp. All those tents and smiles seem like a return to civilization to us.

Another day. Farewell to our new friends in camp, around Windy Corner and heading down toward the Kahiltna airstrip. As we descend, the view of Mount Foraker is awesome. Mount Hunter and Huntington equally so. The scenery goes on forever. I can see green some 12,000 feet below. Gorgeous. Paradise. We arrive at the Kahiltna Glacier late in the day. I will never eat Hamburger Helper or use snow shoes again in my life! Another group flies in and we fly back to Talkeetna.

After spending days in the numbing whiteness of snow and ice, the valleys never looked so green and inviting.

TRAVEL INFORMATION

◆ GETTING THERE

The hub of this area is Fairbanks which is serviced by major air carriers. To reach Fairbanks by car from the Lower 48 via the Alaska Highway, a several thousand mile trip, see page 186. If you fly into Anchorage, you can reach Fairbanks by driving north on the scenic George Parks Highway, or by taking the train.

◆ GETTING AROUND

By Car

Major car-rental companies operate from Fairbanks with rates starting around $50 per day; most without unlimited mileage. The 358-mile scenic **George Parks Highway** connects Anchorage and Fairbanks, and provides access to Denali National Park. The **Dalton Highway,** a 400-mile-plus limited-access gravel road from near Fairbanks to Prudhoe Bay, is off limits for most rental cars, but a few companies will rent four-wheel drives for just such a road. For highway snow conditions call the **State Department of Transportation in Fairbanks;** *907-456-7623.*

By Train

Daily passenger service is offered between Anchorage and Fairbanks by way of Talkeetna and Denali National Park in the summer season (May through September). **Alaska Railroad.** *Anchorage, 800-544-0552.*

By Plane

From Fairbanks it is possible to travel to rural towns and scenic areas by commuter carriers offering intrastate scheduled air service, or chartered air service provided by local pilots. The Federal Aviation Administration has a list of certified air-taxi operations throughout Alaska. The following serve this area:

Frontier Flying Service flies to 23 Interior and Arctic villages. *907-474-0014*

Larry's Flying Service flies to Anaktuvuk Pass, Bettles, Fort Yukon, and 13 other villages. *907-474-9169*

Warbelow's Air Ventures, Inc. offers service to the Interior, bush mail-plane trips, Arctic Circle tours, hot-springs fly-ins, and sightseeing charters. *907-474-0518*

Bus Tours

Bus tours throughout the Interior offer excursions to Circle Hot Springs and into the Yukon Territory. There is an excursion into the Arctic along the Dalton Highway between Fairbanks and Deadhorse; travelers go one way by air, the other by bus. The route crosses the Brooks Range, the Arctic Circle, and the Yukon River.

Gray Line of Alaska. *Fairbanks; 907-456-7741 or Seattle, WA; 206-281-3535.*

Northern Alaska Tour Company. *Fairbanks, 907-474-8600.*

Climate

SUNLIGHT			
SUMMER MAXIMUM	SUNRISE	SUNSET	# OF HOURS
Fairbanks	2:59 AM	12:48 AM	21:49
WINTER MINIMUM	SUNRISE	SUNSET	# OF HOURS
Fairbanks	10:59 AM	2:41 PM	3:42

Only the Siberian heartland has a more extreme climate than the interior valleys of Alaska. In the winter the cold air settles as in a bowl, and week-long spells of 40 or even 50 below zero are not uncommon. When the temperature rises (above 0°) it snows. Spring and fall last about a week in May and September, respectively. July brings warm, even hot, temperatures and occasional thunderstorms.

TEMPS (F°)	AVG. JAN. HIGH	AVG. JAN. LOW	AVG. APRIL HIGH	AVG. APRIL LOW	AVG. JULY HIGH	AVG. JULY LOW	AVG. OCT. HIGH	AVG. OCT. LOW	RECORD HIGH	RECORD LOW
Denali N.P.	10	-8	38	15	67	42	32	13	94	-60
Fairbanks	-2	-20	40	19	72	52	36	19	99	-66
Fort Yukon	-13	-31	38	17	75	53	33	10	100	-78

PRECIPITATION (INCHES)	AVG. JAN.	AVG. APRIL	AVG. JULY	AVG. OCT.	ANNUAL RAIN	ANNUAL SNOW
Denali N.P.	0.7"	0.4"	3.2"	1.1"	16"	80"
Fairbanks	0.5"	0.3"	2.0"	0.8"	11"	67"
Fort Yukon	0.4"	0.3"	1.1"	0.6"	7"	41"

Food, Lodging, & Tours

◆ Regional Information

Alaska Bed and Breakfast Association.
369 S. Franklin, Suite 200, Juneau, AK 99801; 907-586-2959
For information on B&Bs throughout Alaska.

Alaska Public Lands Information Center.
250 Cushman St., #1A, Fairbanks, AK 99501; 907-465-0527
Information on cabins, camping and hiking.

Restaurant Prices
Per person, without drinks, tax, or tip:
$ = under $12; $$ = $12–$20; $$$ = over $20

Room Rates
Per night, per room, double occupancy:
$ = under $70; $$ = $70–$100; $$$ = over $100

= lodging
= restaurant
= campground
= wilderness lodge

CIRCLE *map page 210, D-2*

population 100

Circle Hot Springs Resort. 134 miles northeast of Fairbanks; 907-520-5113 $–$$

Family resort featuring an olympic-size swimming pool, bubbling with hot spring water. Guests can choose from lodge rooms, furnished cabins, or hostel type (bring your sleeping bag) accommodations. Campers and RVx welcome. Winter activities include cross country skiing, dog sled rides, and watching the Aurora borealis.

Snow machine rental available. Facilities include small plane landing strip, ice cream parlor, saloon, and restaurant.

DELTA JUNCTION *map page 210, C-3*

population 652
visitors information 907-895-9941

Pizza Bella. Mile 265 Richardson Hwy., across from the visitors center; 907-895-4841 $

A taste of Italy a la Americana in the tundra.

Rika's Roadhouse. Mile 275, Richardson Hwy.; 907-895-4201 $

Historic landmark; homemade soups and sandwiches served cafeteria-style. Only open until 5 pm.

Black Spruce Lodge. Accessible by shuttle boat; 907-388-2409 $$

Rustic lodge with ten cabins situated near Quartz Lake, where the rainbow trout are plentiful. Open May–September; reservations necessary.

Kelly's Country Inn Motel. Downtown Delta Junction on the Richardson Hwy.; 907-895-4667 $$

Newly remodeled. Kitchenettes available.

DENALI NAT'L PARK *map page 210, A&B-2&3*

Also see Talkeetna, Page 205

population 171
visitors information 907-683-2294

Talkeetna/Denali Visitor Center. At the junction of the Parks Highway and the Talkeetna spur road; 800-660-2688.
If you're traveling to Denali from Anchorage, the log cabin visitors center is an excellent place to make reservations and plans. The helpful staff will show you pictures of accommodations, call ahead and make reservations, and give you practical advice.

Lynx Creek Pizzaria. One mile north of the park entrance on the George Parks Hwy.; 907-683-2547 $–$$
American-style tomato, cheese, and meat pizza. Thick bean and meat (no veggies or rice) burritos. Beer. Checkered tablecloths. Informal and convivial.

The Perch. Mile 224, Parks Hwy.; 907-683-2523 $$–$$$
Breakfast, dinner, and packed box lunches are available, all served with home-baked breads and desserts. Many consider this the best restaurant in the area, with large ortions and great value for your money. Breakfast, dinner, and packed box lunches available.

Camp Denali. 90 miles west of the George Parks Hwy. on a private parcel within Denali National Park. P.O. Box 67, Denali National Park, AK 99755; 907-683-2290 $$$
Log-cabin enclave in the heart of the park noted for rustic charm, home-cooked meals. Family-owned and operated log cabin complex deep in the park, with spectacular views of Mt. McKinley. Resort emphasis is on natural history, education, and tranquility. Expert naturalists on staff, leading guided hikes and evening programs.

CAMP DENALI

Carlo Creek Lodge. Off highway at Carlo Creek about Mile 224; 907-683-2573 $–$$
About the nicest campground in the area. Each site is under a log roof, a wonderful protection during frequent rainstorms. By the creek and owned by a nice couple; several cabins also available.

INTERIOR

Carlo Heights Bed and Breakfast. On private road one mile off Mile 224 off George Parks Hwy.; 907-683-1615 $$
An appealing modern wood cabin on a hill overlooking a river valley. Comfortable and private. Fifteen minutes south of park entrance.

Denali Backcountry Lodge. P.O. Box 810, Girdwood, AK 99587; 800-841-0692 or 907-783-1342. $$$
Complete package for lodging deep within the park, including guided hiking, wildlife viewing, bicycling, photography, and natural history programs.

DENALI BACKCOUNTRY LODGE

Denali Dome Home Bed & Breakfast. 137 Healy Spur Rd., 12 miles from park entrance; 907-683-1239 $$
A beautiful, clean home. Four levels, open and airy, big living room and fireplace. Full breakfast. Jacuzzi and sauna. Open year round.

Denali Grizzly Bear Cabins and Campground. Mile 231.1 George Parks Hwy.; 907-683-2696 $-$$$
Old Alaskan establishment offering tent cabins, hookups, tent sites, and rv hookups, as well as a grocery store. A 6-mile drive to the Denali National Park entrance. Make reservations early.

Denali National Park Hotel. Just inside Denali National Park. Follow signs from visitors center; 907-276-7234 or 800-276-7234 $$$
Comfortable, government-issue-style buildings; inside are restaurants and gift shops.

Denali Princess Lodge. Off Parks Hwy. near park entrance. 907-683-2282 or 800-426-0500 off season $$$
Overlooking the Nenana River with 280 rooms; shuttle service to park, airport, and railroad station; spa, restaurant, and a gift shop on premises.

Denali River Cabins. Just south of the park entrance along the highway on the Nenana River; 800-230-7275 $$$
Lovely location, 54 wood cabins, hot tub, and river-side sauna. RV park.

Denali West Lodge. Reservations: Dept. VP, P.O. Box 40, Lake Minchumina, AK 99757; 907-674-3112 $$$
Spectacular Mount McKinley view, private log cabins; mush your own dogsled team; trek upland forest and alpine tundra; paddle creeks, rivers and wetland marshes; photograph wildlife.

DENALI NAT'L PARK *continued*

Denali Wilderness Lodge. Reservations summer: P.O. Box 50, Denali Park, AK 99755; winter: P.O. Box 120, Trout Lake, WA 98650; 509-395-2711 $$$

Built on the site of a turn-of-the-century mining camp, this rustic lodge is expensive, in part because you must fly in to get there, but the flight itself is spectacular and the experience of staying in this historic spot in the wilds may prove worth the splurge. Horseback riding, naturalists, good food, private cabins.

DENALI WILDERNESS LODGE

Grandview Bed and Breakfast. Located in Healy. 12 miles north of park entrance; follow signs from highway; 907-683-2468 $$

Light and airy space; decorated in light colors; big windows and scenic mountain view. Continental breakfasts, full kitchen available to guests. Owners live in a separate home.

Kantishna Roadhouse. P.O. Box 130, Denali National Park, AK 99755; 800-942-7420/ winter: P.O. Box 81670, Fairbanks, AK 99708 $$$

Located 95 miles west of the George Parks Highway on a private parcel within Denali National Park and Preserve. One of the oldest roadhouses in Alaska. You'll find modern cabins, good food three times daily, and day hikes with trained naturalists. Good mountain biking, wildlife observation in the area. Just a few miles from Wonder Lake.

McKinley Chalet Resort. Reservations: Dept. VP, 241 W. Ship Creek Ave., Anchorage, AK 99501; 800-276-7234 $$$

Features suites, restaurants, beer and wine bars, indoor pool, hot tub, sauna, Cabin Dinner Theater, wildlife and natural history tours, and rafting.

McKinley RV Park Campground. Mile 248.4 on the George Parks Hwy. (about 10miles north of Denali National Park); 800-478-2562 or 907-683-2379 $

True, the campground is right on the busy highway, but it is convenient—both to the park entrance, and to the adjacent restaurant, gas station and store.

North Face Lodge. Located 90 miles west of the George Parks Hwy. on a private parcel within Denali National Park and Preserve. Reservations: P.O. Box 67, Denali National Park, AK 99755; 907-683-2290 $$$

Comfortable rooms in a modern lodge.

Hiking, canoeing, and fishing all nearby. Flightseeing trips also available, as well as nature walks with a naturalist. Stunning views of Mt. McKinley.

NORTH FACE LODGE

The Perch. Mile 224, Parks Hwy.; 907-683-2523 $$

Attractive modern cabins off the highway in the forest. The resort has a good restaurant.

◆ Tours

Denali Raft Adventures. 907-683-2234

All-day, two- and four-hour scenic and whitewater floats available on the Nenana River.

FAIRBANKS *map page 210, C-3*

population 31,850
visitors information 907-456-5774

Alaska Salmon Bake. Northeast corner of Airport Way and Peger Rd.; 907-452-7274 $

This is a great deal—a huge outdoor barbecue every day in the summer; buffet with grilled halibut, salmon, ribs, baked beans, potato salad, garden and caesar salad, sourdough rolls, blueberry cake, iced tea, lemonade, and other hearty foodstuffs. Everybody stops here at least once, and many people park their RVs overnight in the parking lot nearby. Located inside Alaskaland historical Park, which features a gold rush ambience and an old-fashioned carousel.

Castle Restaurant. 4510 Airport Rd.; 907-474-2165 $$–$$$

Restaurant, bar, and night club. Dinner only, featuring steak and seafood, a billiard room, and live music after nine.

Chena's Restaurant. 4200 Boat St.; 800-770-3343 $$–$$$

Bar and restaurant with pleasant outside deck, featuring smoked ribs and chicken, top steaks and Alaska seafood.

Gambardella's Pasta Bella. Corner of 2nd Ave. and Barnette St. downtown; 907-456-3417 $

Good Italian food, though often crowded at lunch hour.

Hot Licks Ice Cream. 3453 College Rd.; 907-479-7813 $

Where college students hang out; homemade ice cream, gourmet coffee.

Palace Saloon. In Alaskaland, corner of Airport Way and Peger Rd.; 907-456-5960 $

Nightly old-fashioned revues with dancers and honky-tonk piano.

FAIRBANKS *continued*

Oriental House. 1101 Noble St.; 907-456-1172 $
Good quality, quickly served, inexpensive Chinese food.

Pike's Landing. 4438 Airport Way; 907-479-7113 $$–$$$
Diners can choose to sit on a large deck overlooking the Chena River, in an elegant dining room, or in a casual sports bar. Open for breakfast, lunch, and dinner, and for Sunday brunch.

The Pump House Restaurant and Saloon. Mile 1.3 Chena Pump Rd.; 907-479-8452 $$
The Pump House is perhaps the in-town restaurant most favored by Fairbanksans. A great place to hang out in the evening, as well. Huge stuffed brown bear at restaurant entrance.

River City Bagels and Deli. 364 Old Chena Pump Rd.; 907-451-8648 $
A friendly place to enjoy classic deli sandwiches and fresh bagels and breads.

Sam's Sourdough Cafe. 3702 Cameron St.; 907-479-0523 $
Excellent breakfasts and hearty lunches and dinners.

Two Rivers Lodge. Mile 16 Chena Hot Springs Rd.; 907-488-6815 $$$
Probably the best food around Fairbanks—plus a nice folksy atmosphere. A trout lake out in front.

Ah, Rose Marie Bed and Breakfast. 302 Cowles St.; 907-456-2040 $$
A 65-year-old farmhouse offers cozy rooms and has northern lights–viewing accommodations in the winter.

Alaska Heritage Inn and Hostel. 1018 22nd Ave.; 907-451-6587 $
Inexpensive rooms; bunkbeds; tent sites.

Alaska 7 Gables Bed & Breakfast. 4312 Birch Ln.; 907-479-0751 $–$$
Pleasant accommodations close to the airport, the university campus, and several small shopping centers. The inn has many nice touches, including Jacuzzi baths and delicious breakfasts. Canoe rentals available. Free for guests.

ALASKA SEVEN GABLES BED & BREAKFAST

Captain Bartlett Inn. 1411 Airport Way; 800-544-7528 outside of Alaska, 800-478-7900 inside Alaska $$$
This mid-size hotel with 200 nicely appointed rooms is across the street from Alaskaland theme park. Also houses the "Dogsled Saloon."

Chena Hot Springs Resort. 65 miles northeast of Fairbanks, at the end of a long paved road bearing the same name; 907-452-7867 $$–$$$

Spa offers winter aurora-watching accommodations and activities that include full-body massages, cross-country skiing, ice fishing, ice skating, and dogsledding. Summer guests can enjoy the endless daylight with camping, picnicking, hiking, horseback riding. The resort also has a restaurant.

Cloudberry Lookout. 310 Yana; 907-479-7334 $$

An extraordinary log and glass structure set on 60 wooded acres just outside Fairbanks and a seven-minute drive from the University of Alaska. The inn's four guest rooms are furnished with family heirloom antiques, and each has a private bath. As for outdoor recreation, an extensive trail system adjoins the property. There is a watchtower where guests have prime-viewing of the aurora (northern lights). Kitchen and laundry facilities available. Rates include full breakfast.

Ester Gold Camp. Mile 351.7 George Parks Hwy.; 907-479-2500 $

Private campground five minutes south of Fairbanks with clean, comfortable sites to park your RV or set up your tent.

Fairbanks Princess Hotel. 4477 Pikes Landing Rd.; 907-455-4477 $$–$$$

Located out by the airport, conveniently close to Pike's Landing, a popular watering hole and restaurant.

◆ Tours

Beaver Sports. 3480 College Rd.; 907-479-2494

Northern Alaska Tour Company—Arctic Circle Adventure. 907-474-8600

All-day (or half-day) bus trips to the Arctic Circle and Yukon River. Also available are 3- and 4-day fly-drive tours to Prudhoe Bay and Barrow, an overnight tour to the Brooks Range, and an evening air tour to the Arctic Circle and back.

Riverboat Discovery III. 1975 Discover Dr.; 907-479-6673

Sternwheeler river cruise; includes tour of an Indian village and viewing of a sled dog team.

Kantishna

See Denali National Park, page 264.

Tok & Vicinity

map page 210, D-4

population 1,400
visitors information 907-883-5887 winter, 907-883-5775 summer

Cleft of the Rock Bed and Breakfast. Sundog Trail; 907-883-4219 or 800-478-5646 $$

Three rooms in-house and three cabins, set in grove of white spruce. Car battery plug-ins for winter visitors. Warm Christian hospitality.

TOK & VICINITY
continued

Fast Eddy's Restaurant. 1313 Alaskan Hwy.; 907-883-4411 $
Good American food—fresh halibut, steaks and potatoes, pizza.

Water's Edge B&B.
Mile 191.4 Richardson Hwy., north of Paxson; 907-482-9001 $$
On the banks of Summit Lake, the inn offers modern, furnished cabins and one duplex. Private baths. Innkeepers arrange guided fishing and boat trips, and berry picking. Tent and RV spaces near the inn.

WATER'S EDGE BED & BREAKFAST

FESTIVALS AND EVENTS

FEBRUARY

1000-mile Yukon Quest. Top mushers compete in a sled-dog race between Fairbanks and Whitehorse. *907-452-7954*

Fairbanks: Festival of Native Arts. Native dance groups and artisans come from across Alaska to the University of Alaska Fairbanks for this three-day event; usually held in the latter part of the month. *For more information, contact the Alaska Native Studies Department, UofA Fairbanks; 907-474-6889*

MARCH

North Pole: Winter Carnival. Events include craft bazaars, music and dancing, a parade, and ice sculptures. 907-488-2242

Iditarod Trail Sled Dog Race. Dogs and mushers cross 1,049 miles of tundra, rivers, mountains, and ice-locked sea coast to reach Nome 11 to 15 days later. Festivities include a reindeer potluck and the Iditarod awards banquet at the finish. *Wasilla, Iditarod Trail Headquarters; 907-376-5155*

April

Fairbanks: Arctic Man Ski & Sno Go Classic. Race competetiors ski down a mountain and then are pulled up a neighboring hill by their partners on snowmachines. *907-456-2626*

Nenana: Ice Classic. Highlight is a lottery where people pay $2 to guess the time the ice breaks (to the day and minute). First prize is a share of the pot, often exceeding $50 thousand. *970-832-5446*

June

Fairbanks: Midnight Sun Baseball Game. Held in late June in celebration of the longest day of the year, the summer solstice.

July

Fairbanks: Golden Days. Reenactment of gold being found near Fairbanks in 1902. Activities include a parade, contests, races, and flower show. *907-452-1105*

Fairbanks: Summer Arts Festival. Late July and early August mark the arrival of this annual festival, which features music, dance, theater, opera, ice-skating, and various lectures and workshops dedicated to the arts. *907-474-8869*

Fairbanks: World Eskimo-Indian Olympics. Participants compete in a varied events including the knuckle hop, blanket toss, and ear pulling. *907-452-6646*

October

Fairbanks: Oktoberfest. Held in late September, early October. Features German food and polka dancing. *907-479-5531*

December

Fairbanks: Athabascan Old-Time Fiddling Festival. Features traditional Native music. *907-452-1825*

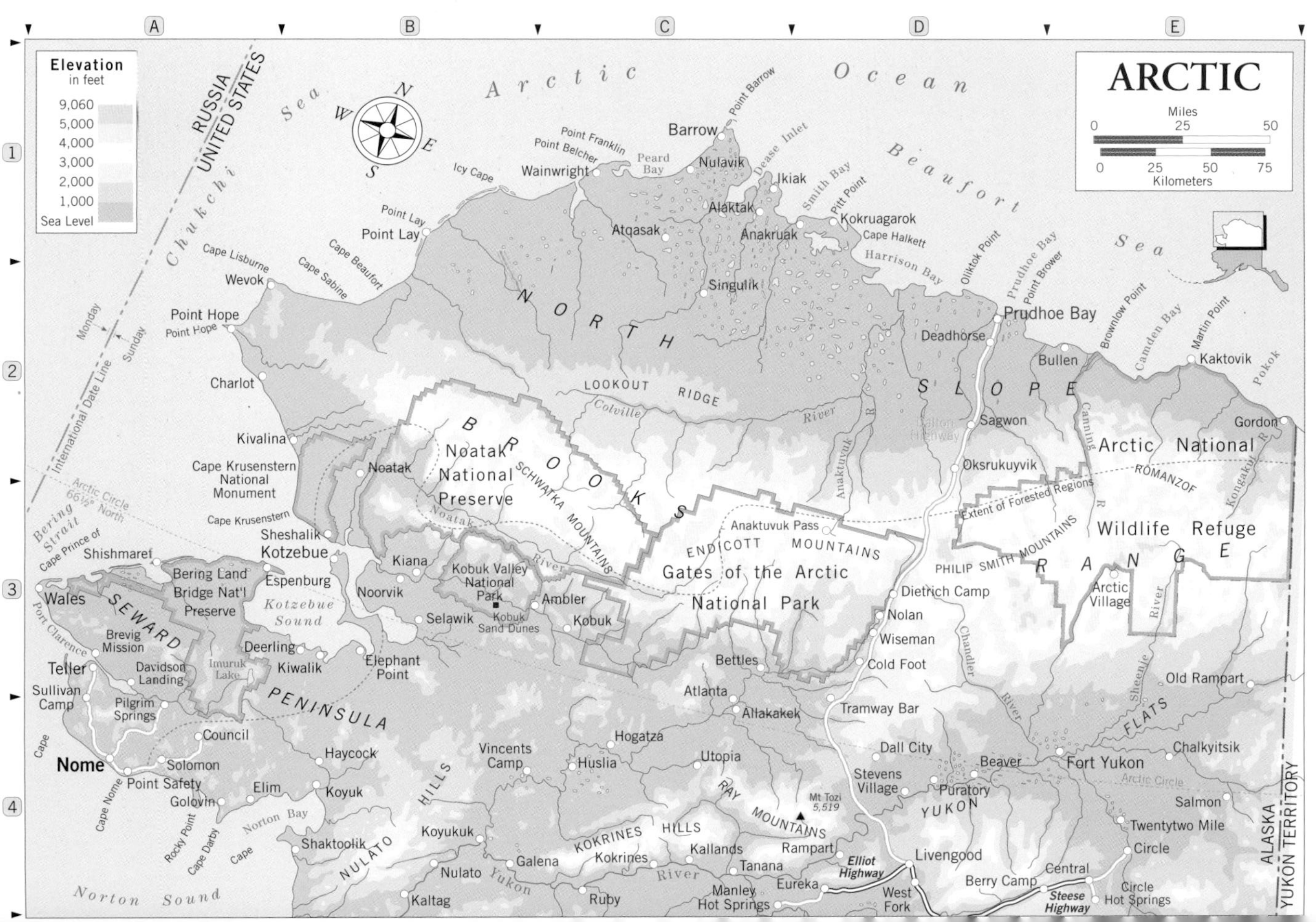
ARCTIC
Miles
0 25 50
0 25 50 75
Kilometers
Elevation
in feet
9,060
5,000
4,000
3,000
2,000
1,000
Sea Level
A
B
C
D
E
1
2
3
4
Arctic Ocean
Beaufort Sea
Chukchi Sea
RUSSIA
UNITED STATES
International Date Line
Monday
Sunday
Arctic Circle 66½° North
Bering Strait
Point Barrow
Barrow
Point Franklin
Point Belcher
Peard Bay
Wainwright
Icy Cape
Nulavik
Dease Inlet
Ikiak
Smith Bay
Pitt Point
Alaktak
Anakruak
Atqasak
Kokruagarok
Cape Halkett
Harrison Bay
Oliktok Point
Prudhoe Bay
Point Brower
Brownlow Point
Camden Bay
Martin Point
Kaktovik
Pokok
Point Lay
Cape Lisburne
Wevok
Cape Sabine
Cape Beaufort
Point Hope
Singulik
NORTH SLOPE
Deadhorse
Bullen
Charlot
LOOKOUT RIDGE
Colville River
Anaktuvuk R
Dalton Highway
Sagwon
Gordon
Canning R
Arctic National Wildlife Refuge
Kongakut R
ROMANZOF
Kivalina
BROOKS RANGE
Noatak National Preserve
Noatak
SCHWATKA MOUNTAINS
Oksrukuyvik
Extent of Forested Regions
Cape Krusenstern National Monument
Cape Krusenstern
Sheshalik
Kotzebue
Shishmaref
Cape Prince of Wales
Anaktuvuk Pass
ENDICOTT MOUNTAINS
Gates of the Arctic National Park
PHILIP SMITH MOUNTAINS
Kiana
Kobuk Valley National Park
Bering Land Bridge Nat'l Preserve
Espenburg
Noorvik
Ambler
Kobuk
Kobuk Sand Dunes
Dietrich Camp
Arctic Village
Wales
SEWARD PENINSULA
Kotzebue Sound
Selawik
Nolan
Wiseman
Port Clarence
Brevig Mission
Deerling
Elephant Point
Teller
Davidson Landing
Imuruk Lake
Kiwalik
Bettles
Cold Foot
Chandler River
Sheenjek River
Old Rampart
Sullivan Camp
Pilgrim Springs
Atlanta
Allakaket
Tramway Bar
FLATS
Council
Haycock
Hogatza
Dall City
Chalkyitsik
Cape Nome
Nome
Solomon
Point Safety
Vincents Camp
Huslia
Utopia
Beaver
Fort Yukon
Stevens Village
Puratory
Arctic Circle
Golovin
Elim
Koyuk
HILLS
RAY MOUNTAINS
Mt Tozi 5,519
YUKON
Salmon
Norton Bay
Rocky Point
Cape Darby
Cape
Shaktoolik
NULATO
Koyukuk
KOKRINES HILLS
Twentytwo Mile
Kallands
Rampart
Elliot Highway
Livengood
Circle
Galena
Kokrines
Tanana
Central
Nulato
Yukon
River
Eureka
Berry Camp
Circle Hot Springs
Norton Sound
Kaltag
Ruby
Manley Hot Springs
West Fork
Steese Highway
ALASKA
YUKON TERRITORY

THE ARCTIC

HIGHLIGHTS

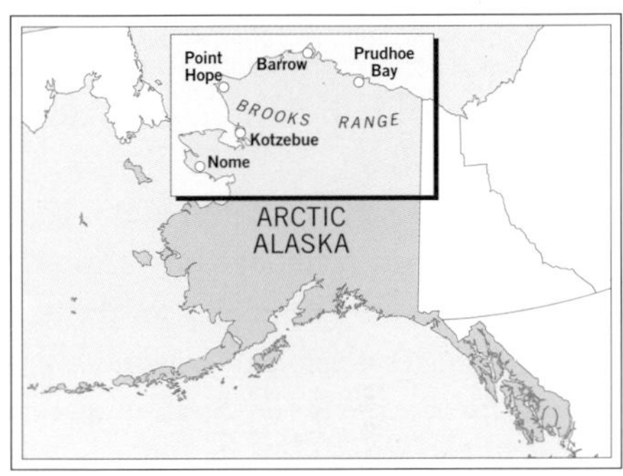

MAPS

PRACTICAL INFORMATION

LANDSCAPE AND TRAVEL

The chief quality of Arctic Alaska is space. This becomes most evident when, as most do, you enter the region by air. Your plane lifts off from a village airstrip which is in itself remote. Gradually, you reach a cruising altitude of 500 to 600 feet, navigating around hills, climbing to thread through passes, descending to cruise above river valleys, all the time advancing over a landscape that has no work of man on it. To the north is the Arctic Ocean; to the west, the Bering Sea and Siberia. The Brooks Range protects the Arctic's southern flank, and what stretches before you as you travel north is spruce taiga, then treeless tundra, and finally, snow- and ice-filled seas.

For most of your flight, as you look down below, you see no cabins, no tents, no boat docks. Not so much as one smoke plume from one campfire. Occasionally you will see animals—an obsidian black bear feeding on some blueberries beside a lake, looking up annoyed at this buzzing overhead, a great bull moose on a bed of sphagnum moss, a herd of caribou running free and wild over a rolling tundra dome. If it is autumn, the colors will amaze—the salmon leaves of the blueberry patches, the purple of the spent fireweed, the orange of the dwarf birch, and the yellow of the alpine willow. If it is summer, you will see a thousand variations on the color green. But rarely in your travels in Arctic Alaska will you see anything that is connected with the human race.

One road leads into the Arctic from the Interior, and that is the Dalton Highway, which follows the Alaska pipeline north from Fairbanks *(see page 278, following)*. Other roads in the region radiate out several miles from small towns before ending in the Bush.

Most of the parks described in this chapter are reached by bush plane. They are, for the most part, without roads, campsites, or visitors centers. Several small arctic towns are worth a visit, if only for the purpose of absorbing their austere isolation. From Nome it's possible to visit and stay overnight in several Eskimo villages, and even to fly over the Bering Strait to spend the night in Siberia.

For listings of airplane companies, wilderness lodges, and accommodations in Arctic towns, see page 308, following.

One place to hide out in during the long, cold Arctic nights is the local saloon (above).
Lichens, bearberry, and other low plants typical of dry, or alpine tundra.

■ Life in the Arctic Wild

Life is difficult for both plants and animals in Arctic Alaska. Summer is painfully brief, and winter is triple its length in much of the Lower 48. Everywhere life clings to a tiny foothold, defending that niche with passion and cleverness, from the alpine forget-me-not growing in the lee of a solitary rock that breaks the wind to a grizzly bear retiring to its den every October, fattened by a summer of feeding. People live along rivers and along the coasts, relying on the fish and the animals drawn to water. Vast areas have no people in them at all. There is much nobility and mystery here, in the way an arctic blossom courageously blooms, despite being half-buried in an early snow, in the hair-raising howl of the wolf down the valley, letting you know it has smelled your campfire, and in the delicate play of the northern lights among the stars of the constellation we call Ursa Major.

Arctic Seasons

Nick Jans is a writer and teacher in Ambler, a Inupiat Eskimo village of 350 people located 50 miles north of the Arctic Circle and 200 miles from the nearest road.

It's not much—a single willow leaf, yellow, curled at the edges. The early August sun rests warm on my back as I work outside the cabin, and white-crowned sparrows flicker through the trees. Forty miles to the east, a thunderhead billows against the dreamwashed bulk of Old Man Mountain. But the leaf knows the truth, and so do I. Summer's over.

It's hard to believe, looking at this vibrant green landscape, that it will burn bright, fade, and drift into snow, all in just three weeks. Arctic seasons blow open and shut like doors in the wind; the change is startling, something I've never gotten used to. There's often a single week you can point to, sometimes a day, that marks an edge.

Still, the old joke about the two Arctic seasons, winter and fall, is off base. Ambler may be among Alaska's cold spots (four winters ago, we held between 40 and 70 below zero for 21 days straight), but you'd never guess that from the almost tropical intensity of a midsummer day. From late May to early August, the sun hardly sets, carving an elliptical path above the horizon. Frost can hit on the Fourth of July—this is, after all, the arctic—but eighty degrees on a cloudless day isn't unusual, and 90s aren't out of the question.

Then there are the manic extremes of light: near total darkness to unending day in just six months, then back again. The whole damn village goes haywire in late spring. Friends drop in to visit at midnight; second graders stagger into school bleary-eyed, bragging they "never sleep yet." You can't blame me, a few years ago, for shooting my alarm clock full of holes.

After the frantic bustle of spring, summer life in Ambler turns languid. High schoolers play basketball outside at 2 A.M.; the women pick berries; men set out at midnight to hook sheefish. The only ones exerting much energy are the kids. Sun-browned and wearing shorts, they ride bikes, play games, and cool off in the Kobuk's bone-chilling waters.

But from the heady week of solstice, when the sun never sets, the light keeps falling away. At first it's just a minute a day, but the pace quickens, the midnight twilights deepen. Winter's coming, though the sun burns down and fireweed blooms.

By mid-August, night is dark enough for stars, and the morning tundra creaks with frost. "Falltime," people say. "Time to get busy." The men set out hunting for caribou and bear. The women fish in earnest, endless cycles of checking net, cutting and drying. It's time, too, to gather cranberries, wild rhubarb, and masru, Eskimo potato. In the still, luminous days between the first cold rains, the cry of wild geese echoes down the sky.

Meanwhile, school's started. Trapped inside, I can't help staring out across the flats, where each leaf blazes red and gold. To the west, snow squalls pile against the Jades, then clear in brilliant rifts of blue.

I rush home, throw my gear together, and head out on the river. If anyone asks why, I don't have a good reason. Sometimes I run downstream a few miles and sit on a high bank, listening to the river, facing into the sun. I know it's only winter coming, but I find myself saying goodbye to all the bright things of this world, to the time that, just a month ago, seemed to last forever.

Leaves fade and fall; shelf ice reaches out into the current, sealing away the water into hard silence, more each day as the river cools, until, sometime in October, only a few steaming runs remain. I watch them close one by one, and feel myself settling with the land, drifting down into the cold, white dream. Far to the south, the sun leans against the Waring Mountains. I open my hand and let it go.

—Nick Jans, *A Place Beyond,* 1996

■ Fairbanks to Arctic Ocean: Dalton Highway

The Dalton Highway officially begins at Mile 73.1 of the Elliott Highway north of Fairbanks and continues over 350 miles of unpaved road to Deadhorse near Prudhoe Bay on the Arctic Ocean. It is a true adventure, a pilgrimage of continual discovery through the last really wild corner of the United States.

◆ Preparing for the Journey

Before you get started, be sure to stop at the BLM office on University Avenue in Fairbanks to obtain the latest information on the road—forest fires, truck or bus accidents, pipeline problems, avalanches, inclement weather, and mud slides can close the road for days. If you are interested—as many are—in fishing and hunting along the Dalton Highway, also make a stop at the **Alaska Department of Fish & Game** office at 1300 College Road in Fairbanks, to obtain necessary licenses and receive some friendly advice on hotspots. Only bow hunting is permitted within five miles of the Dalton Highway, which has created a game-rich corridor.

Coldfoot road sign speaks for itself.

When I made my trip up the Dalton Highway, I took all of the ordinary precautions. In the back of my small Subaru station wagon, I packed as many tools and spare parts as I could, from crescent wrenches to needle-nosed pliers, battery-operated tire pumps to reinforced tow-straps, fuses to air hoses, alternator belts to spark plugs. There were also two full-sized, wheel-mounted spare tires (the Dalton has few services and you are guaranteed at least one completely destroyed tire) and four 5-gallon gas containers, as well as enough food and bottled water for two weeks. Not to mention hip-waders, shovels, winter clothing, boxes of 35-mm film, spare cameras, and enough ammunition to bring meat into camp for years, if necessary. Most rental contracts specify the vehicle cannot be taken off the paved road, and the Dalton currently is not paved, but a few rental agencies (Hertz, for instance) will rent four-wheel drives specifically for the Dalton Highway. Always drive very slowly and always pull over for trucks (to save your windshield). Expect snow at any time of the year and carry tire chains.

◆ Along the Pipeline

For much of its length, the Dalton Highway runs parallel to the trans-Alaska pipeline, which is owned and operated by the Alyeska Pipeline Service Company. You will see their vehicles and helicopters every once in awhile, but don't count on them for assistance in an emergency. They regard travelers on "their" road—which was finally opened to the general public only by a lawsuit that was appealed all the way to the Alaska Supreme Court—as unwelcome intruders. You'll notice the pipeline is elevated on metal support structures—this keeps the pipe from making contact with the permafrost, the permanently frozen ground that is synonymous with arctic Alaska. Melt the permafrost and you'd have a big problem with shifting pipeline supports and 30-inch pipes suddenly spewing their hot contents out on the pristine arctic tundra. This would constitute an environmental and public relations nightmare and has fortunately only happened a few times—each time the mess has been quickly cleaned up.

The Dalton Highway follows the trans-Alaska pipeline for much of the distance from Fairbanks to Prudhoe Bay.

◆ Fairbanks to the Yukon River *map page 272, D-4*

For the first 55 miles from Fairbanks to the Yukon River, the Dalton Highway crosses a gentle hill and valley country, densely forested with white spruce, quaking aspen, and paper birch. Only occasionally will you see evidence of human civilization—normally related to old gold-dredging operations. More and more, you are leaving civilization behind. At Wickersham Dome (Mile 29.7) there is a pull-out and several nice trails on the tundra (good blueberry picking each August). You can count on spotting black bears and moose in this area near dawn and dusk, as well as the occasional coyote, fox, grizzly, and wolf.

There's a pull-out above the **Yukon River bridge,** a nice place to stop, stretch your legs, and meditate on one of the world's great rivers. The Yukon is Alaska's largest river, the fifth longest on the continent, and the 20th longest on the planet. The river drains an immense area, and when you look at that 2,300-foot-long steel girder bridge, you comprehend something of the huge volume of water traveling beneath it toward the Bering Sea. Prior to the bridge's construction—which was an expensive and major obstacle on the Dalton Highway—earth-moving equipment and supply trucks had to be ferried across the Yukon River in hovercraft.

King, silver, and chum salmon arrive here in July to spawn where they themselves were born, after having traveled here from the Bering Sea, 1,000 river miles away.

The gas station and tire repair shop on the north side of the Yukon bridge is one of the last on the highway—be forewarned. Also available at the crossing are a restaurant, motel, phone, and emergency communications; east of the highway, there's a campground. The Yukon Crossing Visitor Contact Station here is operated seven days a week, June through August.

◆ North of the Yukon River *map page 272, D-4*

After crossing the Yukon, the Dalton Highway climbs through a tumbled hill and valley country similar to that on the southern approach. Gradually, forests give way to grassy meadowlands, and eventually tundra.

At Mile 98 you pass by **Finger Mountain,** which is distinguished by many exposed rock escarpments or "tors." Nearby are thermokarst lakes (meltwater pooled over permanent ice fields) as well as soft mounds in which tundra vegetation covers glacial sand, old dune fields, or ice blocks. Ten or twelve thousand years ago, this landscape would have had woolly mammoths and steppe bison on it. Forty million years earlier Alaska was closer to the equator, and dinosaurs roamed the valley. Fossils from both periods abound in the area.

◆ CROSSING THE ARCTIC CIRCLE *map page 272, D-3*

An old Alaska saying: "There's no law above the Yukon River, and no God above the Arctic Circle." The Arctic Circle is crossed at Mile 115.3. There is a pull-out here and a campsite (many people stop to photograph the nice view to the west), but, to my way of thinking, the Arctic does not truly begin until the last upright tree is left behind, and that does not occur until you reach the Chandalar Shelf at about Mile 236.

By about Mile 166, you are driving in the valley of the **Middle Fork of the Koyukuk River.** This is historic country, if only because Bob Marshall (father of the American wilderness system) explored this country earlier in the century, writing his influential books *Arctic Village* and *Alaskan Wilderness.*

A vivid Arctic sunset illuminates the fall sky. (Photo by Nick Jans)

Coldfoot, a village with a 3,500-foot unimproved airstrip, is encountered at Mile 175. This is the last place before the Arctic Coast where you can take on fuel or get some hot food not cooked over a campfire. Its amenities include several motels, a 24-hour restaurant, a store, trading post, laundromat, gas station, emergency medical service, and the most northerly saloon in North America. The **Visitors Center for the Gates of the Arctic National Park** is here, as basically everything to the west for 400 miles is national park or preserve.

Wiseman is passed at Mile 188.6. Robert Marshall spent some time here, studying the inhabitants, which consisted of Inupiats and white miners. Today, about 25 year-round inhabitants live in the Wiseman community.

Once past the Chandalar Shelf, you are really in the Arctic Country. From Mile 194 is a view to the north of Sukakpak Mountain, the traditional boundary between Inupiat and Athabaskan Indian territories. At Mile 236.8 you pass the last white spruce. The tree is less than six inches wide a foot from the ground, and yet is several hundred years old—slow growing this far north. The climb up through

(above) Along the Dalton Highway one encounters Coldfoot, a town whose claim to fame is the record low temperature of -82°F, and we're not talking wind chill effect.

(right) A landscape typical of Gates of the Arctic National Park. Here a crystal clear river cuts through the Schwatka Mountains. (Photo by Nick Jans)

the Brooks Range to Atigun Pass (Mile 244.7) is long, arduous, and dangerous. Keep your eyes open for oncoming trucks, which may, if their brakes give out on the far side, need quite a bit of road in order to navigate a tight turn. And remember all this is on loose gravel, which has a way of lengthening braking distances. On top of Atigun Pass you can expect to see Dall sheep right by the road.

In summer, **Atigun Valley** is covered in varying shades of green, opening to the wide expanse of the Arctic coastal plain beyond. You will see lots of Dall sheep and barren-ground caribou here, as well as the occasional grizzly bear or wolf. It's difficult to believe, but true, that for over ten thousand years people have made their living in this land that has no upright trees or natural shelter from the elements.

The rest of the journey features an enormous tundra plain with gorgeous skies and limitless vistas. Try doing as local animals do, and travel in the bright summer evenings. The light can be magical. If it is early-summer, you will encounter more and more caribou as you approach the coast. This is their summer range, and they prefer to be as close to the water as possible. For insect relief they actually stand in the water. If you forget your insect repellent, you may be inclined to join them. You will also encounter large numbers of songbirds and waterfowl who happily devour the same insects that mammals are trying to escape from. The road ends at Mile 414. You are in the vicinity of Deadhorse, which is associated with the Prudhoe Bay operation. *(For more on facilities here, see page 312.)* The best thing about turning around at this point is that you get to see it all again.

■ GATES OF THE ARCTIC NATIONAL PARK *map page 272, C&D-2&3*

For quite a stretch on the Dalton Highway north of Wiseman, the Gates of the Arctic National Park is only five miles west of the road. But for the foreseeable future, that is as close as you can get by car to this eight-million-acre national park. For the most part, travel into the park is limited to bush plane charters, most commonly out of Bettles, Ambler, and Kotzebue *(see page 308)*. Catching a bush mail plane from Fairbanks to the Eskimo village of Anaktuvuk Pass will also put you in the center of some breathtaking country. Popular drop-off points include Wild Lake and near the headwaters of any of six National Wild Rivers that course through the park—the Alatna, John, Kobuk, Noatak, North Fork of the Koyukuk, and the Tinayguk. The number of possible hiking or float trips is close to infinite.

Inflatable raft, collapsible kayak, or pack canoe (all of which can be carried inside aircraft) are the choices of most experienced travelers. A typical scenario involves being flown to the upper stretches of a river and traveling downstream anywhere from 50 to several hundred miles, taking side hikes or backpacking excursions as opportunities present themselves. It's often possible to take out at a downstream village and catch a mail plane, thereby saving the considerable cost of a pick-up charter.

Probably the biggest attraction in the park, other than the actual Gates of the Arctic between Frigid Crags and Boreal Mountain, are the **Arrigetch Peaks,** which are reached via a floatplane trip to Circle Lake west of Bettles. These abrupt granite spires lure mountain and rock climbers. To the north are lovely mountain lakes, a scattering of cottonwoods, and a vast wilderness of pale-green tundra.

My sole excursion into Gates of the Arctic National Park occurred just south of Atigun Pass on the Dalton Highway and consisted of a long pack over **Oolah Pass,** a popular cross-country walk en route to the park. If you've ever hiked on tundra overlying permafrost, you can picture the following scenario—a man and woman, each with an 80-pound pack, surrounded by a cloud of mosquitoes, trying to hike on a moving waterbed (water-logged tundra is anything but stable) while keeping an eye out for tussocks (grass clumps that can pitch you to the ground) and grizzly bears. The scenery may be out of this world, but the going is rough, and only for the hardy, experienced, and well-equipped.

■ ARCTIC NATIONAL WILDLIFE REFUGE *map page 272, D&E-2&3*

Most rivers run clear and cold over smooth beds of cobblestone, with even the deepest pools as transparent as glass. Wildflower beds extend for miles toward glaciers, glacial lakes, and quiet bogs of sphagnum moss. Birds fly across the tundra in massive flocks like something out of the dawn of creation. Salmon fill entire streams from bank to bank, and brilliant green northern lights flicker over a snow-covered valley. This is the Arctic National Wildlife Refuge, the largest wildlife refuge in the world, which extends from the Yukon border more than 250 miles west to the Dalton Highway, and south from the Arctic Ocean hundreds of miles to the foothills above the Yukon River. Notably moved by his visit here, Edward Abbey wrote:

> Well, I'm thinking, now I'm satisfied. Now I've seen it, the secret of the riddle of the Spirit of the Arctic—the flowering of life, of life wild, free and abundant, in the midst of the hardest, cruelest land on the northern half of Earth.

Most visitors enter ANWR by air charter via Fort Yukon, Bettles, or Kaktovik on Barter Island. Such trips are expensive and often delayed because of weather problems. My own introduction to ANWR occurred rather unexpectedly, when one of my graduate students invited me on a hunting trip. We flew together to Fort Yukon on a commercial prop plane, then transferred our gear to a bush plane, a two-seat Piper Supercub. One at a time, we were ferried north a hundred miles to the mountains west of the Sheenjek River. The pilot landed quite literally on top of a nameless mountain in a maneuver I will never forget—a controlled crash, throttle just above stall. At the last minute, I muttered some sort of quick prayer in which I made a number of heart-felt promises about being a good person in the

Moose cow and calf, common sights in this part of the world. (Photo by Nick Jans)

service of noble causes. We came to a halt, wings bobbing back and forth, and caribou scattering out of the way. (The pilot died at the controls of his plane two months later in the Yukon Flats National Wildlife Refuge, as did a USFWS biologist riding in the back seat.)

We spent five days hunting there. It rained the whole time (thank God it didn't snow), and I must say the trip was unlike anything else in my experience. Images of that trip will always linger—the rock ptarmigan huddling in the lee of a wind-flagged spruce at timberline, the river otter that wandered into camp one day, the grizzly I encountered as I was packing the caribou meat from the kill site to camp. The bear approached at a leisurely but determined walk to a distance of about 30 yards. I took off my pack and fired one round into the tundra in front of it, and it ambled off at the same measured, dignified pace in the other direction. After all, there was a steaming gut pile (the viscera) to be had for free back at the kill site.

My second visit to ANWR was less exciting, but no less spectacular in terms of the scenery. I simply walked east from the Dalton Highway in the vicinity of the

Migrating caribou in the Arctic region. (Photo by Nick Jans)

lower Atigun Canyon. This little adventure gave me a vivid sense of the arctic coastal environment and of the foothills that are so important to wildlife in the area, especially caribou. Over 130,000 caribou comprise the Porcupine Caribou Herd, which has been at the center of a long-running debate over oil and gas exploration and development on the coastal plain.

Bush Etiquette

Bush residents are generally helpful and friendly, but may seem distant in dealing with an outsider. Being relaxed, smiling, and polite goes a long way. Being overly loud or inquisitive is frowned on by many Native people; long comfortable silences often punctuate everyday conversation. By no means brag of your own recent exploits; listen instead. Always ask permission before pointing a camera at someone, or exploring an apparently deserted cabin or fish camp. If you find yourself in the presence of people who make it clear they resent outsiders, withdraw as gracefully as possible, and move on to the next experience. Be aware that some Native villages actively encourage visitors, while some just as actively discourage them. Most are somewhere in the middle. Ask around in advance.

Out on the river, approaching a Native camp with a friendly wave and a smile can often lead to an invitation to stop for coffee or a shared meal—and a truly memorable experience. People who sometimes won't give you the time of day in town are often expansive hosts to fellow travelers, in the best Bush tradition. But if things seem busy or you feel ignored, take the hint. Subsistence fishing or hunting is serious work, and folks may not have time to chat with strangers.

Lower sections of the Kobuk, Noatak, and Koyukuk Rivers sometimes are quite busy with local motorboat traffic and camps. Accept the occasional floating Pepsi can as part of the reality in modern Bush Alaska. While it may seem wilderness to you, the rivers are the local highways between villages. Relax and enjoy the traffic as part of the local ambience. If it's a more remote, secluded experience you seek, spend as much time as possible off the main rivers, backpacking or floating one of the many remote tributary valleys.

—Nick Jans

Anaktuvuk Pass has one of the most beautiful settings of any bush village in Alaska, nestled in the heart of the Brooks Range some 260 miles northwest of Fairbanks. (Photo by Nick Jans)

Brooks Range Communities

North of the Arctic Circle, villages are few and far between. They are extremely important to the wilderness traveler, for they provide airstrips, river access, last-minute supplies, and reliable communications in the event of an emergency. As in other bush areas of Alaska, life proceeds at a slow and relaxed pace in these remote villages, a laid-back ambiance that can come as quite a shock to the visitor. In the Bush, appearances are considered far less important than function. Today's oil drum is tomorrow's wood stove, and this sort of philosophy pervades the lives of most residents, Native and non-Native alike.

◆ Ambler *map page 272, B/C-3*

This Inupiat village of 325 on the upper Kobuk, offers a small, comfortable (if expensive) lodge and restaurant, well-stocked village stores, and an expertly run flying service (including floatplane charters into the Brooks Range). Ambler and its sister village upriver, Shungnak, are famous for their hand-crafted birch bark baskets. It's often possible to arrange in both places for fish trips, dropoffs, or boat rides on the main Kobuk River, though regular guided services are nonexistent.

◆ Anaktuvuk Pass *map page 272, D-3*

Anaktuvuk Pass has the most beautiful setting of any bush village in Alaska. Located 260 miles northwest of Fairbanks in the central Brooks Range, it sits on a broad divide between the John River, which drains south, and the Anaktuvuk River, which drains north. Anaktuvuk Pass is an area of unusual historic importance to the Inupiat. For untold ages, the arctic caribou have used the wide pass in their annual migrations, and it is here the Eskimo once waited for their prey. Even today, the Natives use the area for subsistence hunting, though they have set their nomadic traditions aside for village life, in this last remaining settlement of the Nunamuit or inland Inupiat Eskimo. Direct scheduled airline flights from Fairbanks to Anaktuvuk are available on a regular basis, which makes the village one of the most accessible in Arctic Alaska. There is a Gates of the Arctic National Park ranger station in Anaktuvuk Pass, as well as a restaurant and a no-frills public campground.

◆ Arctic Village *map page 272, E-3*

Arctic Village is located about 100 miles northwest of Fort Yukon and provides a jumping-off point for explorations of the central Brooks Range, including the Wind River, the Philip Smith Mountains, and the headwaters of the Sheenjek River. A direct air charter to Arctic Village can also be obtained from Fairbanks, about 300 miles to the south. The village maintains a cabin for overnight visitors and guided, one-day tours are available by prior arrangement, but little else in the way of facilities is available. Unless you're part of a tour, staying here is not recommended. The village maintains jurisdiction over a 1.4-million-acre reservation, where hunting and fishing can be pursued with a tribal permit; inquire in advance. *(See page 311.)*

◆ **Bettles** *map page 272, C-3*

Located nearly 200 air miles north and west of Fairbanks, Bettles is best known as the main jumping-off point for the 7.9-million-acre Gates of the Arctic National Park to the north. Visitors also use the town as a base of operations for summer fishing and autumn hunting trips, as well as for winter dogsled excursions. There are a number of large national wildlife refuges nearby (Kanuti, Yukon Flats, Nowitna, Koyukuk, and Selawik), as well the Kobuk Dunes National Park to the west. Overnight accommodations are available in Bettles, and there are state and federal offices representing wildlife and land management agencies. A number of outfitters operate out of Bettles. Air service to Bettles is offered from charter companies in Fairbanks *(see page 261 for suggestions).*

◆ **Kiana** *map page 272, B-3*

This Eskimo village on the middle Kobuk, once a gold mining camp, offers a picturesque mountain setting at the mouth of the Squirrel River. Facilities include two well-stocked stores, a local flying service, and two Native-run guiding operations offering riverboat trips, fishing, and wildlife viewing, and a lodge a few miles north of town.

◆ **Shungnak and Kobuk** *map page 272, C-3*

These two Eskimo villages on the upper Kobuk River, just eight river miles apart, are common take-out places for float trips on the upper Kobuk. Below Kobuk, the current slows and motor skiff and low-flying aircraft traffic can be heavy at times. Both villages offer small stores and gasoline sales. Overnight accommodations are available by prior arrangement in Shungnak *(see page 315),* as well as boat rides.

■ Arctic Coast Communities

◆ **Barrow** *map page 272, C-1*

Asking a resident of Anchorage if he's ever been to Barrow is like asking a resident of Santiago if he's been to the South Pole, for the setting in which Barrow (pop. 3,470) goes about its business is austere, to say the least. It is set on vast treeless, bushless tundra near a gravel beach at the edge of the Arctic Ocean. The ground is usually frozen and snow covered, or, if the permafrost melts, slushy. Author Annie

The treeless city of Barrow, which lies haphazardly along the shores of the Arctic Ocean.

Dillard, in her essay "An Expedition to the Pole," described the surrounding arctic coast as a land of icebergs and water and cold blue sky. Winter is almost a full-time season here, and the brief green of summer is an anomaly in an otherwise cold and dark landscape.

Eighty years ago, Barrow was a traditional Eskimo settlement; 30 years ago it was traditional and poor but modernizing, with few outsiders. Twenty years ago revenues from the trans-Alaska pipeline began flowing into the coffers of the governing borough, itself the center of Inupiat business and government for a huge section of the Arctic. Traditional Eskimo life has largely disappeared since. Tribal members now receive enough money to live on. Most still hunt, but there's a dreariness to the place. Dwellings are drab, prefab houses, yards dominated by drying caribou hides and broken machinery. There is, however, a beautiful new school that's a center of community life.

In the fall of 1988, media attention became focused on three whales trapped in the early ice. The rescue eventually involved a Soviet icebreaker and resulted in the liberation of two of the three whales. Heart-warming as this story was, it had an odd resonance in Barrow, since the Inupiat have traditionally hunted whales.

The most public arguments lately have been those between community leaders, who are trying to keep the town dry, and those who want to make liquor legal.

Why visit Barrow? Well, it has the distinction of being the northernmost town in the Western Hemisphere. Scheduled daily jet airline service is available from both Anchorage and Fairbanks, and a taxi driver (probably an immigrant from the Third World who can't wait to get home again) can take you from the airstrip to the Top of the World Hotel. If you come in summer, bring earplugs, so you can get to sleep. Otherwise, you'll be kept awake by children playing and dogs barking outside in the sunlight of midnight. There are several restaurants in Barrow *(see page 311)*, and those are the northernmost places in America where you can eat or drink whatever you are eating or drinking there. A tour company will take you down to the beach in a four-wheel-drive vehicle to see the Arctic Ocean, possibly a polar bear, and a monument to humorist Will Rogers and aviation pioneer Wiley Post, who died here in an airplane accident in 1935.

◆ Prudhoe Bay *map page 272, D-2*

Prudhoe Bay is the center of operations for the Alyeska Pipeline Company, which sends the oil drilled here south via the Alaska pipeline to the coastal town of Valdez where it is piped onto oil tankers. In his book *Arctic Dreams,* Barry Lopez writes about his journey to this stark landscape, now tamed by the region's major industry:

> *I* look up at Pump Station #1, past the cyclone fencing and barbed wire. The slogging pumps sequestered within insulated buildings on the tundra, the fields of pipe, the roughshod trucks, all the muscular engineering, the Viking bellows that draws and gathers and directs—that it all runs to the head of this seemingly innocent pipe, lined out like a stainless-steel thread toward the indifferent Brooks Range, that it is all reduced to the southward journey of this 48-inch pipe, seems impossible.
>
> No toil, no wildness shows. It could not seem to the chaperoned visitor more composed, inoffensive, or civilized.

Public access to Prudhoe Bay is limited. In recent years a number of tour companies have offered packaged bus tours via the Dalton Highway. Accommodations are available in Deadhorse *(see Travel Information, page 312)*.

A whalebone arch (top) designates Point Barrow, the northernmost point of the U.S. The Inupiat blanket toss (above), now a ritual presentation, formerly was employed to enable hunters to spot game above the flat and desolate landscape. Ceremonial drummers perform in Barrow (right).

■ Seward Peninsula Communities

◆ Kotzebue *map page 272, B-3*

map page 272, B-3

The Eskimo community of Kotzebue, located on Kotzebue Sound north of the Seward Peninsula, and 26 miles above the Arctic Circle, is an important regional town providing access to the Noatak National Preserve, Kobuk Valley National Park, and the western aspects of Gates of the Arctic National Park. The National Park Service maintains an office in Kotzebue, and park managers will assist travelers in planning a journey in the parklands. Kotzebue is serviced by jet from Nome and Anchorage, and a number of bush flying services offer connections to Gates of the Arctic, the Noatak Preserve, Cape Krusenstern, and Kobuk Valley Park.

Kotzebue is a sizable town of 3,500 people (with another 4,200 living in nearby villages), and is the largest Native settlement in the state. The Northwest Alaska Native Association (NANA) has its headquarters here and funds the **Living Museum of the Arctic** on Second Avenue. Museum programs emphasize Native culture and include folk dances, crafts demonstrations, slide shows, story telling, and the traditional blanket toss (the latter imitates the early custom of throwing hunters high in the air from seal-skin blankets). Visitors will find many of the amenities of town life in Kotzebue, including a hotel, restaurants, stores, and a bank. During the summer the sun does not set for 36 continuous days.

What remains of the Council City and Solomon Railroad near Nome.

Small Adventures

And I think over again
My small adventures
When from a shore wind I drifted out
In my kayak
And thought I was in danger.
My fears,
Those small ones
That I thought so big,
For all the vital things
I had to get and to reach.

And yet, there is only
One great thing,
The only thing:
To live to see in huts and on journeys
The great day that dawns
And the light that fills the world.

— Song from the Kitlinguiharmiut. Copper Eskimo.

—Recorded and translated by Knud Rasmussen, *The Report of the Fifth Thule Expedition, 1921–1924, the Danish Expedition to Arctic North America*

◆ Nome *map page 272, A-4*

Surrounded by treeless arctic tundra, Nome is located on the southeastern corner of the Seward Peninsula north of Norton Sound. Nome supposedly got its name when an early cartographer, unsure what to call this remote spot, wrote on an early map: "Name?" Later a draftsman copied this out as "Nome." Today the city's motto is, "There's No Place Like Nome."

Nome has long been a major town in this area, beginning originally as a mining camp in 1898, and at one time serving as home to more than 20,000 gold prospectors. Those days are gone now—thankfully—and Nome has evolved into the business and governmental hub for this part of Arctic Alaska. It's remote:

Gold Dust Soup

Everybody in Nome was prospering in those days. The Third Beach Line seemed inexhaustible. Gold was flowing freely, and a platter of ham-and-eggs cost four dollars. Even the stew bums in Nome were getting their share. The swamper in the Northern Saloon offered to polish the brass spittoons for nothing, in exchange for the privilege of panning the sawdust in the front of the bar, where patrons paying for drinks spilled gold dust on the floor. In the Arctic Restaurant on Front Street the cook kept a pot of soup bubbling on the stove all winter, using the greasy wooden spoon to measure out a customer's dust. He rinsed the spoon in the soup. By winter's end he had amassed a comfortable stake at the bottom of the pot, and went back to the States in the spring.

—Klondy Nelson with Corey Ford,
Daughter of the Gold Rush, 1955

Up to 20,000 prospectors flooded into Nome in 1899 and 1900, creating massive tent cities on the town's beaches before fanning out over the Seward Peninsula in search of elusive pay dirt. (Underwood Photo Archives, San Francisco)

(previous pages) One of the natural wonders of the northern skies are the lights of the aurora borealis, which band the sky about 200 nights of the year in central and northern Alaska.

539 miles northwest of Anchorage and 165 miles from the coast of Siberia; and it has a raw, frontier look to it. Weathered wooden houses, low commercial buildings, and saloons curve about a stony Arctic shore. An important new building here is the headquarters of the Sitnasauk Native Corporation, which owns and operates a gas station, a parts store, apartments, and a hardware-grocery store.

This is a friendly, close-knit town, where locals don't lock their houses or cars. The architecture is typical rural Alaskan—low cinderblock buildings, but some new structures have copied gold rush–era architecture. Fast-food restaurants and stores offer many of the items that you can get in the Lower 48. Drinking is a problem here, as it is elsewhere in the Arctic.

Nome is noted for being at the finish line of the 1,049-mile Iditarod dogsled race that begins in Anchorage the first Saturday in March. Twenty years ago it took mushers 20 days to complete this trip. In the past few years, the winning time has been shortened to about nine days and two hours, and stragglers take an additional week. First prize? $52,000. Nome celebrates Memorial Day with a "Polar Bear Swim" in 35 degree F water.

Several longish gravel roads (up to 80 miles) originating in Nome lead into the backcountry of Seward Peninsula. One hundred and eighty species of birds are seen here, and the tundra in the summertime is quite beautiful. Nome can also be used as base of operations for explorations of the remote and quite striking Seward peninsula. You can also fly on Bering Air to Siberia and stay in the home of a Russian family *(see pages 308 and 314).*

■ Kobuk Valley National Park *map page 272, B-3*

In 1980, just as he was leaving office, President Jimmy Carter signed the bill that made this 1.7-million-acre area the Kobuk Valley National Park. This parkland is one of the prettiest areas in Alaska, replete with clear running streams and rivers, the northernmost sand dune field in the hemisphere, ancient archaeological sites, and all of the diverse fauna and flora typical of a vast province of the Brooks Range. Depending on season, Kobuk Valley, like other parks of northwestern Alaska, sees light to moderately heavy traffic along the main river corridor.

One of the most fascinating sites in Kobuk Valley National Park is known as **Onion Portage** near the Kobuk River, which has been studied by archaeologists since 1940. Scientists have found chiseled stone spear points and tools, ancient hearthbeds, Siberian-style pit houses, and other artifacts. Data suggests that Native people used this game-rich area for at least 12,000 years. Like their modern descendants, these ancient folk based their culture on caribou, moose, furbearers, wild berries and roots, and, especially, the plentiful annual runs of spawning salmon.

The other main attraction of the Kobuk Valley National Park is the 25-square-mile **Kobuk Sand Dunes,** some of which rise to more than 100 feet in height.

■ Bering Land Bridge National Preserve *map page 272, A-3*

The Seward Peninsula reaches far from the mass of the North American continent, and of Alaska, straining, it would seem, to join up with the nearby coast of Asia. Between the extreme point of this peninsula near Cape Prince of Wales and Cape Deshnev on Russia's Chukotsk Peninsula is the shallow Bering Strait, a narrow region which, in ancient times, was not covered by water. It was over this exposed sea bed that the first Siberian immigrants ventured eastward into the New World. Eventually, these people walked, canoed, rafted, kayaked, and dogsledded deeper into the continent, ultimately reaching the tip of South America. If there is ever an

Fall colors (above) in Kobuk Valley National Park. The park's sand dunes (right), encompassing more than 25 square miles, rise as high as 100 feet in places. (Both photos by Nick Jans)

epic poem written of the Americas, it will begin here, in Bering Land Bridge National Preserve, with the first Asians walking into the Great Land, amazed at the abundance of wildlife and at the complete absence of human life.

A large portion of the northern Seward Peninsula has been designated as Bering Land Bridge National Preserve. In the preserve are thousands of lakes, several hot springs, ancient lava flows, extinct volcanoes, beautiful Imuruk Lake, prehistoric camping sites, Jurassic fossil sites, active Eskimo villages and reindeer herding camps, 3,000-foot mountains, and subsistence fishing sites. Wildlife includes everything from grizzly bears, wolves, and caribou to bearded seals, walrus, and bowhead whales. The reintroduced musk ox is also found in the preserve. Bering Land Bridge National Preserve lies just below the Arctic Circle, with access from nearby Kotzebue and Nome. The Taylor Highway reaches within 20 miles of the preserve.

■ Cape Krusenstern National Monument *map page 272, B-2&3*

Cape Krusenstern is among the least visited, distant outposts of the National Park System. Access is by air charter from Kotzebue, possibly by boat, or by snowmobile in winter. The monument is not particularly large—at 66,000 acres only about twice the size of Grand Teton National Park—but the wildlife and plant associations found here are unique, the windswept coastline starkly spectacular. Relatively nearby villages include Noatak (30 miles inland) and Kivalina (on the coast). There are no accommodations outside or restaurants outside of Kotzebue.

Summer is short and sweet at Cape Krusenstern, and winter long and brutal. This is the land of polar bears and bearded seals, wolves and musk ox. The monument is not particularly large—at 660,000 acres only about twice the size of Grand Teton National Park—but it is full of wildlife and plant associations found in few other locations.

It is also a country inhabited by that ubiquitous symbol of the far north—the grizzly bear. One of my former graduate students once spent a summer conducting research at Cape Krusenstern National Monument with her husband, a University of Alaska biologist, and she reported an amazing observation. The local grizzly bears would boldly climb down the steep cliffs where the seabirds lived in order to rob the eggs and hatchlings from the seabird nests. I must confess I was somewhat skeptical until shown a sheet of 35-mm color slides clearly demonstrating this unique behavior.

Nome Childhood, Early 1900s

Nome was a perfect place for a little girl to grow up; Mother knew I was safe anywhere, the miners were always watching over me, and it was daylight around the clock. I rode Dad's horse Napoleon by the hour around the flower-dotted countryside. On the spongy tundra, Napoleon would feel his way as though he were treading on eggs, but when he struck the hard-packed sand of the beach he would gallop excitedly along the surf, kicking up water as he raced toward the sandspit.

There the Eskimos always made their summer camp, netting tomcod and humpback and dog salmon, which they peddled around town or hung on racks to dry in the sun for their winter food. Every day the hunters came in from the Bering Sea, paddling skin-covered kayaks heaped high with hair seals and eider ducks. Sometimes when the wind blew from the Siberian shore, we could hear the bellowing herds of walrus riding the drifting ice. Picked crews would launch their big umiaks through the surf and disappear into the fog. Hours later they would sail back chanting a triumphant "Ai-yi-yi," their boats loaded to the water line with gore-spattered blubbery hulks weighing more than a ton each, and toss armloads of yard-long ivory tusks to the squaws wading out into the surf.

Napoleon and I were always welcomed as friends. The Eskimo would shout a merry "Allooo!" when we showed up for a visit, and I would loop Napoleon's reins over a fish rack where he could nibble at the dried salmon. I loved to wander from one sod igloo to another, watching the old men of the village carving ivory in the shelter of an upended umiak.

—Klondy Nelson with Corey Ford,
Daughter of the Gold Rush, 1958

Minnie Gray of Ambler and her grandson Erik gather blueberries. (Photo by Nick Jans)

While the terrestrial interior of Cape Krusenstern is not exactly an oasis of life, (supporting a few moose, musk oxen, foxes, and brown bears, plus seasonally migrating caribou), the coastline is rich. Bearded seal, beluga, and seabirds are abundant in summer, and occasionally walrus or bowhead whales wander close to shore. When sea mammal carcasses wash ashore, sizeable congregations of scavenging bears and foxes can sometimes be observed. Fishing in the various coastal lagoons and spring-fed streams can be excellent for pike and sea-run Dolly Varden, known to the Natives as "trout."

The coastal region of the monument contains a wealth of prehistoric sites, as this area was used intensely during the Bering Land Bridge period, and subsequently by Eskimo people attracted to the rich marine resources. Eskimos still maintain hunting and fishing camps here. Seals are particularly valued, providing meat, oil, and skins, as are the chum salmon available in local waters. Access is, by Arctic Alaska standards, relatively easy, with daily jet service to Kotzebue from both Fairbanks and Anchorage, and then charter aircraft available for the 20-minute flight north to Cape Krusenstern. The major negative factor at Cape Krusenstern is the weather, which is like coastal seaside weather anywhere in the northern latitudes—heavy on the rain and fog and quite unpredictable. All visitors should be prepared for total self-sufficiency, and for the distinct possibility that weather may extend the visit many days beyond any scheduled departure time.

■ Noatak National Preserve *map page 272, B–D-2&3*

The 6.5-million-acre Noatak National Preserve is part of an integrated complex of parklands including the Kobuk Valley National Park and Gates of the Arctic National Park. Together, these three immense parks protect the entire central and western Brooks Range west of Atigun Pass and the Dalton Highway. If you started walking west at Atigun Pass, you could trek continuously on national park land for nearly 500 miles (a distance as great as that between San Diego and San Francisco). What you would notice on such a journey is that, as you advance westward, the fauna, flora, and even geographic features become increasingly like those of northern Asia. In fact, the wild Noatak River basin is rich in anthropological and fossil evidence of the interplay between the North American and Asian continents. Over these lands traveled plants, animals, and people, and not only in an easterly direction, but also westward back into Asia, cross-fertilizing life there as well.

The Noatak National Preserve is remote—more than 350 air miles north and west of Fairbanks. To get there you'll have to catch a mail plane from Fairbanks or the villages of Ambler or Bettles where bush plane charters are available. Many visitors use Kotzebue as a jump-off point, and the park staff there will be happy to help you plan your journey. The Noatak River itself is 450 miles long and drains almost due west from the Schwatka Mountains to Kotzebue Sound on the Chukchi Sea, which is south of the Arctic Ocean.

A trip down the Noatak will lead you through jagged peaks, rolling tundra plains, canyons, a few rapids, quiet pools, and in the lower reaches, spruce forests. It's considered one of the finest wild rivers in the world. You may see many other travelers or you may have long stretches virtually to yourself, depending on the season. Wildlife, though often spread thin, can be highly visible to a keen observer. Dall sheep, moose, caribou, swans, falcons, eagles, foxes, and grizzlies are fairly common, and you might just glimpse a wolf. The Noatak also offers fine fishing for grayling, chum salmon, and Dolly Varden. Try mouths of tributary streams and deeper pools. Take out at a Noatak village, or paddle all the way to Kotzebue. Note: exercise extreme caution crossing Hotham Inlet.

A yellow birch leaf rests on a bed of bearberry leaves (red), lingonberry leaves (green broadleaf), and the pine-like leaves of crowberry which carpet the arctic landscape. (Photo by Nick Jans)

TRAVEL INFORMATION

Alaska's Arctic region, characterized by its vast, frozen, sparsely populated tundra, is largely inaccessible by road. Aside from the lone Dalton Highway (a 415-mile limited-access gravel road connecting Fairbanks to Prudhoe Bay), the Arctic has no major thoroughfares. Air travel is the lifeline to the north and the domain of the Alaskan bush pilot.

The major airlines have established routes and offer package deals such as a one- or two-day trip to Barrow from Fairbanks complete with a guided bus tour for around $400, but these tours are of short duration and fairly limited in scope. Independent travelers may prefer a customized tour provided by smaller tour-package companies which feature the air services of experienced bush pilots and guarantee a room at the end of the flight. Reservations made at least six months to a year in advance are recommended for travel during the peak season (late May through early September). Package tours and air taxi services are popular and numerous in the Arctic, a small percentage of which are listed below.

Alaska Airlines Vacations. *Seattle, WA;* 800-*468-2248.* Package tours to Barrow, Prudhoe Bay, Nome, and Kotzebue; local arrangements are handled by Native ground operators.

Ambler Air Service. *Ambler; 907-445-2121.* Floatplane service to Noatak, Gates of the Arctic, and Kobuk Valley National Park.

Arctic Air Guides. *Kotzebue; 907-442-3030.* Air-taxi and flightseeing tours of the Arctic region.

Bering Air Inc. *907-443-5464.* Bush- based air-taxi service offering flightseeing tours. Also service Nome and Kotzebue.

Brooks Range Aviation. *Bettles; 800-692-5443.* Serves entire Brooks Range and ANWAR with both float planes and wheels.

Frontier Flying Service. *907-474-0014.* Fairbanks to Nome and Bettles.

Gray Line of Alaska. *Seattle, WA, 206-281-3535 or* 800-*544-2206.* Package tours up the Dalton Highway between Fairbanks and Deadhorse, traveling one way by air, the other by coach.

Lee's Sea Air. *Keana; 907-474-0518.* Locally operated bush air charters in Kobuk Valley area. Wheels only.

Warbelow's Air Ventures. *Fairbanks; 800-478-0812.* Scheduled and chartered flights to throughout the upper Yukon, central and eastern Brooks Range bush tours.

Wright's Air Service. Fairbanks, *907-474-0518.* Scheduled and chartered flights to the upper Yukon, central and eastern Brooks Range.

■ Climate

This region, much of it north of the Arctic Circle, marks the northern extent of Alaska's great forests and the beginning of the dry tundra zone which extends to the shores of the Arctic Sea. This is the driest region of the state, with precipitation comparable to the driest areas of the American Southwest such as Yuma and Death Valley. It is cold but dry year round north of the Brooks Range. Inland areas, to the south of the Brooks and Endicott Mountains (as represented by Kobuk National Park), have warmer summers and in some years quite heavy precipitation. Nome, on the Seward Peninsula, has a climate slightly modified by its proximity to the Bering Sea. This entire region undergoes periods of complete darkness from November through January and non-stop daylight from May through July. Temperatures in July may exceed 90° F and fall in January to –60° F.

SUNLIGHT			
SUMMER MAXIMUM	SUNRISE	SUNSET	# OF HOURS
Barrow	84 DAYS OF CONTINUOUS DAYLIGHT		
WINTER MINIMUM	SUNRISE	SUNSET	# OF HOURS
Barrow	67 DAYS WITHOUT DAYLIGHT		

TEMPS (F°)	AVG. JAN.		AVG. APRIL		AVG. JULY		AVG. OCT.		RECORD	RECORD
	HIGH	LOW	HIGH	LOW	HIGH	LOW	HIGH	LOW	HIGH	LOW
Barrow	-9	-20	5	-10	43	33	20	10	79	-56
Kobuk NP	-2	-20	28	7	66	48	27	15	90	-64
Nome	13	0	27	10	57	45	34	21	86	-54

PRECIPITATION (INCHES)	AVG. JAN.	AVG. APRIL	AVG. JULY	AVG. OCT.	ANNUAL RAIN	ANNUAL SNOW
Barrow	0.2"	0.2"	0.9"	0.5"	5"	28"
Kobuk N.P.	0.7"	0.8"	2.7"	0.9"	16"	60"
Nome	0.9"	0.7"	2.3"	1.3"	16"	56"

■ Food, Lodging, & Tours

◆ Regional Information

U.S. Forest Service Information Center. For information on cabins, camping and hiking in Alaska. *101 Egan Dr., Juneau, AK 99801; 907-586-8751.*

Restaurant Prices
Per person, without drinks, tax, or tip:
\$ = under \$12; \$\$ = \$12–\$20; \$\$\$ = over \$20

Room Rates
Per night, per room, double occupancy:
\$ = under \$70; \$\$ = \$70–\$100; \$\$\$ = over \$100

= lodging
= restaurant
= campground
= wilderness lodge

Ambler *map page 272, B/C-3*

population 325
for information try Kobuk River Lodge

Kobuk River Lodge. 907-445-2165 \$\$\$
Three cozy, rustic rooms upstairs from store and (in summer) two efficiency cabins. Includes home-cooked meals.

Anaktuvuk Pass *map page 272, D-3*

population 340
visitor and campground information
National Park Service; 907-661-3520

Arctic Village

map page 272, E-3

population 120
visitors information and day tours if arranged in advance; 907-587-5328

Parish Hall. Reservations; 907-587-5328 $
Bring your own sleeping bag.

Barrow *map page 272, C-1*

population 3,470
visitors information; 907-852-5211

Arctic Pizza. 125 Apayuak St.; 907-852-4222 $$$
Full service dinners in family restaurant. Fine dining area upstairs with ocean view.

Brower's Cafe. Stevenson St. and the beach; 907-852-3435 $$–$$$
A rustic beach-front cafe located in the oldest building in Arctic Alaska. Menu includes reindeer sausage.

Ken's Restaurant. Above the airport terminal building; 907-852-8888 $$
Reasonably priced hamburgers and Chinese food, with daily specials.

Pepe's North of the Border. 1204 Agvik St.; 907-852-8200, next door to Top of the World Hotel $$$
Enchiladas, taco, and chiles rellenos in the northernmost Mexican restaurant in the U.S. Also serves seafood and steaks.

Teriyaki House. Ahkovah St.; 907-852-2276; opposite Alaska Airlines $$
Serves Japanese and Chinese fare.

Barrow Airport Inn. Near the airport, 1815 Momeganna St.; 907-852-2525 $$$
Modern hotel offering such amenities as cable TV, telephones, full kitchenettes (in nine of the rooms), and complimentary morning coffee served in the lobby.

Top of the World Hotel. 1200 Agvik St.; 907-852-3900 or 800-882-8478 $$$
Forty-six rooms in the ultimate polar community, with a restaurant. A comfortable hotel with a stuffed polar bear in its frontier-style lobby. Rooms have baths, TV, telephones.

◆ Tours

Tundra Tours. Top of the World Hotel tours (see above). 800-882-8478
Half-day $58 bus tours of the town and surrounding sites; includes presentations of Eskimo dancing and mask-making.

BETTLES *map page 272, C-3*

population 56
visitors information; 907-692-5191

Bettles Lodge. Reservations address: Dept. VP, P.O. Box 27, Bettles, AK 99726; 800-770-5111 $$$
Fly-in lodge offering private rooms, efficiency apartments, and bunk house. Aircraft fuel, gift house, restaurant, and liquor store also located here. Arctic tour packages from Fairbanks.

◆ TOURS

Sourdough Outfitters. 907-692-5252
Cross-country dogsled trips in Gates of the Arctic National Park and Preserve; backpacking/canoe trips.

COLDFOOT *map page 272, D-3*

population 35
visitors information; 907-678-5209 (summer only)

Coldfoot Services and Arctic Acres Inn. Mile 175 Dalton Hwy.; 907-678-5201
The only visitors facilities in this historic mining camp and last-of-the-frontier town. At the restaurant ($–$$), frequented mainly by truckers, diners sit side by side at long wooden tables and benches. Motel rooms are bare-bones but expensive ($$$). Northern lights viewing from September through March.

COUNCIL *map page 272, A-4*

population 10

Camp Bendeleben. Reservations: Box 1137; Nome, AK 99762; 907-443-2880 $$$
Originally a 1900s gold-mining post, now a year-round, reservation only camp featuring fishing for Arctic char, grayling, and salmon; also ice-fishing, bird-watching, and photography. Three-night minimum, rates include all meals and transportation between the lodge and Nome. *Also see White Mountain Lodge in Nome.*

DEADHORSE (PRUDHOE BAY) *map page 272, D-2*

population 8,600 (including Prudhoe Bay)

Arctic Caribou Inn. Reservations: P.O. Box 340111, Prudhoe Bay, AK 99734; 907-659-2368 summer only $$$
Located near Deadhorse airport; 75 rooms with private or shared facilities, lounge and dining areas. Departure point for tours to the oilfields and the Arctic Ocean.

◆ TOURS

Prudhoe Bay Adventures. Reservations: Northern Alaska Tour Company, Box 82991-MD96, Fairbanks, AK 99708; 907-474-8600
Travel up the Dalton Highway, visit a rural Alaskan homestead, cross the Arctic Circle, view caribou and other wildlife on the Arctic tundra; tour Prudhoe Bay oilfields.

FORT YUKON
map page 272, E-4

population 675
visitor information: try Alaska Yukon tours, below.

◆ TOURS

Alaska Yukon Tours. 907-662-2793
Native run fish-camp tours.

KAKTOVIK (BARTER ISLAND) *map page 272, E-2*

population 227
visitor information; 907-640-6313

Visitors to the Arctic National Wildlife Refuge often fly into Kaktovik. Contact Alaska Air or Frontier Flying Service *(see page 308).*

Waldo Arms. 907-640-6513 $$
Meals and accommodations found here—13 rooms. If you're a guest, meals are included in rate.

◆ TOURS

Alaska Flyers. 907-640-6324
Flying tours and air charters to ANWR and elsewhere.

KIANA *map page 272, B-3*

population 350
for visitor information try Kiana Trading Post 907-475-2138

◆ TOURS AND LODGING

Kobuk River Jets. 907-475-2149 $$$
Lori Scheurch has opened a rustic, out of town lodge on the river that's received good reviews. Food and boat trips included in price. Native operated.

Don Smith 907-475-2186. $$
Native operated boat tours, fishing, and lodging.

KOTZEBUE *map page 272, B-3*

population 2,750
visitor information; 907-442-3401

Kotzebue Pizza House. 2nd and Bison St; 907-442-3432 $-$$
Despite its name, locals come here for the the burgers and Asian food.

Nullagvik Hotel Restaurant. 308 Shore Ave.; 907-442-3331 $$
Coffee-shop–style restaurant.

◆ TOURS AND LODGING

Nullagvik Hotel. 308 Shore Ave.; 907-442-3331 $$$
Owned by local Native corporation, very busy in peak season. Overlooks Hotham Inlet and built on pilings to keep it from melting underlying permafrost. Recently redecorated.

Tour Arctic. 907-265-4118
Bus tours of Kotzebue. Visits to local Eskimo fish camp, Kiana village tour.

NOME *map page 272, A-4*

population 4,400
visitors information 907-443-5535

Fat Freddie's. Front St.; 907-443-5899 $–$$
Overlooking the Bering Sea. Burgers and sandwiches.

Fort Davis Roadhouse. 1.5 miles east of town on the Nome-Council Rd.; 907-443-2660 $$$
Specializes in steak (including reindeer steak) and seafood.

Milano's. 907-443-2924 $$
Pizza and Italian food.

Nacho's Mexican Restaurant. Front St.; 907-443-5503 $$
Mexican fare, popular for breakfast.

Polar Cub Cafe. Front St.; 907-*443-5191* $-$$
Standard breakfast fare served all day, as well as lunch and dinner entrees. Very friendly waitstaff.

Aurora Inn. 907-443-3838 $$
New hotel, nicely appointed, with view of Bering Sea.

Betty's Igloo B&B. 907-443-2419 $$
Three units available; continental breakfast provided.

June's B&B. 907-443-5984 $$
Recalling the gold rush era, this cozy inn has two double rooms, each with handmade quilts and pretty stenciled walls.

Nugget Inn. Front St.; 907-443-2323 $$$
With 47 rooms, this is one of the larger hotels in Nome; a convenient place to stay pending your departure to the hinterlands for fishing, rafting, hunting, exploring. Restaurant, gift shop, and bar.

Trails End. 907-443-3600 $$–$$$
Downtown apartments offering maid service, laundry facilities, and private cooking facilities.

White Mountain Lodge. 80 miles east of Nome. Reservations : Box 149, White Mountain 99784; 907-638-3431 $$$
Located in an Eskimo village accessible by boat from Council or plane from Nome, the lodge provides modern accommodations and meals prepared with Native delicacies. Native guides available to show guests the best fishing spots.

◆ TOURS

Circumpolar Expeditions. 907-272-9299
Will arrange for you to fly across the Bering Straits on Bering Air and spend the night with a Russian family in Siberia.

Flat Dog Kennels. 914 East Sixth St.; 907-443-2958
Leads sled dog rides; offers lessons and overnight trips.

INUA **Expeditions.** 195 Steadman Ave.; 907-443-4994, winter 907-642-4161
Kayaking and bicycle trips arranged.

SHUNGNAK (KOBUK) *map page 272, C-3*

population 275
for visitors information try Shungnak Clinic, opposite

Shugnak Clinic. 907 437-2138 $
May have beds available for $20.

FESTIVALS AND EVENTS

MARCH

Nome: Bering Sea Ice Classic Golf Tournament. Only in Alaska—a golf tournament played in mid-March on the pack ice of the Bering Sea near Nome. *907-443-5535*

Nome: Iditarod Trail Sled Dog Race. Dogs and mushers cross tundra, rivers, mountains, and ice-locked sea coast to reach Nome 11–15 days later. Festivities include a reindeer potluck and the Iditarod Awards Banquet. *907-376-5155*

MAY

Nome: Polar Bear Swim. On Memorial Day, ice permitting, Nomites dip into the 35°F frigid waters of the Bering Sea to test their hardiness (fool-hardiness). *907-443-5535*

JUNE

Nome: Midnight Sun Festival. In northern Alaska the summer solstice means that the longest day of the year is 22 hours long. Activities change every year, but can include a street dance, BBQ, Eskimo dances, and a parade. *907-443-5535*

JULY

Kotzebue: Northwest Native Trade Fair. Eskimo games, dances, and other activities. *907-442-3401*

AUGUST

Nome: Rubber Ducky Race. Rotary Club's annual fundraiser includes rubber duck race from the river to the harbor, bathtub race, and parade.

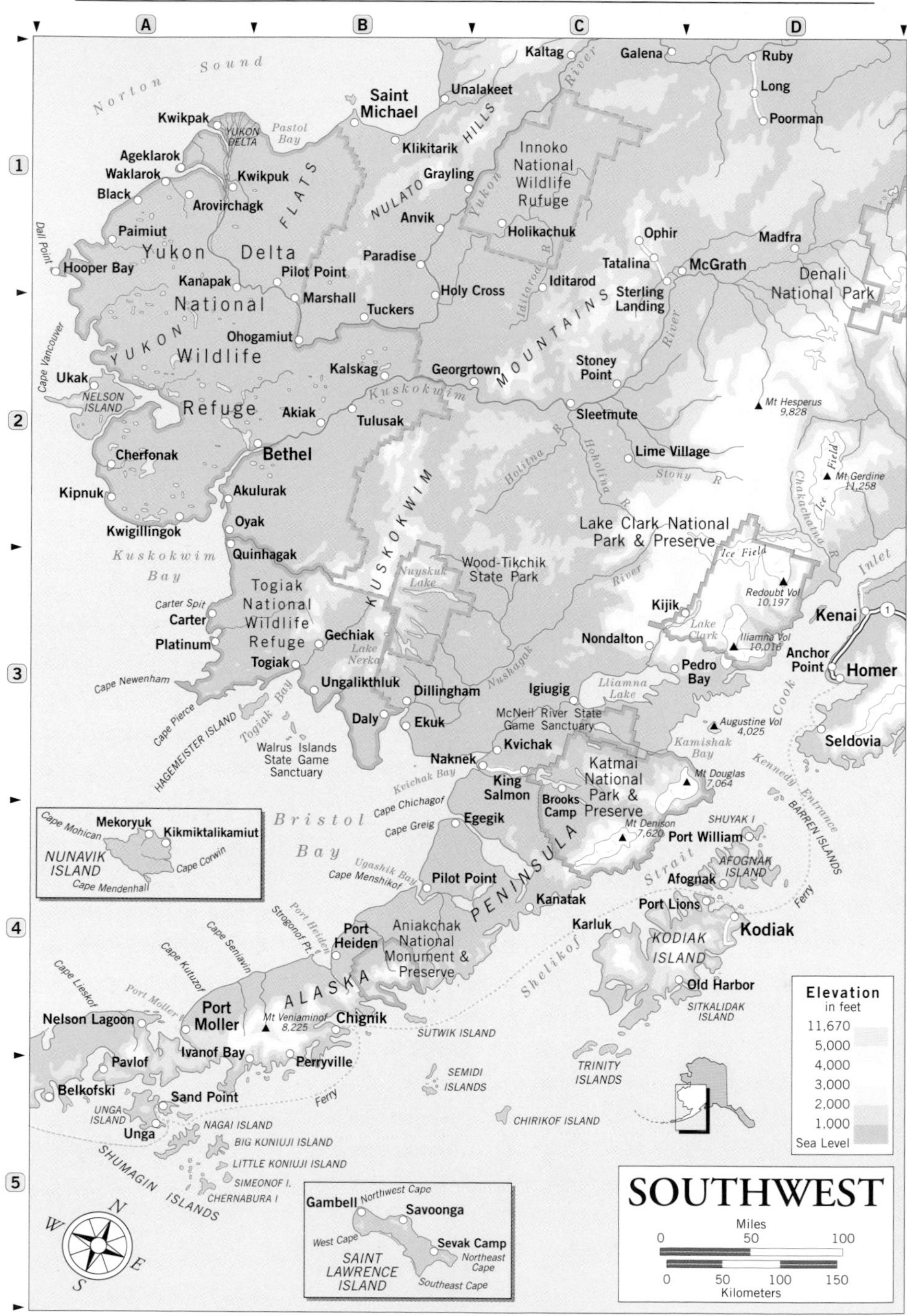
A
B
C
D
1
2
3
4
5
Norton Sound
Kwikpak
YUKON DELTA
Pastol Bay
Saint Michael
Unalakeet
Kaltag
Galena
Ruby
Long
Poorman
Ageklarok
Waklarok
Black
Kwikpuk
Arovirchagk
FLATS
Klikitarik
NULATO HILLS
Grayling
Anvik
Innoko National Wildlife Rufuge
Holikachuk
Yukon
Iditarod R
Dall Point
Paimiut
Hooper Bay
Yukon Delta National Wildlife Refuge
Kanapak
Pilot Point
Marshall
Paradise
Holy Cross
Tuckers
Iditarod
MOUNTAINS
Ophir
Tatalina
McGrath
Sterling Landing
Madfra
Denali National Park
River
Cape Vancouver
YUKON
Ohogamiut
Ukak
NELSON ISLAND
Kalskag
Georgrtown
Kuskokwim
Akiak
Tulusak
Stoney Point
Sleetmute
Mt Hesperus 9,828
Cherfonak
Bethel
Kipnuk
Akulurak
Oyak
Kwigillingok
Quinhagak
Kuskokwim Bay
KUSKOKWIM
Holitna R
Hoholitna R
Lime Village
Stony R
Mt Gerdine 11,258
Ice Field
Chakachatna R
Lake Clark National Park & Preserve
Inlet
Togiak National Wildlife Refuge
Nuyskuk Lake
Wood-Tikchik State Park
River
Redoubt Vol 10,197
Carter Spit
Carter
Platinum
Gechiak
Lake Nerka
Kijik
Lake Clark
Nondalton
Iliamna Vol 10,016
Kenai
Anchor Point
Homer
Togiak
Cape Newenham
Ungalikthluk
Dillingham
Nushagak
Igiugig
Iliamna Lake
Pedro Bay
Cook
Cape Pierce
HAGEMEISTER ISLAND
Togiak Bay
Walrus Islands State Game Sanctuary
Daly
Ekuk
McNeil River State Game Sanctuary
Augustine Vol 4,025
Kamishak Bay
Seldovia
Kvichak
Naknek
Kvichak Bay
King Salmon
Brooks Camp
Katmai National Park & Preserve
Mt Douglas 7,064
Kennedy Entrance
BARREN ISLANDS
Mekoryuk
Kikmiktalikamiut
Cape Mohican
NUNAVIK ISLAND
Cape Corwin
Cape Mendenhall
Bristol Bay
Cape Chichagof
Cape Greig
Egegik
Mt Denison 7,620
SHUYAK I
Port William
Ugashik Bay
Cape Menshikof
Pilot Point
PENINSULA
Strait
AFOGNAK ISLAND
Afognak
Kanatak
Port Lions
Ferry
Strogonof Pt.
Port Heiden
Port Heiden
Aniakchak National Monument & Preserve
Karluk
KODIAK ISLAND
Kodiak
Cape Seniavin
Cape Kutuzof
Cape Lieskof
Port Moller
ALASKA
Shelikof
Old Harbor
Elevation in feet
11,670
5,000
4,000
3,000
2,000
1,000
Sea Level
Nelson Lagoon
Port Moller
Mt Veniaminof 8,225
Chignik
SUTWIK ISLAND
SITKALIDAK ISLAND
Ivanof Bay
Perryville
Pavlof
SEMIDI ISLANDS
TRINITY ISLANDS
Belkofski
Sand Point
Ferry
UNGA ISLAND
Unga
CHIRIKOF ISLAND
NAGAI ISLAND
BIG KONIUJI ISLAND
SHUMAGIN ISLANDS
LITTLE KONIUJI ISLAND
SIMEONOF I.
CHERNABURA I
Gambell
Northwest Cape
Savoonga
West Cape
Sevak Camp
Northeast Cape
SAINT LAWRENCE ISLAND
Southeast Cape
N
W
E
S
SOUTHWEST
Miles
0
50
100
0
50
100
150
Kilometers

SOUTHWEST

HIGHLIGHTS

MAPS

PRACTICAL INFORMATION

LANDSCAPE AND TRAVEL

West of Kodiak and Afognak islands on the Alaska Peninsula is a vast wilderness of marshy tundra and more than 60 smoldering volcanos. Much of this territory now lies within the boundaries of Katmai National Park, Lake Clark National Park, Aniakchak National Park, and Wood-Tikchik State Park. From the southern end of the peninsula begins the thousand-mile-long Aleutian Island chain with its wild, barren coasts and colonies of fur seals, walrus, puffins, and murres.

Comparatively few travelers make it out to sparsely populated Southwestern Alaska, and most of those who do travel by plane. Although prices vary, it's standard for a roundtrip plane flight from Anchorage to Kodiak and on by bush plane to an isolated park to cost $500 or more per person in transportation fees. A marine ferry follows the coastline and stops at many of the Aleutian islands, but travel is time-consuming and dependent on good weather. Most people visit the Peninsula and its neighboring mountains and islands to visit the McNeil River or Brooks Camp bear-viewing platforms, for sport fishing, or for big-game hunting. The region evokes superlatives in either regard. This area also has much to offer river rafters, sea kayakers, hikers, campers, and wildlife photographers.

No roads lead from Anchorage into this area; weather can sock in the Kodiak airport for days at a time in the middle of summer. The largest town, Dillingham, is a major fishing port.

■ Earthquakes, Tidal Waves, and Fish-Filled Seas

Much of southwestern Alaska rests on top of one of the most active tectonic areas in the world. In 1946, for example, a tidal wave generated by seismic activity in the Aleutians completely swept a local U.S. Coast Guard lighthouse out to sea. The reinforced concrete structure had been located on a rocky point ten stories above the high tide mark. The 14 men inside were never accounted for. Five hours later the same wave struck Hawaii, killing 159 and causing $25 million in damage. It then sped south over the Equator to slam into Chile, rebounding back and hitting the other side of Hawaii, where it caused more damage. The Good Friday earthquake of 1964 wrecked salmon canneries on Kodiak, and the subsequent tidal wave destroyed the harbor and the city.

The World's Most Dangerous Job

Among the many dangerous professions Alaska has to offer one is the deadliest of all: Tanner (or snow crab) and king crab fishing. Every year dozens of men and women lose their lives when the 120-foot crab boats are caught in the ferocious storms raking the Bering Sea and Gulf of Alaska. Winds over 100 miles per hour and seas of 50 feet are not uncommon. Sea spray can freeze so quickly and become so thick on deck that boats capsize from top weight before crews can clear the ice with sledgehammers and baseball bats.

Iron crab pots weigh 750 pounds and must be maneuvered by hand on deck night and day while the boat pitches and rolls in howling gales and ice storms. Roughly 15 percent of the crabbers are incapacitated each year. But the lure of big money provides ever-fresh recruits for the skippers and canneries of Kodiak Island and Dutch Harbor. In the boom years of the late seventies and early eighties each crew member could pocket more than $20,000 after a successful catch lasting six weeks. A precipitous drop in the king crab population between 1981 and 1985 weakened the industry for a few years. Fishermen then began harvesting tanner (snow) crab and opilio crab.

The human spirit is tough, though, and resilient, and Kodiak was soon rebuilt into what it is today—a bustling, thriving economic center for the North Pacific fishing industry. The seas are filled with gold in the form of salmon, halibut, pollack, and other edible species. So rich are these resources that other nations—especially those along the Pacific Rim—bring their factory fleets into the area. The Alaskan Congressional delegation is forever petitioning the White House to impose sanctions on those countries (such as Taiwan) that employ rapacious and/or outlawed fishing practices. There is the very real concern that some of these fisheries may soon disappear. The lessons in this respect are even more recent—the once-thriving king crab industry in Kodiak and Dutch Harbor is now but a shadow of its former self.

■ KODIAK ISLAND *map page 316, C-4*

In 1899 naturalist John Burroughs described Kodiak Island as a "pastoral paradise," and, nearly one hundred years later, if you visit Kodiak during the summer you'll probably agree with him. Located strategically on the edge of the warming Japanese current, Kodiak is 100 miles long and is located 252 air miles south of Anchorage and the Kenai peninsula. Bathed in continual precipitation, Kodiak and its sister islands are every bit as green as Ireland, and if you come, as Burroughs did, from icy Prince William Sound or from the dry forests and tundra of the Interior, the sudden wash of green across the landscape will be quite startling. One of my colleagues at the University of Alaska used to refer to Kodiak as the "northernmost Hawaiian Island" and sometimes when you are on Kodiak, hiking in a dense jungle world of green beside a clear running stream, the description does not seem too far off the mark.

Because of its moisture and greenery, Kodiak supports an incredible proliferation of wildlife: brown bear, Sitka black-tailed deer, elk, mountain goats, pink salmon, sockeye salmon, coho salmon, king salmon, chum salmon, arctic char, steelhead, arctic grayling, bald eagles, otters, weasels, foxes, and more than 200 species of birds (from tundra swans to golden plovers). And the wildflowers—fireweed, shooting stars, wild blue iris—are out of this world. The place is like an enormous greenhouse where the humidity and temperature have been carefully controlled by Mother Nature to make conditions perfect for growing flowers. Thankfully, almost all of Kodiak Island—all 1,865,000 acres—is forever protected

Beautiful Kodiak

For naturalist John Burroughs, who only a few weeks earlier had explored cold and misty Prince William Sound, the transition from the realm of frozen glaciers and granite rock to Kodiak Island, warmed by the Japanese current and drenched in rain, was profound:

Never before had I seen such beauty of greenness, because never before had I seen it from such a vantage ground of blue sea. . . . At one point we passed near a large natural park. It looked as if a landscape gardener might have been employed to grade and shape the ground and plant it with grass and trees in just the right proportion. . . . Our course lay through narrow channels and over open bays sprinkled with green islands, past bold cliffs and headlands, til . . . we reached the village of Kodiak, called by the Russians St. Paul. . . . How welcome the warmth! We swarmed out of the ship, like boys out of school, longing for a taste of grass and of the rural seclusion and sweetness!

—John Burroughs, *The Harriman Expedition,* 1899

from development as Kodiak National Wildlife Refuge. Because of the rugged coastline, no place on Kodiak Island is more than 15 miles from the sea, a favorable geographic situation that fosters three habitats—rain forest, grass meadowland and tundra, and glaciated high country.

You will probably reach Kodiak Island either by air (direct flights from Anchorage) or via the Alaska Marine Ferry. In either case, you will find yourself in the town of Kodiak, which is quite large by Alaskan standards (6,365 souls in the 1990 census). The town was rebuilt after the tidal wave from the 1964 earthquake washed over it; consequently Kodiak is quite modern in appearance. Here are all the amenities—hotels, motels, restaurants, stores, campgrounds, post office. You will notice quite a few boats docked in the harbor—Kodiak is the third-largest commercial fishing port in the country. Stroll along the harbor, smelling the sea on one side, while the warm and friendly aroma of coffee and cooking food coaxes the other nostril to pull you into one of the waterfront cafes.

The island of Kodiak was considered an emerald paradise by sea-weary explorers and traders.

◆ In the Town of Kodiak

Visitors Center

There are several worthwhile attractions in the town of Kodiak. First, the **visitors center** is located on the corner of Tagupa Road and Center Street on the waterfront. I'd highly recommend a stop here to learn more about the diverse recreational possibilities on the island—the visitors center is loaded with brochures, pamphlets, and information on tours, air charters, fishing lodges, and so forth.

Baranof Museum

Nearly everyone who visits Kodiak stops in at the **Baranof Museum** which focuses on the Russian period of Kodiak's history. The museum is located across the street from the visitors center.

Holy Resurection Church

Also nearby is the beautiful **Holy Resurrection Church,** which serves a parish established in 1794 (when Colorado was still known only to a few French trappers and Montana had yet to be explored by Lewis and Clark).

Alutiq Culture and Heritage Center

Located 100 yards west of the intersection of Marine Way and Rezanof Drive, the center features artifacts made by Native

Kodiak is perhaps best known for its large brown bear population (above) and its Russian heritage. Ascension of Our Lord Russian Orthodox Church (left) is in Karluk.

Americans. One of my students at the University of Alaska—Sven Hakkanson—has been quite active in the effort of his people, the Aleut, to recover their past. Two things are important in this respect—the preservation of language, which is synonymous with culture, and the maintenance of traditions through the education of younger generations. Museums are vitally important in this effort.

◆ Kodiak Island Excursions

Buckskin River

There is an unusually good road system (for Alaska) around Kodiak, and you can use it to reach some interesting sites. Only six miles west of downtown on the Chiniak Road is the **Buskin River,** which has excellent fishing in season—the Buskin River Recreational Site has camping sites and short nature trails.

Fort Abercrombie State Park

East of town, the state park has hiking trails around the old military installation. Past Fort Abercrombie, there is a trail at the end of the road to Termination Point, which offers a nice view of the surrounding headlands and sea. More extensive explorations can be undertaken to the south, on the road that passes the Buskin River Recreational Site to such places as **Womens Bay, Happy Beach, Cape Greville,** and **Pasagshak Bay.** During the deer hunting season, these roads will be very busy with hunters. (Rifle hunting seasons for bear are in April and September, those for deer and elk, in the autumn.)

Backcountry

Those with an interest in seeing the backcountry can arrange to be transported by boat or air to any one of a number of remote wilderness locations, both in Kodiak National Wildlife Refuge (recreational cabins available for rent) and in nearby Shuyak Island State Park. Afognak Island and Raspberry Island to the north are very popular with sea kayakers, sport fishermen, and big-game hunters. Kodiak also has its share of fishing lodges, many on Native corporation land and some run by the corporations. Bear in mind through all this that you can put your car on the ferry at Homer and be driving around Kodiak 12 hours later, watching from your front seat as brown bears feed on sea-run Pacific salmon. That's pretty incredible.

■ Lake Clark National Park *map page 316, C&D-2&3*

The name of Dick Proenneke, a pioneering homesteader, will forever be associated with Lake Clark National Park, located across the Cook Inlet from the Kenai Peninsula. Proenneke arrived in 1967, fell in love with the rugged wildness of the place, and eventually found some good land and built a sturdy cabin from hand-felled logs. He became a modern Thoreau, a man who went out and actually did what most only dream of—building a wilderness cabin and living off the bounties of the northern land—berries, fish, big game. His experiences inspired the book *One Man's Wilderness: An Alaskan Odyssey:*

> What was I capable of that I didn't know yet? What about my limits? Could I truly enjoy my own company for an entire year? Was I equal to everything this wild land could throw at me? I had seen its moods in late spring, summer and early fall, but what would winter bring? Would I love the isolation then with its bone-stabbing cold, its brooding ghostly silence, its forced confinement? At age 51, I intended to find out.

Today, Proenneke is a living legend at Lake Clark (as is former governor Jay Hammond, who also has a log home in the area) and his book is *must* reading for anyone contemplating a visit to this beautiful park.

It is no longer possible to settle at Lake Clark, which is now a national park, but you may still visit the place and appreciate the vast solitude and wilderness that is now forever protected from further development. At 3,653,000 acres, Lake Clark National Park is approximately 12 times larger than Grand Teton National Park in northwestern Wyoming—plenty of country to hike, camp, fish, photograph, and boat in. Regular commercial flights from Anchorage to Iliamna provide one of the most popular means of access. Another alternative is to fly a charter from Anchorage, Kenai, or Homer west over Cook Inlet into the park. As you drive the Sterling Highway from Kenai to Homer, the two volcanoes you see across Cook Inlet—Redoubt and Iliamna—are within Lake Clark National Park. They often harmlessly steam, but in recent years, the volcanos have erupted on several occasions. In 1992, a Boeing 747 flying through the ash cloud of one of these eruptions lost power in all four engines and, after restarting one engine, made an emergency landing in Anchorage. Sometimes, during an eruption, the towns of the Western Kenai are coated with enough acidic ash to destroy the paint finish of a car. Still, the view is sublime.

In Lake Clark you will find everything from coastal rain forests to alpine tundra, from active volcanoes to serene fjords, from high mountain lakes to saltwater estuaries. The wildlife is just as diverse, ranging from belugas and killer whales at the mouth of the Tuxedni River on the east to grizzly bears and Dall sheep on the tundra slopes above Port Alsworth on the west. The salt and fresh waters in and around Lake Clark National Park offer some of the greatest fishing opportunities in North America—the Newhalen River is as famous for its fantastic runs of red salmon, as the Iliamna River is for its 10- and 12-pound rainbow trout (which you can catch and release all day, or until your arm falls off, whichever comes first). Lake Clark and nearby Lake Iliamna support the world's largest runs of sockeye salmon—fish that eventually go on to live in Bristol Bay (on the northwest side of the Alaska Peninsula) and form the basis for the most productive commercial salmon fishing waters on the planet.

If you can visit only one place in Alaska, and are concerned about the crowds on the Kenai Peninsula or in Denali National Park, Lake Clark National Park may be the place for you. Here you will experience much of the same beauty—both of landscape and of wildlife—but with a fraction of the people around you. Because of the additional air travel it will be more expensive, but having come this far, you may decide a little extra is worth it in order to have a truly once-in-a-lifetime experience.

Iliamna is located on the north end of Iliamna Lake (the largest in the state) about 225 miles southwest from Anchorage. It is also one of the most strategically located communities—fly north and you are soon in Lake Clark National Park, turn south and within a short time you are flying over Katmai National Park. Also this—some of the largest rainbow trout in the world can be found in the Kvichak River system. You'll also run into some of the best salmon fishing in the state. In the autumn berry-picking in the area is excellent, as well as hunting in the national wildlife refuges for black and grizzly bear, moose, and caribou. Accommodations are limited to several lodges and bed-and-breakfasts in Iliamna. There are some stores featuring local native crafts. Various outfitters, guides, and aircraft charter companies can quickly get you into the backcountry.

Fishing is the biggest industry and employer in Southwest Alaska. The ports of Kodiak (right) and Dillingham are where most of the action takes place.

MALKA
MYSTIC
LADY

■ Katmai National Park *map page 316, C-3&4*

On June 6, 1912, following a week of severe earthquakes, the Novarupta Volcano south of Iliamna Lake suddenly exploded as if it had been hit by a nuclear bomb. The entire top of the mountain was violently blown off, throwing enormous quantities of pumice, ash, and rock across the Alaskan landscape. Scientists estimated the total volume of displaced planetary material in this event was in excess of seven cubic miles—two times that expelled in the great 1883 Krakatau explosion in Indonesia. A nearby river valley was buried in 700 feet of solid debris. There followed hellish blasts of superhot gas, lava, pumice, and ash. The whole northern hemisphere of the planet was wrapped in a haze for weeks from this single catastrophic eruption. On Kodiak Island, high noon was turned into blackest midnight for two days. A thousand miles away, in Vancouver, Canada, acid rain from the blast caused drying clothes to fall apart on laundry lines. A year later, sunsets and sunrises were still brilliantly colored from the volcanic particles that had not settled out of the atmosphere.

Four years later, exploring the still-smoldering area for the National Geographic Society, Robert Griggs discovered the primary scene of destruction, an area now referred to on maps as the **Valley of Ten Thousand Smokes.** In his book of the same name, Griggs describes "one of the most amazing visions ever beheld by mortal eye":

> The whole valley as far as the eye could reach was full of hundreds, no thousands—literally, tens of thousands—of smokes curling up from its fissured floor. . . . Some were sending up columns of steam which rose a thousand feet before dissolving.

Many of you reading this book have been to Yellowstone National Park and have seen the famous Old Faithful geothermal geyser, which periodically shoots 100 feet in the air. Every summer people drive halfway across the country just to see this unusual geological phenomenon. Imagine a steam vent that reaches 1,000 feet in the air—10 times the height of Old Faithful. Now imagine hundreds of them on that order, and a thousand ascending to 500 feet, and thousands more the size of Old Faithful. The sight of these geysers in the remote Katmai Valley must have convinced all who saw them of the ultimate power and authority of Mother Nature on this world.

SHISHALDIN (8000 FEET), FROM OONEMAK PASS.

Although the activity of the steam vents has ceased, the valley remains a sight to amaze. Wisps of steam still rise from the volcanoes, some with acidic cauldrons still boiling. Today, the Valley of Ten Thousand Smokes forms the centerpiece of this crown jewel park, which was first designated a national monument by presidential proclamation in 1918. Under the 1980 Alaska Lands bill, Katmai reached its final configuration, with a total of 4,268,000 acres under protection as park or preserve. This makes the park almost twice the size of Yellowstone—the largest national park in the Lower 48. Eight major river systems are included in the park. In addition to its importance as a geological preserve, with

15 volcanoes within park boundaries, Katmai also protects one of the largest populations of brown bears in the world. These bears, which feed on the spawning salmon, grow to mind-boggling size, with adult males regularly reaching weights in excess of 1,000 pounds.

In Katmai the bears are easily viewed at **Brooks Camp** on Naknek Lake, where there are observation platforms, and at nearby **McNeil River State Game Sanctuary**, which has similar viewing areas *(see "WILDLIFE," page 59, for more detailed information on these sites)*. In both cases, near salmon streams that are heavily used by the bears in the summer months, park rangers have constructed bear observation facilities. At times, up to 60 bears can be seen at one time at Brooks Falls and on the McNeil River.

In either case, people access the area by flying from Anchorage to King Salmon, and then catching local floatplane charters to these specific destinations. In addition to the wildlife viewing opportunities, Katmai offers some of the finest sport fishing for grayling, northern pike, rainbow trout, and sockeye salmon in Alaska.

Photographing brown bears from a bear observation platform at Brooks Camp (above). Children make the most of a wooden box sleigh in the largely Yupik town of Bethel (right).

There are also some fantastic opportunities for rafting, kayaking, hiking, and camping in this extraordinary park. All plans for such undertakings, however, must be made from six to seven months in advance. *See Travel Information, page 340, following.*

The most important village in this area, in terms of access to nearby national parks and wildlife refuges, as well as to numerous fishing lakes, rivers, and streams, is **King Salmon.** (*See page 343 for more information.*)

■ Aniakchak National Monument *map page 316, B-4*

Imagine walking through a giant outdoor diorama of the moon and witnessing the same sort of other worldly scenery that Neil Armstrong and Buzz Aldrin observed on the Sea of Tranquillity in 1969. Imagine trekking across a valley of cinders and lava and pumice, with nothing connected to the human race anywhere in sight—a desolate landscape out of the parables of Heraclitus or the mind of Thomas Merino. Imagine that you are walking across the ruins of a volcano so large that its collapsed caldera forms a basin six miles across, with a total area of 30 square miles (larger than Manhattan Island). Imagine all this, and you have Aniakchak National Monument—bizarre, oddly beautiful, and remote. So remote, in fact, that the caldera was unknown to all but the few Native people who lived in this area until 1922.

Aniakchak is literally at the end of the world—400 miles southwest of Anchorage. It is accessed in stages, first by flying commercially from Anchorage to King Salmon, and then from King Salmon to Meshik (Port Heiden), and then in a charter from Meshik into the national monument. This initial journey, just to reach a wilderness launching point, can take anywhere from two to five or six days, depending on the weather (which is notoriously unreliable on the Peninsula). Visitors normally head for Surprise Lake, a short flight from Port Heiden, to go fishing or on a float trip. **Surprise Lake,** stunning emerald green in color, is fed by geothermal springs and lies just inside the collapsed caldera near The Gates through which the Aniakchak River flows. Picture a circular sand castle with one small notch caved in, through which a river runs, and you have Aniakchak Caldera.

In the caldera you'll see much wildlife, including grizzly bears, caribou, golden and bald eagles, red foxes, and other common Peninsular fauna. The volcano last erupted in 1931, and most geologists believe there is currently no danger in visiting the area. Primitive camping and backpacking are permitted here.

■ Dillingham and Vicinity *map page 316, B-3*

Dillingham is located about 320 miles southwest of Anchorage, on the shores of Bristol Bay. More than 500 boats are based in Dillingham—part of the great fleet that annually fishes for salmon in productive Bristol Bay. Because of its commercial importance, Dillingham has regular commercial airline service from Anchorage, which makes it more accessible than many other parts of Southwestern Alaska. Visitors will find an array of hotels, restaurants, and stores. The town provides access to two world-class natural sights: Walrus Islands State Game Sanctuary and Wood-Tikchik State Park.

◆ Walrus Islands State Game Sanctuary *map page 316, B-3*

Walrus Islands State Game Sanctuary is located about 70 miles southwest of Dillingham and is normally reached by boat charter from Dillingham via the small Eskimo village of Togiak. More than 10,000 walruses summer at the Walrus Islands, as well as up to 1,000 Steller sea lions and hundreds of thousands of puffins, auklets, gulls, cormorants, kittiwakes, and murres. There is also a small population of red foxes. This place is a mecca for wildlife photographers, but is somewhat difficult to reach. Once you're there, though, it's worth it.

◆ Wood-Tilchik State Park *map page 316, B-3*

At 1.4 million acres, Wood-Tikchik State Park is about three times larger than Rocky Mountain National Park in Colorado. Its vast system of lakes is interconnected by various rivers and streams, and steep snowy peaks tower over the still, clear glacial waters. Wildlife is abundant—moose, black and grizzly bears, wolf, fox, lynx, marten, and beaver. Hunting is permitted in Alaskan state parks. The fishing is the primary attraction of the area, though, with most species you'd expect found here—Dolly Varden, rainbow trout, northern pike, arctic grayling, and, of course, red salmon. There are quite a few excellent (but *very* expensive) fishing lodges in the area.

■ Aleutian Islands —Alaska Maritime National Wildlife Refuge

The sheer geographic immensity of this preserve is beyond the ability of most of us to comprehend. First of all, the refuge is not in one place but consists of more than 2,400 scattered pieces of real estate. To the arctic north, for example, on Cape Lisburne, there is a parcel at about 70 degrees north latitude. On the south, by contrast, is tiny Forrester Island in the Panhandle, about the same latitude as Prince Rupert, British Columbia (54 degrees north latitude). Forrester Island is at longitude 133 degrees. Attu Island—on the far west and nearly to Russia—is at longitude 174 degrees. Amazing. That is an east-to-west distance as great as that from Jacksonville, Florida to San Diego, California, and a north-to-south distance that would span the entire east coast of the Lower 48.

These islands, headlands, coves, bays, inlets, passages, beaches, estuaries, reefs, rocky islets, cliffsides, mountains, lakes, rivers, streams, and volcanoes preserve wildlife—Steller sea lions, walrus, sea otters, northern fur seals, polar bears, whales, orcas, grizzly bears, wolves, wolverines, deer, caribou, eagles, and most of all, seabirds. It is estimated that the immense refuge supports more than 40 million birds. One of the most popular sites in this respect is also one of the most remote—Attu Island (where the bloodiest Aleutian battle was fought in World War II). Here die-hard birders flock early each summer in the hope of identifying rare Asian species as they migrate north to the arctic. You will find the visitors center for this refuge in Homer, Alaska *(see page 173)*. Here staff personnel will be happy to outline the many recreational possibilities—birding, hiking, camping, boating, sport fishing, big-game hunting—available in this remote and unusual refuge.

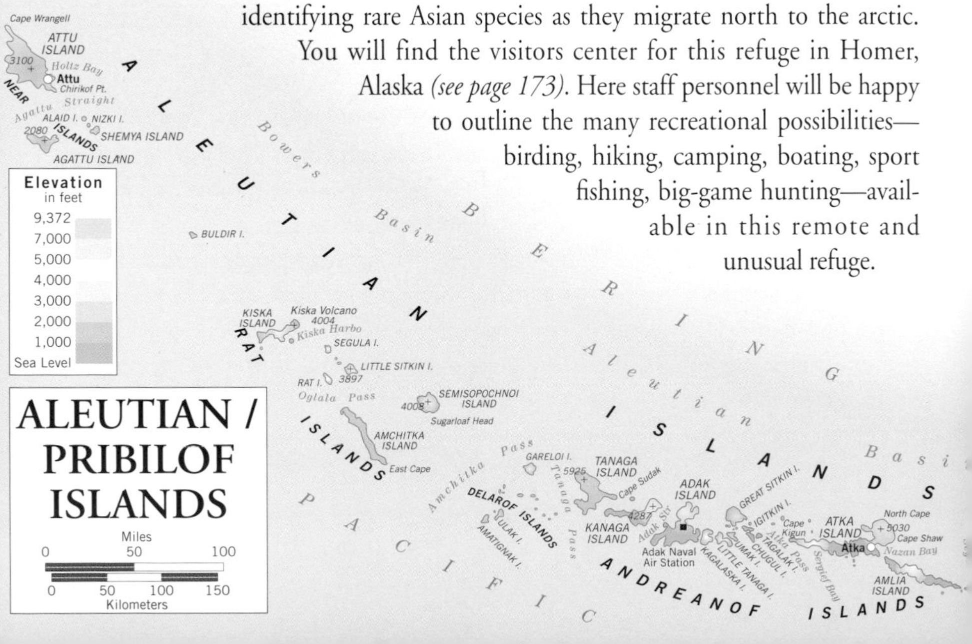

ALEUTIAN / PRIBILOF ISLANDS

■ Pribilof Islands

Of special interest to the visitors of the Pribilof and Aleutian islands were the fur seals, the extent of the herds illustrated by Henry Wood Elliot in this 1872 painting. (Anchorage Museum of History and Art)

The Pribilof Islands are an increasingly popular destination for wildlife lovers, with commercial airline access from Anchorage during the summer months. (This 'scheduled' service is often subject to weather delays which may last for days, however.) St. Paul Island hosts the world's largest colony of northern fur seals, and both harbor seals and Steller sea lions are easily seen during the summer season. These islands also support some of the largest seabird colonies on the planet, including puffins, auklets, murres, kittiwakes, cormorants, fulmars, and rare species from the Russian Far East. The constant rains and fog in this area make the tundra wildflower displays, which peak around the summer solstice, particularly magnificent. Virtually every wildlife photographer of note in North America—from Tom Mangelson to Galen Rowell—has made a pilgrimage to this wildlife paradise.

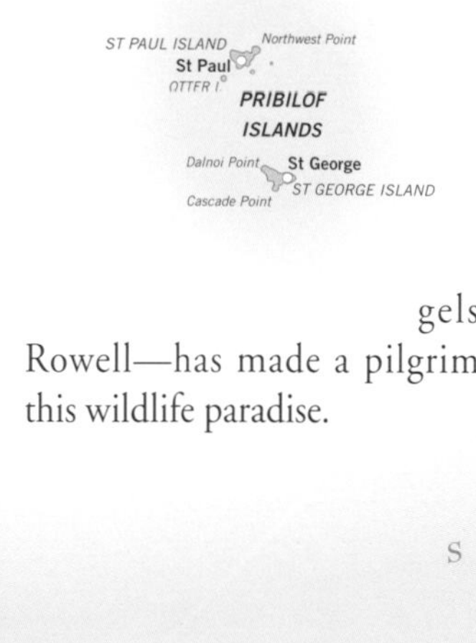

A MAN of OONALASHKA.

Artist J. Webber's drawing of an Aleutian Native, 1778. (Bancroft Library)

THE HUNT

I am not entirely comfortable on the sea ice butchering walrus like this. The harshness of the landscape, the vulnerability of the boat, and the great size and power of the hunted animal combine to increase my sense of danger. The killing jars me, in spite of my regard for the simple elements of human survival.

No matter what sophistication of mind you bring to such events, no matter what breadth of anthropological understanding, no matter your fondness for the food, your desire to participate, you have still seen an animal killed. You have met the intertwined issues—what is an animal? What is death? . . .

It is easy to develop an affection for the Yup'ik people, especially when you are invited to participate in events still defined largely by their own traditions. The entire event—leaving to hunt, hunting, coming home, the food shared in a family setting—creates a sense of well-being easy to share. . . .

—Barry Lopez, *Arctic Dreams,* 1986

Quest for Avuk *by Fred Machetanz, 1973. (Anchorage Museum of History and Art)*

(following pages) Unalaska is one of the Aleutian Islands' principal towns.

■ Travel Information

The Southwest comprises the Aleutian and Pribilof Islands, the Kodiak Island group, and the Alaska Peninsula. Geographically, this vast area is characterized by windswept grassy tundra and some spruce forests. Most is undeveloped wilderness, without roads. Most visitors travel to the Southwest from Anchorage.

◆ Getting There

By Ferry

Travelers can reach Kodiak Island from Homer on the Kenai Peninsula in 10 hours on the ferry *Tustumena* for around $48, from Seward for $54. From Valdez or Cordova on Prince William Sound it is $98. For those wishing to travel out to the Aleutians, this same ferry will make the week-long journey from Kodiak to Dutch Harbor once a month in the summer for about $400 round-trip. *Tustumena, 100 Marine Way, Kodiak; 907-486-3800.*

By Plane

Air is the most popular way to see the Kodiak National Wildlife Refuge and its neighboring sites. There are many floatplane companies that access the numerous remote attractions not served by road. A typical fare from Anchorage to Kodiak runs $225–$290 round-trip. Another well-traveled air route is the flight into Katmai National Park from Anchorage along Cook Inlet. Some transfer to smaller amphibious planes that can take them to remote accommodations.

Traveling from Anchorage to Kodiak, and on to the Alaskan Peninsula by bush plane varies in cost depending on what part of the peninsula you visit. One-day round-trip flightseeing tours for bear viewing are also available and cost around $400 per person.

Era Aviation; 800-866-8394
Sea Hawk Air; 907-486-8282

■ CLIMATE

SUNLIGHT			
SUMMER MAXIMUM	SUNRISE	SUNSET	# OF HOURS
Adak	6:27 AM	11:10 PM	16:43
WINTER MINIMUM	SUNRISE	SUNSET	# OF HOURS
Adak	10:52 AM	6:38 PM	7:46

This region encompasses the enormous barely populated interior region of Alaska's southwestern quadrant, lined by busy coastal fishing ports and canneries along the Bering Sea. However, it is the Aleutian Island chain and the great national parks of Lake Clark and Katmai that most people know best. The moderating influence of the Japanese current keeps the climate of most Aleutian Islands mild and rainy as represented by Adak (midway along the island chain) in the chart below. In fact, it has been colder in northern Florida than it has been in the Aleutians. The isolated Pribilof Islands, in the middle of the Bering Sea, are fog-shrouded and chilly year-round. Kodiak Island has a climate similar to the Aleutian Islands and fog and storms may ground air transport for several days at end. Lake Clark National Park has a climate more closely associated with interior Alaska, with harsher winters but warmer summers.

TEMPS (F°)	AVG. JAN.		AVG. APRIL		AVG. JULY		AVG. OCT.		RECORD	RECORD
	HIGH	LOW	HIGH	LOW	HIGH	LOW	HIGH	LOW	HIGH	LOW
Lake Clark	24	3	41	22	67	45	41	25	90	-50
Kodiak	38	23	48	39	60	52	50	39	85	-12
Adak	41	30	46	40	52	48	48	43	80	8
Pribilofs	33	22	41	35	47	43	42	34	64	-26

PRECIPITATION (INCHES)	AVG. JAN.	AVG. APRIL	AVG. JULY	AVG. OCT.	ANNUAL RAIN	ANNUAL SNOW
Lake Clark	2.1"	2.4"	2.2"	3.1"	29"	100"
Kodiak	4.7"	3.9"	3.6"	7.6"	61"	40"
Adak	6.5"	5.2"	5.5"	7.7"	70"	102"
Pribilofs	2.3"	1.4"	2.7"	3.3"	28"	56"

■ Food, Lodging, & Tours

Restaurant Prices
Per person, without drinks, tax, or tip:
$ = under $12; $$ = $12–$20; $$$ = over $20

Room Rates
Per night, per room, double occupancy:
$ = under $70; $$ = $70–$100; $$$ = over $100

= lodging
= restaurant
= campground
= wilderness lodge

BETHEL *map page 316, A/B-2*

population 4,868
visitors information; 907-543-2047

Diane's Cafe. 1220 Hoffman Hwy.; 907-543-4305 $$–$$$
Housed in the Pacifica Guest House, Diane's features vegetarian dishes, Alaskan salmon and halibut, and steaks.

Pacifica Guest House. 1220 Hoffman Hwy.; 907-543-4305 $$$
For quiet elegance in the Bush, stay in a Queen Anne-style suite or a standard room. Hot tub, an exercise room, a meeting room, travel services, and an airport shuttle.

DILLINGHAM
map page 316, B-3

population 2,200

Muddy Rudder. On Main St. between the grocery stores; 907-842-2634 $–$$
Popular restaurant for locals, open for breakfast, lunch, and dinner.

Ricardo's. Located on Wildmill Hill; 907-842-1205 $–$$
Restaurant and bar.

Beaver Creek Bed and Breakfast. Aleknagtik Dr., 907-842-5366 $$
Comfortable home, nice folks. Rooms and cottages.

Bristol Inn. 104 Main St. 907-842-2240 $$
Popular, in-town lodge.

Katmai National Park & Preserve

map page 316, B-3

visitors information; 907-543-2047

Brooks Lodge.
Reservations: Katmailand, 4550 Aircraft Dr., Anchorage 99502; 907-243-5448 or 800-544-0551 $$$
Modern cabins circle the quaint main lodge. Activities include fly fishing, brown bear viewing, and tours of the Valley of Ten Thousand Smokes. Packages range from one-day standard to four-day deluxe. Three-night air and lodging package is about $870 per person for double occupancy (meals not included).

Grosvenor Lodge.
Reservations: Katmailand, 4550 Aircraft Dr., Anchorage 99502; 907-243-5448 or 800-544-0551 $$$
This lodge, accessible by floatplane, is surrounded by streams and rivers that are a sports fisherman's paradise. Cabins have electricity and shared baths.

Kulik Lodge.
Reservations: Katmailand, 4550 Aircraft Dr., Anchorage, AK 99502; 907-243-5448 or 800-544-0551. $$$
Accessible by floatplane and especially popular with fly fishermen, these two-person cabins are equipped with electricity and baths.

◆ Tours

Coastal Outfitters. 907-235-8492
Brown bear photography excursions in the Shelikof Coast of Katmai National Park; also customized fishing tours.

Katmai Air Service.
P.O. Box 278, King Salmon 99613; 907-246-3079 or 907-243-5448
A bird's-eye view of bear and moose, abandoned Native villages, and early trade and hunting routes.

King Salmon

map page 316, C-3/4

population 434
visitors information; 907-246-4250

King Ko Inn. 907-246-3378 $
Simple rooms, with shared and semiprivate bath. Cafe, and jet boat service to Katmai.

◆ Tours

Branch River Air. P.O. Box 545, King Salmon, AK 99613; 907-248-3539 or 907-246-3437
Floatplane service, guided or unguided trips, and lodging in remote areas of the Alaska peninsula.

KODIAK (KODIAK ISLAND) *map page 316, C-4*

population 7,229
visitors information; 800-789-4782

Cactus Flats. 338 Mission Rd.; 907-486-4677 $
The Kodiak vegetarians are catered to here with fresh juices and sandwiches.

El Chicano. 103 Center St. in the Old Bakery Mall; 907-486-6116 $
Surprisingly authentic, dishing up such Mexican favorites as homemade tamales, chiles rellenos, and menudo.

Henry's. 512 Marine Way; 907-486-8844 $
Popular with the local fishermen. Dishes range from chow mein to hamburgers.

King's Diner. Beside Lilly Lake; 907-486-4100 $
Locals come for standard American fare, especially hamburgers.

RED LAKE CABIN OF THE ALASKA DEPARTMENT OF FISH AND GAME ON KODIAK

Afognak Adventure. Reservations: Dept. VP, P.O. Box 1277, Kodiak, AK 99615; 907-486-6014 or 800-770-6014
Rustic, fully equipped, remote cabins offer nearby hiking, fishing; some cabins have banya (Native steam bath).

Alaska State Parks, Kodiak District. Reservations: SR Box 3800, Kodiak AK 99615; 907-486-6339 $
Four cabins with eight bunks on Shuyak Island are available for $25 per person, per night. Reservations can be made in writing up to six months in advance.

Buskin River Inn. 1395 Airport Way; 907-487-2700 $$$
Located by the airport, with a restaurant on the premises known for its good seafood. Guests can fish for salmon in the river that runs past the hotel.

The Shelikof Lodge. 211 Thorsheim Ave., Kodiak; 907-486-4141. $$
Modern hotel in downtown Kodiak with airport shuttle. Lounge, restaurant, 34 rooms.

Kodiak National Wildlife Refuge. Reservations: 1390 Buskin River Rd., Kodiak, AK; 907-487-2600 $
Nine rustic cabins sleeping four. Maximum seven-day stay; assigned by a lottery; write for application and return it by January 2 for April–June dates, and by April 1 to stay July–September.

Best Western Kodiak. 236 Rezanof St.; 907-486-5712 or 800-544-0970 $$–$$$
Comfortable lodging, with a restaurant.

◆ Tours

Alutiiq Tours and Transportation. 907-486-4997
Custom tours and sightseeing in Kodiak.

Dig Afognak. Afognak Native Corporation, Box 1277, Kodiak, AK 99615; 800-770-6014
Hands-on participation in an archaeological excavation; 6-day programs at remote, comfortable sites on Afognak Island.

Kodiak-Katmai Outdoors Inc. 907-486-2628 or 800-762-5634
Tour packages including Kodiak Island and Katmai National Park.

Kodiak Native Tourism Association. 888- 288-5736
Package tours on Kodiak Island. Birding, bear watching, kayaking, fishing, city and village tours, custom requests.

Kodiak Island Charters. 907-486-5380
Ocean fishing and sightseeing for up to 16 passengers; giant halibut and king salmon are their specialities.

Kodiak Island Ultimate Adventures. 800-544-2202
Tour packages and adventure excursions

Kodiak Treks. 907-487-2122
Hiking and wilderness adventures.

Munsey's Bear Camp. 907-847-2203
Five-day fishing cruises of the Kodiak Island coastline with spectacular views of the abundant wildlife, including brown bears, whales, bald eagles, and puffins.

Mythos Expeditions. 907-486-5536
Kayak trips.

Unalaska Island/Dutch Harbor (Aleutian Islands) *map page 335*

population 3,800
visitors information; 907-581-2612

Stormy's Restaurant. 2nd Ave. and Broadway; 907-581-1565 $$
Serves a range of ethnic dishes including Mexican, Greek, Italian, and American.

Ziggy's. Off Airport Beach Rd., Dutch Harbor; 907-581-2800 $$
A range of American and Mexican food served.

Grand Aleutian Hotel. Dutch Harbor; 907-581-3844 $$$
This luxury hotel has 106 rooms, six suites, two restaurants, and a three-story atrium lobby with a stone fireplace.

Unisea Inn. Dutch Harbor; 907-581-1325 or 800-891-1194 $$$
Waterfront hotel with 44 rooms, two restaurants, two lounges with music six nights a week, and a beauty parlor and liquor store on site.

St. Paul (Pribilof Islands) *map page 336*

population 600
visitor information; 907-546-2331

Trident Seafoods Galley. 907-546-2377
Cafeteria style dining. Seafood and American dishes. Has the recommendation of being the only game in town.

King Eider Hotel. Downtown St. Paul; 907-546-2477 $$$
Dating back to the 1880s, this simply decorated but comfortable hotel caters mostly to tour groups who come to the remote island to see the fur-seal rookeries and seabirds. The 25 rooms all have shared baths.

Yupik natives selling dolls in Bethel.

A handful of King crab. (Underwood Photo Archives, San Francisco)

FESTIVALS AND EVENTS

JANUARY

Kodiak: The Russian New Year and Masquerade Ball. Mid-January; celebrates Alaska's Colonial heritage. *907-486-3524*

MAY

Kodiak: King Crab Festival. Held on Memorial Day weekend, the event includes a parade, survival-suit races, a blessing of the fleet ceremony, and musical performances. *907-486-5557*

SEPTEMBER

Kodiak: State Fair and Rodeo. Alaskan-style cowboys compete; also features stock car races and a crafts fair. *800-789-4782*

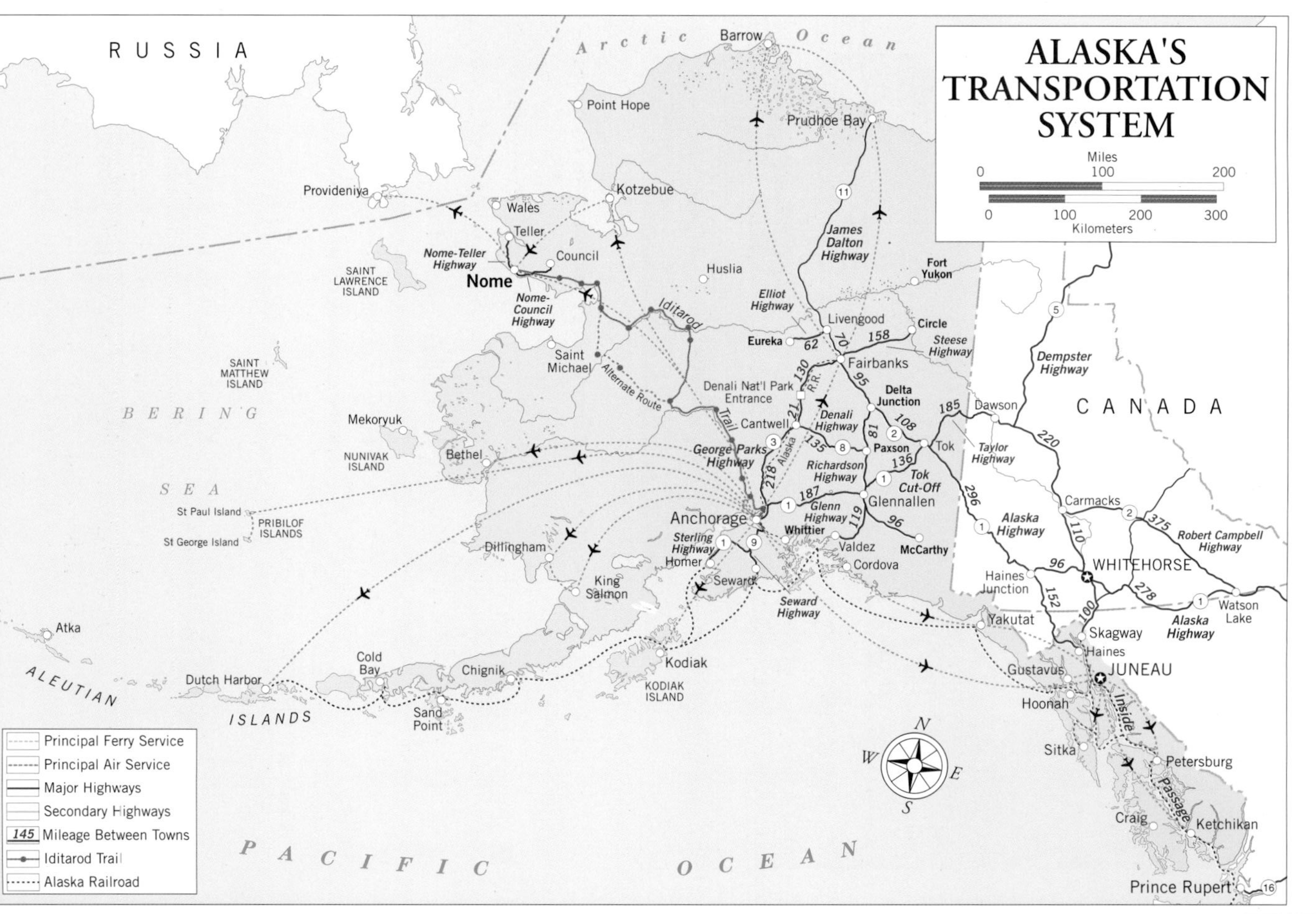

ALASKA'S TRANSPORTATION SYSTEM
Miles
0
100
200
0
100
200
300
Kilometers
RUSSIA
Arctic Ocean
CANADA
BERING SEA
PACIFIC OCEAN
ALEUTIAN ISLANDS
Barrow
Point Hope
Prudhoe Bay
Provideniya
Kotzebue
Wales
Teller
Council
Nome-Teller Highway
Nome
Nome-Council Highway
SAINT LAWRENCE ISLAND
Huslia
James Dalton Highway
Fort Yukon
Elliot Highway
Livengood
Circle
Eureka
Steese Highway
Iditarod Trail
Saint Michael
Alternate Route
Fairbanks
SAINT MATTHEW ISLAND
Denali Nat'l Park Entrance
R.R.
Delta Junction
Dawson
Dempster Highway
Mekoryuk
Cantwell
Denali Highway
Alaska
Tok
Taylor Highway
NUNIVAK ISLAND
Bethel
George Parks Highway
Paxson
Richardson Highway
Tok Cut-Off
Glennallen
Carmacks
St Paul Island
St George Island
PRIBILOF ISLANDS
Anchorage
Glenn Highway
Alaska Highway
Robert Campbell Highway
Dillingham
Sterling Highway
Whittier
Valdez
McCarthy
Homer
Cordova
WHITEHORSE
King Salmon
Seward
Haines Junction
Seward Highway
Watson Lake
Yakutat
Alaska Highway
Atka
Skagway
Haines
Cold Bay
Chignik
Kodiak
Gustavus
JUNEAU
Dutch Harbor
KODIAK ISLAND
Hoonah
Sand Point
Inside Passage
Sitka
Petersburg
Craig
Ketchikan
Prince Rupert
N
W
E
S
Principal Ferry Service
Principal Air Service
Major Highways
Secondary Highways
145 Mileage Between Towns
Iditarod Trail
Alaska Railroad

STATEWIDE
TRAVEL INFORMATION

Listings

NOTE: Much of Alaska is a wilderness and travelers proceed at their own risk. Compass American Guides cannot ensure the safety of any tour or mode of transportation listed in this book for the readers' convenience. We recommend that readers contact the local visitors bureaus for the most up-to-date information (see "Useful Addresses," page 358), as conditions and prices change frequently.

■ Area Code and Time Zone

The area code for the entire state of Alaska is 907, except for the town of Hyder, on the Canadian border, which is 604.

Alaska has two time zones. Southeast to the western tip of the mainland is on Alaska Time, one hour earlier than Pacific Time. The western Aleutians are two hours behind Pacific Time. British Columbia and Yukon are on Pacific Time.

■ Metric Conversions

1 foot = .305 meters
1 mile = 1.6 kilometers
Centigrade = Fahrenheit temp. minus 32, divided by 1.8

■ Climate and Clothing

Alaska has just about everything in the way of weather, from temperatures of 80 below zero to temperatures of 90 degrees Fahrenheit, from torrential downpours to blizzards, from gale-force winds to perfect calm. During the summer, rain is frequent. I reccommend a quality rain suit and rubber knee boots. The main thing, whenever taking a hike or venturing forth into the wilderness, is to dress in layers. Remember that it is always colder on water—streams, rivers, lakes, bays, the ocean—than on land, and prepare appropriately. Binoculars, a folding umbrella, insect repellent, and sunscreen are good to have on hand. Mosquito-net hats are recommended in marshy areas.

In winter, six or seven layers of clothing is advisable, including a parka with a good fur (wolverine, wolf) ruff, a wool scarf, a ski mask or balaclava, mittens with liners, and boots with liners. In the winter be certain to drink a lot of water, as frostbite often occurs when tissue has become dehydrated. Cover your cheeks and nose with a scarf or face-mask to prevent frostbite (even a slight wind dramatically lowers the air temperature).

These sled dogs are being transported to Anchorage to partake in the famous Iditarod race which runs over one thousand miles from Anchorage to Nome.

Cruise ships and floatplanes line the waterfront of Juneau.

GETTING THERE AND GETTING AROUND

By Plane

Several **major air carriers** serve the major cities of Anchorage and Fairbanks with daily flights.

Alaska; *800-426-0333*
Delta; *800-221-1212*
Northwest; *800-225-2525*
United; *800-241-6522*

Juneau is served only by Alaska Airlines. Smaller airlines serve the smaller towns that are scattered about the state, and light planes can be chartered to virtually any point in the state.

Bush planes are used by sports fishermen, big-game hunters, wildlife photographers, river rafters, and other passionate nature lovers. The rates for these bush planes can be quite high—several hundred dollars per hour on up (and the rate is computed both ways, for each trip, because the pilot has to return to the original point). Bush planes offer Alaskan travelers the chance to leave the road system behind and see the wild corners of the state. Flying in bush Alaska is generally quite safe; reduce the risks to a minimum by choosing reputable, established flying services.

Ice houses were used as temporary shelters by hunters in remote areas. Alaska's Eskimos lived in sod igloos. (Underwood Photo Archives, San Francisco)

By Ferry

The **Alaska Marine Highway**—an excellent ferry system from Bellingham, Washington, to Skagway, Alaska, and points in between—offers another option, for those with more time. Information on the summer schedule can be acquired by getting in touch with the Alaska Marine Highway; *www.state.ak.us/amhshome.html; P.O. Box R, Juneau, Alaska 99811, 907-465-3941.* The toll-free number *800-642-0066* can be used for reservations—always book six months in advance of the next summer season.

By Car

Another option is to drive to Alaska along the Alaskan Highway, also known as the alcan. With more than 1,500 miles from Dawson Creek, British Columbia (itself hundreds of miles north of the U.S. border), this is a major undertaking for both car and driver. The road is no longer the gravel washboard it once was; it's virtually all paved and well-engineered, but hardly a high-speed thruway. Pavement breaks frost heaves, or potholes are present in certain stretches. Allow a week to ten days for a leisurely trip. Order a copy of the *Milepost* for a mile-by-mile, detailed guide. *907-272-6070.*

By Train

There is an excellent railroad line from Anchorage to Fairbanks, which features stops in such interesting places as Denali National Park. This can be a comfortable and relaxing means of reaching the park. Further information can be obtained from: Alaska Railroad, *P.O. Box 107500, Anchorage, AK 99510; 907-265-2623 or 800-544-0552.*

By Bus

There are a number of guided bus tours available in Alaska, run by the various cruise ship lines and sightseeing companies. These private tours—any of which can be learned about by calling your local travel agent—are popular with many travelers, especially elders and international travelers for whom language poses difficulties.

The Alaska Railroad connects Anchorage to Fairbanks via Denali National Park.

■ About Accommodations and Wilderness Lodges

See travel information following each chapter for listings of places to stay throughout the state. Modern accommodations, small lodges, and budget motels are plentiful in Alaska. Make reservations as early as possible. Wilderness lodges provide rustic but comfortable accommodations (ranging from primitive cabins to very nice guestrooms in a main lodge) and good, occasionally excellent, cuisine. Most of these lodges are associated with sport fishing and/or big-game hunting, but they are also a great place for a leisurely vacation far from the madding crowd. Some are relatively close to civilization—as with the Kantishna Roadhouse, Camp Denali, or the North Face Lodge in Kantishna, at the end of Wonder Lake Road in Denali National Park. Others are located in the most obscure locations you can imagine—the Unalakleet River in northwestern Alaska, the headwaters of the Wood River in the Alaska Range, the far reaches of the Alaska Peninsula. For a list of all statewide wilderness lodges contact the **Alaska Division of Tourism:** *P.O. Box 110801, Juneau, AK 99811, phone 907-465-2010.*

Forest Service cabins are one of the best buys of Alaska, usually costing about $25 a night. For a list of these call the **U.S. Forest Service Information Center,** *Centennial Hall, 101 Egan Drive, Juneau, AK 99801, 907-586-8751.*

For **chain lodging**, refer to page 190 in the "South-Central" chapter.

■ Fishing

I can think of no other place in North America that offers the diversity or quality of fishing as Alaska, whether it is salt water or fresh water, fly or lure or even bait. Most fishermen practice catch and release, especially in trophy waters, but there is also the opportunity for you to ship home (on dry ice) large quantities of halibut, salmon, or pike.

Use a guide if you can possibly afford it. *(See listings of tour outfits at the end of individual chapters or call the information number listed under the name of each town to get advice about local operators.)* This will be the smartest money you ever spent in your life. Guides provide you with the appropriate fishing rod (who among us owns a rod strong enough for a 90-pound salmon or a 250-pound halibut?), the correct lures or legal bait, the safe drift boat or ocean-going craft, and, most importantly, the expert guidance that will put you into the best areas at the best times.

■ HUNTING

Imagine a place where the state resident license enables you to kill three black bears, a grizzly bear, a bull moose, a Dall sheep ram, five caribou per day, three wolves, and so forth. Imagine a herd of 135,000 caribou (the Central Arctic herd) that only has 400 sport hunters per year, a ratio of 337 animals per hunter. In Alaska you can hunt for 30 days and never hear another rifle shot or spot the smoke from another campfire—and see game every day.

There are laws regulating what type of game you can hunt. Nonresidents without a guide (but with a license) can hunt black bear, caribou, or moose. With a guide, nonresidents can hunt Dall sheep or grizzly bear. Hiring a guide, however, is costly: a guided 10-day hunt may cost as much as a new car.

If you decide on a non-guided hunting expedition, I suggest you be flown into an area like the Mulchatna River west of Anchorage. You and your buddies (don't even think of hunting alone in the Alaskan outback) will be able to hunt in an excellent area, as well as partake of some of the finest fishing in the state on the Mulchatna River and its tributaries. Get set up in a drop-camp where they fly in to check on you every couple of days, and transport the meat and antlers out (remember that it costs a lot to ship the meat out and that if you don't salvage all the meat you will be seeing the inside of an Alaskan jail, not to mention paying fines that will shock you).

If you are a bow-hunter, one of the best places to hunt is the Dalton Highway road corridor, which runs north from Fairbanks to Prudhoe Bay for more than 400 miles. Beyond five miles, rifle hunters may partake, but five miles over tundra is too far to pack anything, even a Boone and Crockett moose—best to fly into an area where you can float a river or hunt from a well-positioned base camp.

Hunting and trapping licenses are required for all nonresidents (and residents with the exception of Alaskans under 16 and over 60 years of age). Licenses may be obtained from any designated issuing agent or by mail from the **Alaska Department of Fish & Game,** *Licensing Division, P.O. Box 25525, Juneau, AK 99802; 907-465-2376.*

River Rafting

Alaska offers some of the finest river rafting in the world, with pristine waters, abundant wildlife and rivers protected along their entire length, from remote wilderness headwaters to terminal confluences. Some of the best river adventures can be had on rivers administered by the Bureau of Land Management.

◆ Beaver Creek

Beaver Creek is popular with the Fairbanks crowd. The river is located in the White Mountains north of town. You put in off the Nome Creek Road on the Steese Highway (milepost 57) and take out near Victoria Creek (accessed only by airplane for return trip), or—if feeling adventurous—you can float all the way to the Yukon River bridge on the Dalton Highway. Total distance in the first case is 127 miles and total distance in the latter is 268 miles. There is good fishing for northern pike and arctic grayling along Beaver Creek, and excellent moose and black bear hunting in the fall. This is considered Class I water (a few riffles and small waves). Further information is available from: **BLM Office Northern District**—*Steese-White Mountains District, 1150 University Ave., Fairbanks, AK 99709; 907-474-2350.*

◆ Birch Creek

Birch Creek is another waterway easily accessed from Fairbanks. Rafters put in at Mile 94.5 on the Steese Highway and take out at Mile 147. This trip offers wilderness aficionados a pleasant 126-mile float through the interior backcountry. Fishing for northern pike and arctic grayling can be quite good. Waters are considered Class I and Class II, with several Class III rapids (long difficult waters for experienced rafters or kayakers only). Travelers often report seeing moose, barren-ground caribou, and black and grizzly bear along Birch Creek, which is popular during the fall hunting season. Further information is available from: **BLM Office Northern District**—*Steese-White Mountains District, 1150 University Ave., Fairbanks, AK 99709; 907-474-2350.*

◆ Delta River

You'll find the put-in for the Delta River float near the Tangle Lakes on the Denali Highway (Mile 22). This is a 35-mile float, with some very dangerous water—Class III rapids—along the way (which makes it popular with experienced kayakers). The take-out point is on the Richardson Highway (Mile 212.5). There is good fishing for lake trout in Tangle Lakes. Further information is available from: **BLM Office Glennallen District**, *Box 147, Glennallen, AK 99588; 907-822-3217.*

◆ Fortymile River

The Fortymile River flows north into the Yukon River from the highlands in east-central Alaska. Access is from the Taylor Highway (Mile 49 or 75). The take-out point is 92 river miles distant at Eagle. There is excellent fishing for arctic grayling and burbot along the Fortymile, as well as good hunting for moose and black bear during the fall hunting season. There is some Class IV (dangerous) water on this stretch. Further information is available from: **BLM Office Northern District**—*Steese-White Mountains District, 1150 University Ave., Fairbanks, AK 99709; 907-474-2350.*

◆ Gulkana River

Gulkana River floats are very popular with Alaskans during the summer. The most common three- to five-day excursion leads down the Main Fork, which is heavily forested, with opportunities to observe moose, eagles, and black and grizzly bears. There is also a salmon run on the Gulkana that peaks around the summer solstice in late June, which makes it attractive with local fishermen. The trip down the Main Fork is accessed at the Paxon Lake Campground on the Richardson Highway (Mile 161). The take-out is at Sourdough Campground on the Richardson Highway (Mile 147.5). There is one Class III rapid on this stretch, which at times can be a very tricky proposition. You will see more people on this route than on others in this section, which is both an advantage and a disadvantage. More people around can mean greater safety. On the other hand, if you want solitude, the crowds would be a distraction. Further information is available from: **BLM Office Glennallen District,** *Box 147, Glennallen, AK 99588; 907-822-3217.*

◆ Unalakleet River

If the crowds on the Gulkana are not for you, then the Unalakleet will be the place. Because it is located in an extremely remote corner of northwestern Alaska, the river is seldom visited by summer travelers. The fishing for arctic grayling, arctic char, and salmon (chinook, coho, chum, and pink) is outstanding. You will probably see moose, bears, and eagles along this river. The Unalaklet is accessible only from the air, with the trip typically beginning at Tenmile Creek and continuing 76 miles to the village of Unalakleet. It is normally a Class I (easiest) float. To get in the area you would fly commercial aircraft from Anchorage to Kotzebue, and then charter an aircraft inland to Tenmile Creek. Further information is available from: **BLM Office, Anchorage District,** *6881 Abbot Loop Road, Anchorage, AK 99507; 907-267-1246.*

■ USEFUL ADDRESSES

Anchorage Convention and Visitors Bureau. 201 East Third Avenue, Anchorage, AK 99501; 907-276-4118

Fairbanks Convention & Visitors Bureau. 550 First Avenue, Fairbanks, AK 99701; 907-456-5774

Homer Chamber of Commerce. P.O. Box 541, Homer, AK 99603, 907-235-5300

Juneau Convention and Visitors Bureau. 369 S. Franklin St.; 907-586-1737

Kenai Peninsula Visitors Bureau. 11471 Kenai Spur Hwy., Kenai, AK 99611; 907-283-1991

Kodiak Island Convention and Visitors Bureau. 100 Marine Way, Kodiak, AK 99615; 907-486-4782

Matanuska-Susitna Convention and Visitors Bureau. Mile 35.5 George Parks Hwy., Wasilla, AK; or write HC01 Box 6166J21, Palmer 99645; 907-746-5000

Sitka Visitors Bureau. Lahmeyer Bldg., 303 Lincoln St., Sitka; or write P.O. Box 1226, Sitka, AK 99835; 907-747-5940

Valdez Convention and Visitors Bureau. 200 Chenega St.,Valdez; or write P.O. Box 1603, AK 99686; 907-835-2984

◆ FEDERAL PARKS, FORESTS, AND REFUGES

Alaska Public Lands Information Center. www.nps.gov/aplic/ 250 Cushman St., Suite 1A, Fairbanks 99701; 907-456-0527

A superb source of information on everything from bear viewing areas to cabin reservations.

Alaska Public Lands Information Center. Old Federal Building, 605 West 4th Ave., Suite 105, Anchorage, AK 99501, 907-271-2737

Department of Fish and Game. Public Communication Section, www.state.ak.us; P.O. Box 25526, Juneau, AK 99802-5526; 907-465-6166.

Excellent general information on planning a trip, fishing and hunting, destinations, and general questions. A highly recommended resource.

Alaska Division of State Parks. www.dnr.state.ak.us/parks; 400 Willoughby Ave., Juneau, AK 99801, 907-465-4563

Excellent resource.

Words of Caution

Bears

Never approach an unattended cub, as the sow is always nearby. Never cook in or around your campsite. Never take food into your tent. Hang food in trees if possible. Dispose of fish entrails as far from your campsite as possible and thoroughly wash your hands. Travel in groups whenever possible. Never hike after dark. Make sounds on the trail that definitely identify you as human. Leave your dogs at home. If a bear attacks, assume a fetal or cannonball position, with your fingers interlocked behind your neck and elbows bent to knees, so you can protect your head.

Getting Lost

If you find yourself lost, do not panic. It is important to relax and stay calm. Sit down, study your surroundings and maps, and listen for sounds that may give you a clue as to your whereabouts. Look for a familiar peak, saddle, or ridge. Remember that the sun and moon rise and set from east to west. If you do not have a compass, examine the foliage to determine the north-to-south orientation of vegetation patterns. Remember that north slopes are generally more heavily forested. If you must spend an unplanned night in the wilderness, take advantage of natural shelters such as caves, rock overhangs, fallen trees, and the bases of large coniferous trees. Look around for edible berries, such as raspberries, blueberries, salmonberries, and rose hips. Always carry emergency gear in your day pack, particularly when you are exploring or scouting from your base camp, which is when people often become lost or disoriented. A day pack should include matches, a candle, lighter fluid, a flashlight, a compass, a poncho, water, food, heavier clothing (hat, gloves, parka, sweater), a map, fishhooks and line, a whistle, a reflecting mirror, and a good knife. Some hikers in Alaska carry sophisticated emergency radios and satellite signalling devices, especially when travelling in remote wilderness areas.

Giardia Lamblia

Giardia is an intestinal parasite common in Alaskan water and causes serious gastrointestinal distress. Symptoms include painful intestinal cramps, severe diarrhea, gas, dehydration, dizziness, and extreme listlessness and fatigue. To avoid giardia, boil, filter, or chemically treat all water.

Hypothermia

The cold is a real killer in Alaska, and it can pose a threat on a sunny July day as easily as on a dark night in January. Each year, people die after falling in the water while fishing or boating. The water of Alaska, much of it glacially fed, is extremely cold. Another situation in which people die of exposure is when they are hiking and suddenly find themselves in a rain, sleet, or snowstorm. Whatever the case, the symptoms are as follows: uncontrollable shivering, cold extremities, and a confused and eventually indifferent mental state. Treatment should never include alcohol, which dilates blood vessels and accelerates heat loss. Treatment should include wrapping the victim in dry warm clothing or placing them in a sleeping bag and warming the individual with the body heat of another individual. To avoid frostbite dress warmly, keep your nose, cheeks, ears, and hands covered, avoid prolonged exposure to the cold, and keep your body fully hydrated.

◆ MOSQUITOES

Bring plenty of bug spray and avoid low-lying areas, especially when there is little wind. Try to stay near windy ridgetops or as near the breezy shoreline as you can. In parts of Alaska, a head net, long-sleeve shirts and gloves are a necessity for up to a month every summer. The worst I ever encountered were at Wonder Lake in Denali National Park. The mosquitoes were so bad around the lake that I ran up a 2,000 foot ridge, trailing a cloud of them, to finally reach a point where there was a strong breeze. I stayed up there, shooting pictures of Denali, until after one in the morning, at which time it was safe to descend.

◆ ROAD TRAVEL

In Alaska, wild animals often venture on to the road and create deadly traffic hazards. Always be alert, particularly at dusk, during the night, and at dawn, when animals are especially active.

A NEW YORKER IN ALASKA

I was celebrating my tenth year as a literary agent in New York when my husband asked if I would like to move to Alaska, much in the same way he would inquire if I would like to split that last bagel. We were sitting in our Hoboken, New Jersey, apartment—seven minutes from the heart of Times Square. Like most denizens of the vast New York Metropolitan area, I harbored a love-hate relationship with the city, a relationship that recognized the problems of the place, but still considered it the center of the universe. A move out of its orbit, we thought, could easily leave us emotionally and culturally deprived, but by the time my husband received a job offer from The Nature Conservancy of Alaska one month later, my mind was made up. "Let's go," I declared. The deciding factor: I was due to give birth to my first child in the spring. I would soon be obliged to reinvent myself as a mother. How much easier that would be, I reasoned, if I also shed the habits of my child-free self, which had been shaped for so long by one environment.

And so, as I clutched a pile of letters from disbelieving well-wishers wryly wondering "if I could continue my career from an igloo," we boarded an airplane and began a series of flights that would take us north and west to Anchorage. During the long series of flights, I reflected on the magnitude of the changes ahead. I realized how much we had been looking forward to introducing our child to Hoboken, the birthplace of Frank Sinatra and organized baseball, and home of the finest mozzarella and cannolis this side of Naples. I knew he would have been stimulated by the riches of Manhattan—the dinosaurs of the Museum of Natural History, the peregrine falcons in Central Park. What would we do in Anchorage?

We planted our feet on the Anchorage Airport tarmac in the middle of the driest January on record and quickly learned that Alaskans are similar to New Yorkers in that small talk often consists of soliloquies on why they love or hate the place. My first encounter with an Anchoragite was the nurse practitioner in the office of my new doctor, who said, "I've put in five years here in Alaska, and I'm getting the heck out next week."

After our son was born I came to learn that one of the greatest joys of motherhood is seeing the world anew from a child's wonder-filled eyes. So much of the world that my son sees for the first time is truly new to me, too: the moose loping down our suburban street, a family of bald eagles standing guard over the post office, the brightly painted Yup'ik masks at the Anchorage Museum of History and Art. I read to him from Cindy Shake's *Alaskan Animal Alphabet:*

N: A NARWALL WATCHES THE NORTHERN LIGHTS OVER NOME

Q: THE QIVIUT QUIVERS WHEN THE MUSK OX SHIVERS.

Images come to both of us from the same lens of inexperience and wonder. As we discover together the abundant attractions of Alaska, so we will encounter its dangers: grizzly and black bears, the sudden, often drastic changes of weather, and winding, one-lane mountain roads. And this city woman-cum-Alaska mother who was once fearless on Manhattan's streets will have to learn a new kind of bravery in order to bring comfort to her son.

—*Anne Dubuisson*

RECOMMENDED READING

Abbey, Edward. *Beyond the Wall, Essays from the Outside.* New York: Holt, Rinehart and Winston, 1984. This book contains a great essay about a river-rafting trip that Abbey took in the Arctic Refuge.

Barker, James H. *Always Getting Ready: Upterrlainarluta: Yup'ik Eskimo Substinence in Southwest Alaska.* Seattle, WA: University of Washington Press, 1993. A beautifully photographed portrait of the Native people of the Southwest delta.

Blackman, Margaret B. *Sadie Brower Neakok: An Iñupiaq Woman.* Seattle, WA: University of Washington Press, 1989. A biography of a fascinating Alaskan figure, the magistrate of Barrow for almost 20 years, as well as an exploration of the unique modern culture of the Arctic.

Brower, Kenneth. *Earth and the Great Weather: The Brooks Range.* San Francisco: Friends of the Earth, 1973. Brower's large-format book is now considered a classic of arctic literature; the photographs are truly outstanding.

Caras, Roger. *Monarch of Deadman Bay: The Life and Death of a Kodiak Bear.* Boston: Little, Brown, 1969 (available in a University of Nebraska Press paperback reprint). Caras is perhaps our best writer of animal stories—this is a must-read for anyone visiting the Pacific Coast islands of Alaska.

Carrighar, Sally. *Icebound Summer.* New York: Alfred Knopf, 1958. Carrighar's wonderful book details her stay one summer in the arctic of the Eskimos.

Crisler, Lois. *Arctic Wild.* New York: Harper & Row, 1958. This book documents the stay of a husband and wife in a remote Alaskan wilderness—essential-reading for all potential cabin builders.

Goetzmann, William H. *Looking Far North, the Harriman Expedition to Alaska, 1899.* New York: Viking, 1982. Both John Muir and John Burroughs were part of this historic expedition and Goetzmann's account is an exciting read, illustrated with lovely photographs by Edward Curtis.

Haines, John. *The Stars, the Snow, the Fire.* Minneapolis: Graywolf Press, 1989. If you can only afford one book buy this one. Haines shows you the real Alaska—he lived in the Bush for nearly 40 years. Other notable works include

Living off the Country: Essays on Poetry and Place (1981) and *Fables and Distances* (1996).

Higginson, Ella. *Alaska, the Great Country.* New York: Macmillan, 1908. An interesting book with some fine passages about the Inner Passage. Author Ella Higginson was the Annie Dillard of her day.

Holthaus, Gary, and Robert Hedin. *Alaska: Reflections on Land and Spirit.* Tucson: University of Arizona, 1989. This is one of the better literary anthologies, with essays by John Haines, Richard Nelson, and others.

Hopkins, David. *Paleoecology of Beringea.* New York: Academic, 1982. A fascinating if highly scientific read about the land bridge between Asia and North America.

Jans, Nick. *A Place Beyond: Finding Home in Arctic Alaska.* Anchorage: Alaska Northwest Books, 1996. Compelling tales of life in the far, far north.

London, Jack. *The Call of the Wild.* New York: Macmillan, 1904. A timeless story about a dog and all that a dog symbolizes of man's atavism.

Lopez, Barry. *Arctic Dreams.* New York: Scribner's, 1986. A scholarly look at life in the far north, by one of our great contemporary naturalists.

The Spirit of an Adventurer

"Now don't," I said, shouting to make myself heard in the storm, "now don't, Stickeen. What has got into your queer noodle now? You must be daft. This wild day has nothing for you. There is no game abroad, nothing but weather. Go back to camp and keep warm, get a good breakfast with your master, and be sensible for once. I can't carry you all day or feed you, and this storm will kill you."

But Nature, it seems, was at the bottom of the affair, and she gains her ends with dogs as well as with men, making us do as she likes, shoving and pulling us along her ways, however rough, all but killing us at times in getting her lessons driven hard home. After I stopped again and again, shouting good warning advice, I saw that he was not to be shaken off. . . . The pitiful wanderer just stood there in the wind, drenched and blinking, saying doggedly, "Where thou goest I will go." So at last I told him to come on if he must, and gave him a piece of the bread I had in my pocket; then we struggled on together, and thus began the most memorable of all my wild days.

—John Muir, *Stickeen: Story of a Dog,* 1909

Marshall, Bob. *Arctic Village.* New York: Smith and Haas, 1932 (available in a University of Alaska reprint edition). Marshall offers a detailed look at life in an Eskimo village in the Brooks Range. *Arctic Wilderness.* Berkeley: University of California, 1956. A memoir of Marshall's pioneering explorations in what is today, thanks to Marshall, Gates of the Arctic National Park.

McPhee, John. *Coming into Country.* New York: Farrar, Straus, & Giroux, 1976. McPhee is one of our best travel writers, and of all his works in the genre, this is my favorite. It's an excellent read.

Merton, Thomas. *Thomas Merton in Alaska: The Alaska Conferences, Journals, and Letters.* New York: New Directions, 1989. Thomas Merton, a Trappist Monk and one of the seminal minds in the twentieth century, chronicles his visit to Alaska in 1968.

Milton, John. *Nameless Valleys, Shining Mountains.* New York: Meredith, 1970. John Milton and Ken Brower crossed the Brooks Range on foot from south to north in the late 1960s—this book is a journal of that incredible adventure.

Muir, John. *Travels in Alaska.* San Francisco: Sierra Club, 1989. Muir's prose is strong and vibrant, especially when he writes of Glacier Bay. This should be read by all those visiting the Southeast. *Stickeen: Story of a Dog.* Chester, CT: Applewood Books. This delightful book is a classic tale of John Muir's journey through Alaska with his half-wild companion, Stickeen.

Murie, Adolph. *A Naturalist in Alaska.* Tucson: University of Arizona Press, 1989. Award-winning collection of informal essays on the wildlife of interior Alaska. Also, a good recommendation for those visiting Denali is *The Wolves of Mount McKinley* (1944).

Murie, Margaret. *Two in the Far North.* New York: Knopf, 1962; reprint edition by Alaska Northwest Books, 1998. Murie tells the story of her marriage to the biologist Olaus Murie, and of their incredible adventure in the Alaskan bush before Alaska became a state.

Murray, John. *A Republic of Rivers: Three Centuries of Nature Writing from Alaska and the Yukon.* New York and Oxford: Oxford University Press, 1990. A collection of works from a journey to the Bering Sea in 1741 to writings from the contemporary period. Murray's works on Alaskan wildlife include *The Great Bear: Contemporary Essays on the Grizzly Bear* (1991). *Out Among the Wolves:*

Contemporary Essays on the Wolf (1992). *Wild Hunters: Predators in Peril.* (1993). *Grizzly Bears: an Illustrated Field Guide* (1995).

Naske, Claus. *Alaska: A History of the 49th State.* Norman: University of Oklahoma Press, 1987. Full of archival photographs from the marvelous collection at the University of Alaska, Fairbanks.

Nelson, Richard. *Hunters of the Northern Forest.* Chicago: University of Chicago Press, 1973. *Hunters of the Northern Ice.* Chicago: University of Chicago Press, 1969. *Make Prayers to the Raven: a Koyukon View of the Northern Forest.* Chicago: University of Chicago Press, 1986. *The Island Within.* San Francisco: North Point Press, 1991. As a cultural anthropologist, no one writes more eloquently of native ethnography than Dr. Nelson.

Proenneke, Richard. *One Man's Wilderness: an Alaskan Odyssey.* Anchorage: Alaska Northwest Publishing, 1973. In his fifties, Proenneke traveled to Lake Clark, built a cabin, and loved it so much he stayed—this is a journal of his first year.

Roberts, David. *The Mountain of My Fear.* New York: Vanguard, 1968. An extremely well-written and moving account of Robert's journey to Denali. Also, *Deborah: A Wilderness Narrative* (1970).

Sheldon, Charles. *The Wilderness of the Upper Yukon.* New York: Scribner's, 1911. Written by one of the first literary naturalist-hunters to visit the northland. Another excellent book, especially in preparation for a trip to Kodiak, is *The Wilderness of the North Pacific Coast Islands* (1912). Also, in *The Wilderness of Denali* (1930) Sheldon, who is considered the father of Mount McKinley, writes of his first trip to Denali.

Sherwonit, Bill and Schultz, Jeff. *Iditarod: The Great Race to Nome.* Anchorage: Alaska Northwest Books, 1991. Everything you ever wanted to know about this spectacular sports event. The color photographs are stunning.

Stuck, Hudson. *The Ascent of Denali (Mount McKinley).* New York: Scribner's, 1914. Reverend Stuck's legendary ascent of Denali is a great read—he was an accomplished writer as well as an indefatigable climber of mountains. *Ten Thousand Miles with a Dog Sled.* New York: Scribner's, 1916. Reverend Stuck toured the interior of Alaska, visiting remote bush villages and spreading his faith. This book is a fascinating account of his adventures in the frosty northland—back in the days before trains, planes, and automobiles had made their way to Alaska.

I N D E X

A

B

S

T

COMPASS AMERICAN GUIDES

Compass American Guides are available in general and travel bookstores, or may be ordered directly by calling (800) 733-3000. Please provide title and ISBN when ordering.

Alaska
(2nd edition)
$19.95 ($27.95 Can)
0-679-00230-8

Arizona
(5th edition)
$19.95 ($29.95 Can)
0-679-00432-7

Boston
(2nd edition)
$19.95 ($27.95 Can)
0-679-00284-7

Chicago
(2nd edition)
$18.95 ($26.50 Can)
1-878-86780-6

Coastal California
(2nd edition)
$21.00 ($32.00 Can)
0-679-00439-4

Colorado
(5th edition)
$19.95 ($29.95 Can)
0-679-00435-1

Florida
(1st edition)
$19.95 ($27.95 Can)
0-679-03392-0

Georgia
(1st edition)
$19.95 ($29.95 Can)
0-679-00245-6

Gulf South
(1st edition)
$21.00 ($32.00 Can)
0-679-00533-1

Hawaii
(4th edition)
$19.95 ($27.95 Can)
0-679-00226-X

Idaho
(1st edition)
$18.95 ($26.50 Can)
1-878-86778-4

Las Vegas
(6th edition)
$19.95 ($29.95 Can)
0-679-00370-3

Maine
(3rd edition)
$19.95 ($29.95 Can)
0-679-00436-X

Manhattan
(3rd edition)
$19.95 ($29.95 Can)
0-679-00228-6

Minnesota
(2nd edition)
$19.95 ($29.95 Can)
0-679-00437-8

Montana
(4th edition)
$19.95 ($29.95 Can)
0-679-00281-2

Nevada
(1st edition)
$21.00 ($32.00 Can)
0-679-00535-8

New Mexico
(4th edition)
$21.00 ($32.00 Can)
0-679-00438-6

New Orleans
(4th edition)
$21.00 ($32.00 Can)
0-679-00647-8

North Carolina
(2nd edition)
$19.95 ($29.95 Can)
0-679-00508-0

Oregon
(3rd edition)
$19.95 ($27.95 Can)
0-679-00033-X

Pacific Northwest
(2nd edition)
$19.95 ($27.95 Can)
0-679-00283-9

Pennsylvania
(1st edition)
$19.95 ($29.95 Can)
0-679-00182-4

San Francisco
(5th edition)
$19.95 ($29.95 Can)
0-679 -00229-4

Santa Fe
(3rd edition)
$19.95 ($29.95 Can)
0-679-00286-3

South Carolina
(3rd edition)
$19.95 ($29.95 Can)
0-679-00509-9

South Dakota
(2nd edition)
$18.95 ($26.50 Can)
1-878-86747-4

Southern New England (1st ed)
$19.95 ($29.95 Can)
0-679-00184-0

Southwest
(3rd edition)
$21.00 ($32.00 Can)
0-679-00646-X

Texas
(2nd edition)
$18.95 ($26.50 Can)
1-878-86798-9

Underwater Wonders of the National Parks
$19.95 ($27.95 Can)
0-679-03386-6

Utah
(4th edition)
$18.95 ($26.50 Can)
0-679-00030-5

Vermont
(1st edition)
$19.95 ($27.95 Can)
0-679-00183-2

Virginia
(3rd edition)
$19.95 ($29.95 Can)
0-679-00282-0

Washington
(2nd edition)
$19.95 ($27.95 Can)
1-878-86799-7

Wine Country
(3rd edition)
$21.00 ($32.00 Can)
0-679-00434-3

Wisconsin
(2nd edition)
$18.95 ($26.50 Can)
1-878-86749-0

Wyoming
(3rd edition)
$19.95 ($27.95 Can)
0-679-00034-8

■ About the Author

John A. Murray worked as an English professor at the University of Alaska, Fairbanks from 1988 through 1994. He has published two dozen nature books, including *A Republic of Rivers* (Oxford University Press), *Grizzly Bears* (Roberts-Rinehart), and *Out Among the Wolves* (Alaska Northwest). In 1994 Murray was named series editor for the Sierra Club nature writing annual. His reviews, interviews, essays and articles have appeared in such periodicals as *The Washington Post, The Bloomsbury Review,* and *Publisher's Weekly.*

■ About the Photographer

After receiving a masters degree in fire ecology from UC Berkeley, Don Pitcher worked on wildlife projects in Wyoming, California, and Alaska. He went on to photograph *Wyoming* (Compass American Guides), and to write three other travel guides: *Wyoming Handbook, Washington Handbook* (Moon Publications), and *Berkeley Inside/Out* (Heyday Books). His photographs have appeared in many books, magazines, posters, and other publications. Don bases his travels around Alaska and the world from his Anchorage home where he lives with his wife and daughter.

Comments, suggestions, or updated information?

Please write:

Compass American Guides
5332 College Ave., Suite #201
Oakland, CA 94618
or e-mail
compassk@a.crl.com

NAGB/11/06